WHAT EXPERTS IN PSYCHOTHERAPY ARE SAYING ABOUT *HOW MASTER THERAPISTS WORK*

"In *How Master Therapists Work: Effecting Change from the First through the Last Session and Beyond*, Len Sperry and Jon Carlson offer an absolutely must-read book for beginners and experienced psychotherapists of all stripes (i.e., psychologists, social workers, counselors, marriage and family therapists, psychiatrists, among others). During a very challenging time for the psychotherapy field, trying to manage the increasing demands for quick fixes, easy answers, and evidence-based interventions along with rapid changes in the health care delivery and insurance reimbursement systems, a thoughtful, wise, consoling voice of reason is critically needed. This book is exactly what the doctor ordered! Sperry and Carlson have many years of experience and reflection on conducting psychotherapy and it certainly shows in this important book. Therapists will be grateful for it. I know I am."
Thomas G. Plante, *PhD, ABPP, professor, Santa Clara University; adjunct clinical professor of psychiatry and behavioral sciences, Stanford University*

"In an era where therapists are increasingly conceptualized as no more than mechanically applying manualized treatments, this volume reminds us powerfully of how the person of the therapist can, and does, make all the difference. Sperry and Carlson each invite the reader to consider how this evidence-based variable, the therapist her- or himself, affects the process and outcome of psychotherapy. This should be required reading for all trainees in the field of psychotherapy, as well as for any group writing practice guidelines for treatment. A true tour de force."
Laura S. Brown, *PhD, ABPP, director, Fremont Community Therapy Project*

"This book is an absolute gem that must be read by everyone who is passionate about being a better psychotherapist. Dr. Sperry and Dr. Carlson provide the reader with a rare behind the scenes tour of the work

of a master psychotherapist along with expert commentary that helps to clearly explain the complex underlying processes that help make it all look so natural and easy when applied by a master psychotherapist. Every psychotherapy educator and clinical supervisor should share this book and its related DVDs with each of their students and supervisees. I can think of no better gift to give them."

Jeffrey E. Barnett, *PsyD, ABPP, professor and associate chair, Department of Psychology, Loyola University, Maryland*

"This outstanding work provides the reader with a rare bird's eye view into how a master therapist facilitates successful transformation with an arduous case. It nicely integrates research with clinical commentary to yield a valuable teaching tool for seasoned clinicians and trainees. Above all, it gives the reader a real taste of what it is like to be a master therapist. I highly recommend it."

Frank M. Dattilio, *PhD, ABPP, Harvard Medical School, Boston, Massachusetts*

"Seldom do we get to look inside the therapy chamber at what really happens, and even less the opportunity to experience a master therapist at work. This book does just that. The authors open the door to the inner chambers of a master therapist at work so we can see healing as it happens, making available to the reader the mental processes of the client and master healer as transformation occurs. This amazing book should be required reading for every psychotherapist. It demystifies the mystery of therapy without reducing it to a set of skillful transactions."

Harville Hendrix, *PhD, author of* Getting the Love You Want *and* Receiving Love

"This wonderful book offers so much hope and promise for the counseling and therapy professions. Here, Sperry and Carlson address the natural confusion, ambiguity and uncertainty about how to develop professionally by illuminating a path to practitioner expertise and mastery. Novices, and experienced practitioners too, will devour these pages with great excitement. Bravo to Sperry and Carlson!"

Tom Skovholt, *PhD, LP, ABPP, professor, University of Minnesota*

"Fundamentally, this is a book about '. . . how psychotherapy can effect significant changes within a limited number of sessions and can sustain those changes for several years.' But more than that, Drs. Sperry and Carlson have elegantly revealed the 'deep structure' of masterful psychotherapy, by exploring the critical importance of the therapist's contribution to the therapeutic alliance. In their eleven characteristics typical of the 'ideal therapist,' Sperry and Carlson provide a useful template for aspiring master therapists, reminding us that '. . . not everything in the human realm follows linear thinking and logic.' Through their analysis of the case of Aimee, Sperry and Carlson allow the reader to follow the flexible yet systematic approach of the master therapist, using actual transcripts. Thus, the reader is not merely 'told,' but engagingly 'shown' the path of excellence in therapy. I can recommend this book with confidence to both beginning and more experienced psychotherapists."

Ronald Pies, *MD, professor of psychiatry, SUNY Upstate Medical University; clinical professor of psychiatry, Tufts University School of Medicine*

"I was impressed with the systematic way the authors described 'the master therapist.' The most important value of the book is the personal insight the reader will gain. This is a must-read for students in the helping professions, clinicians immersed in therapy with clients and for supervisors who direct others toward their eventual goal of becoming a 'master therapist.'"

Roy Kern, *PhD, scientific professor, Department of Theoretical Psychology, Vytautas Magnus University, Kaunas, Lithuania*

"This is a deeply thought-provoking and exciting book! It puts into words what effective therapy is and how it is operationalized in session by the masters. This is a great book for clinicians, teachers and trainers of novice counselors, and counselors-in-training. In a field where brief treatment models have become the norm, it will revolutionize how counselors think about their clinical work and the impact they can have on their clients in a short period of time."

Katherine M. Helm, *PhD, professor of psychology, director of graduate programs in psychology, Lewis University*

"Finally, a book that not only identifies what master therapists do, but offers a step-by-step guide for developing into one. This book is an essential guide for pre-practicum, practicum, and internships in all concentration settings (schools or universities, clinical mental health settings, or working with couples, families, or larger systems). It re-focuses students and faculty away from the mandate to 'do no harm' and toward the supreme goal of becoming a highly competent practitioner. No one should settle for being just 'ok' at their job when truly competent is both possible and teachable."

James Robert Bitter, *EdD, professor of counseling, East Tennessee State University*

"Students are eager to see the practical applications of theory to case examples. This book demonstrates how theory comes alive as Dr. Jon

Carlson works with one client. I found the commentaries by both Drs. Sperry and Carlson in each of the chapters to be interesting and informative. Through these commentaries the reader is able to gain insight into what the therapist was thinking and doing at the various stages of the therapeutic process. This work is an excellent blend of research, theory, and interventions illuminating how change can occur."
  Gerald Corey, *EdD, ABPP, professor emeritus of human services and counseling, California State University, Fullerton*

"The process of psychotherapy is an inevitable blend of art and science. A treatment may be empirically supported, but the artistry necessary to be a master therapist simply can't be found in a manual. Jon Carlson's therapeutic elegance, presented here in his work with his client Aimee, is a profound reminder of how much sophistication goes into a successful treatment that comes from the deeper Self of the therapist. With this book, Sperry and Carlson have made a great contribution to all those therapists who aspire to be master therapists themselves one day."
  Michael D. Yapko, *PhD, clinical psychologist and author of* Trancework *and* Depression Is Contagious

"This book is a must-read for all those who are interested in the effectiveness of psychotherapy and in psychotherapy training. By including not only the expertise of experienced psychotherapists, but also by providing information from basic psychology and psychotherapy research, we learn a great deal about expertise in psychotherapy, a topic that has been understudied."
  Clara E. Hill, *PhD, professor, Department of Psychology, University of Maryland*

"If you want to understand the characteristics and competencies of a master therapist, as well as the process of becoming one, this book is for you. Both thorough and accessible, *How Master Therapists Work* is a valuable resource for mental health professionals regardless of their level of clinical experience. I recommend highly."
  Richard E. Watts, *PhD, distinguished professor of counseling, director, Center for Research and Doctoral Studies in Counselor Education, Sam Houston State University*

"Every so often a book comes along that radically changes the way we think about the practice of psychotherapy. This is that book. I only wish it had been available when I was in training."
  Richard Sauber, *editor of the* American Journal of Family Therapy *and former professor in the departments of psychiatry at Brown University, Columbia University, and the University of Pennsylvania*

"This text by Sperry and Carlson is an excellent and engaging journey through the psychotherapy process. While placing today's practices in an historical context by reviewing relevant research, they identify how therapy has become refined by master therapists to be today's effective treatment model. By case illustration and expanded commentary the authors present the structural and practical aspects of the current practice of psychotherapy, but even more importantly, their incisive case analyses manage to convey the intricate and subtle aspects of master therapists that result in them being seen as artists in healing people's lives. This text is exceptional for students just beginning, master therapists with decades of experience, and to all in between."
      Arthur M. Horne, *distinguished research professor,*
            the University of Georgia

"In the last decade much emphasis has been placed on evidence-based treatment, and rightly so, if it had not been at the neglect of the role of the psychotherapist. Ultimately, it is the skill and understanding of the therapist that determines the success or failure of therapy. The authors have restored the rightful emphasis on the therapist, delineated its parameters, and expertly demonstrated it in detail in a brilliantly conducted six session brief psychotherapy from which every practitioner can learn much."
    Nicholas A. Cummings, *PhD, ScD, former president,*
   American Psychological Association; distinguished professor,
            University of Nevada, Reno

"Something very important to know about Len Sperry and Jon Carlson is not only are they master therapists, they are also master educators. In *How Master Therapists Work* they have crafted a text of exceptional clarity in making explicit the steps in facilitating client change. Anchored by Carlson's brilliant series of interviews with Aimee and underscored by Sperry's incisive commentary, this book is a tremendously valuable comprehensive competency-focused resource for instructors, students, and practitioners."
   Brian A. Gerrard, *PhD, associate professor, Counseling Psychology*
        Department, University of San Francisco

"Want to watch a master therapist at work, hear why he did what he did, and learn numerous ways to incorporate valuable skills and lessons into your own practice? Sperry and Carlson have provided us with an excellent guide to making first-order, second-order, and third-order change—in our clients and in ourselves. I strongly recommend it!"
  Michael F. Hoyt, *PhD, author of* Brief Psychotherapies: Principles &
   Practices, *editor of* The Handbook of Constructive Therapies

"Ostensibly this book analyzes how a master psychotherapist effects change with one client. However, it quickly engages readers in examining their own pattern of practice from the perspectives of first-order techniques, second-order transformations, and third-order truths. The resulting insights promise to clarify and even change the reader's pattern of practice."
  Mark L. Savickas, *professor of family and community medicine, Northeast Ohio Medical University*

"*How Master Therapists Work* is a clear, concise, and well-referenced guide to the orientations and practices of Jon Carlson, an acknowledged master psychotherapist. Discover how to bring out the best in your clients . . . and yourself. Important for the pro; invaluable for the tyro."
  Jeffrey K. Zeig, *PhD, director, the Milton Erickson Foundation*

"Observing how a 'master therapist' works offers an unparalleled reference point for discovering the characteristics associated with effective psychotherapy. The expanding literature on therapist expertise typically represents a nomothetic perspective: looking for common elements across the work of many master therapists. Len Sperry and Jon Carlson have taken a fresh, idiographic approach, involving one master therapist (Sperry) studying in detail an entire therapy conducted by another master therapist (Carlson). The reader feels present in each session and, then, present as the two master therapists discuss their observations and experiences. Sperry and Carlson offer the reader a virtual apprenticeship in the conduct of masterful psychotherapy, as well as an innovative conceptual framework for understanding how master therapists facilitate a therapeutic process qualitatively superior to less skillful clinicians. By reading this book, psychotherapists of all skill levels can enhance their comprehension of the therapist's contribution to therapeutic change."
  Jeffrey L. Binder, *PhD, ABPP, professor of psychology, Georgia School of Professional Psychology, Atlanta, Georgia*

"Psychotherapy is a combination of both a science and an art form. Len Sperry and Jon Carlson have provided an incisive anatomy of psychotherapy and outlined the critical steps in becoming a master therapist. This book is a primer for beginning and seasoned clinicians. KUDOS!"
  Donald Meichenbaum, *PhD, research director, Melissa Institute for Violence Prevention, Miami, Florida*

"Understanding the characteristics of 'super shrinks' and their impact on client outcomes is a hot topic in psychotherapy training and research, which Len Sperry and Jon Carlson's volume *How Master Therapists Work: Effecting Change from the First through the Last Session and Beyond* addresses beautifully. Based on an actual short-term course of transtheoretical psychotherapy from APA's Psychotherapy Video Series, Sperry and Carlson present verbatim transcript material, complete with 'color commentary.' In proceeding through the chapters of this compelling book, the reader is able to comprehend clearly how the expert therapist quickly and genuinely connects with and understands the client, ascertains and highlights the core issues, creates a credible and energizing treatment plan, copes gracefully and caringly with inevitable obstacles, measures progress, and facilitates transformative change in the client via teaching her to become adept at constructive self-reflection. The result is a marvelous text that provides a concise illustration of how to teach clients to become their own therapists, such that clients benefit from treatment not only while it occurs, but onward from the termination of formal sessions. This is the essence of masterful therapy."

Cory F. Newman, *PhD, ABPP, professor of psychology, Psychiatry, Perelman School of Medicine, University of Pennsylvania, and director, Center for Cognitive Therapy*

"There are a lot of books about doing therapy from a particular model. This book is about therapeutic mastery that cuts across models. Beginners and experienced therapists alike will learn from how Jon Carlson works with focus, nuance, and skill. Nothing showy here, just masterful therapy. You will love the client Aimee and wish that Jon was your own therapist!"

William J. Doherty, *PhD, professor and director, Minnesota Couples on the Brink Project at the University of Minnesota, St. Paul*

"Sperry and Carlson weave together a brilliant tapestry of the moment-to-moment therapeutic process, elegantly interspersing case material from the case of Aimee to highlight key points. This is a valuable resource for therapists at all stages of professional development, from the student who has yet to see her or his first client to the seasoned therapist."

Craig S. Cashwell, *PhD, LPC, NCC, ACS, CSAT, professor, Department of Counseling and Educational Development, the University of North Carolina at Greensboro*

"Len Sperry and Jon Carlson have written a wonderful book that has something for everyone in this field. It is a treat to 'see'—through transcript—and 'hear'—through commentary on the sessions—a master therapist, Jon Carlson, at work. This book shows us just how therapeutic change that's substantive and lasting takes place. The text analyzes and de-mystifies the process by which master therapists effect therapeutic changes in people's lives. The exposition is clear, readable, rooted in empirical research, and yet presented through the wisdom and experiences of two authors with decades of experience between them. I highly recommend this book to beginners and expert clinicians alike, and everyone in between."

Diana Fosha, *PhD, author of* The Transforming Power of Affect *and editor of* The Healing Power of Emotion: Affective Neuroscience, Development & Clinical Practice

"*How Master Therapists Work* instructs and inspires! Clearly written and comprehensive, this book illuminates the process of becoming a supremely effective psychotherapist. By presenting both transcripts and commentary it brings the reader into the therapy room to watch the movement toward increasing health and wellbeing and to understand how this change comes about. With the belief that it is the therapist and not the treatment that influences therapeutic change, the authors explore the 'best of the best' in a way that develops increasing skill and competence in practitioners. A must-read for beginners and experienced therapists alike, *How Master Therapists Work* will transform your practice of psychotherapy!"

Judith V. Jordan, *PhD, ABPP, founder, Relational-Cultural Therapy; assistant professor, Harvard Medical School, Cambridge, Massachusetts*

"Within their book on how master therapists work, Dr. Sperry and Dr. Carlson have shared literature pertaining to psychotherapy as well as transcripts from multiple sessions with a client, along with commentary on the process of therapy. Views expressed include remarks pertaining to topics like the therapeutic alliance, case conceptualization, assisting clients with some level of initial change, facilitating 'corrective experiences', considering first and second order change as well as third order change, and termination of therapy. This book has the potential to help students better understand the therapeutic process and to help practitioners evaluate and reconsider their practice."

John D. West, *professor, Counseling and Human Development, Kent State University*

"This compelling book written in collaboration by two close friends and master clinicians offers an intimate view of the process of psychotherapy and how change occurs over the course of brief treatment. An in-depth case, with extensive transcripts, illustrates the process of effective psychotherapy and how second and third order change necessary for enduring effects occurs. The theory of change is clearly articulated and cases and commentary are provided in a seamless and engaging manner.

Anyone interested in learning how master therapists utilize complex pattern recognition skills and create opportunities for transformational experiences will want to read this volume."
Jeffrey J. Magnavita, *PhD, ABPP, independent practice, Glastonbury, Connecticut; lecturer in psychiatry, Yale University; founder, Unified Psychotherapy Project*

"This inspiring book will be of value to all students of therapy, whatever their orientation and level of experience. In following so closely the actual collaboration of a seriously suffering patient and a highly skilled clinician, it demystifies the complex endeavor of psychotherapy, demonstrates its effectiveness, and leaves the reader caring deeply about both participants in this absorbing human drama."
Nancy McWilliams, *PhD, ABPP, Rutgers University Graduate School of Applied and Professional Psychology*

"If you aren't teaching a course where you can use this book, create one! We have long known that observing and modeling master therapists could add to our clinical competency, but now Sperry and Carlson have put such an opportunity at our fingertips. These authors have deftly presented the art and science of effecting change in a format that will appeal to the neophyte as well as the experienced practitioner."
Hanna Levenson, *PhD, professor, Wright Institute, Berkeley, California; director, Brief Therapy Program, California Pacific Medical Center, San Francisco*

"Len Sperry and Jon Carlson have provided an invaluable resource for therapists, both beginners and veterans. It is ideal for consultations and seminars focusing on the need for achieving rapid outcomes in therapy. Upon learning the principles contained in this book, neophyte and experienced practitioners will be able to implement the orders of change and integrate them into their counseling and therapy. Specific dialogues, therapist client interchanges, illustrate the authors' excellent and sensible discussions. Neophyte and experienced practitioners will feel led to new insights and an eagerness to implement the skills demonstrated by the authors. Additionally, an underlying message is contained: that the authors demonstrate a profound respect for readers who seek skills that can be integrated into all major theories of psychotherapy."
Robert Wubbolding, *PhD, Center for Reality Therapy, Cincinnati, Ohio*

"In the age of evidence-based treatments, we often forget that psychotherapy is an exceedingly difficult craft to master and that deliberate and sustained effort is needed to be an expert. Like any craft, the practitioner needs to see psychotherapy in action. Jon Carlson, the therapist, and Len Sperry, the commenter, in *How Master Therapists Work*, present the reader with a beautiful analysis of a single case, providing a rare combination of theory, practice, and analysis, which brings psychotherapy to life, quite brilliantly. This is the way to learn about psychotherapy!"

Bruce E. Wampold, *PhD, Patricia L. Wolleat Professor of Counseling Psychology, University of Wisconsin, Madison; director, Modum Bad Psychiatric Center, Vikersund, Norway.*

HOW MASTER THERAPISTS WORK

Effecting Change from the First through the Last Session and Beyond

Len Sperry and Jon Carlson

NEW YORK AND LONDON

First published 2014
by Routledge
711 Third Avenue, New York, NY 10017

and by Routledge
27 Church Road, Hove, East Sussex BN3 2FA

Routledge is an imprint of the Taylor & Francis Group, an informa business

© 2014 Taylor & Francis

The right of Len Sperry and Jon Carlson to be identified as authors of this work has been asserted by them in accordance with sections 77 and 78 of the Copyright, Designs and Patents Act 1988.

All rights reserved. No part of this book may be reprinted or reproduced or utilized in any form or by any electronic, mechanical, or other means, now known or hereafter invented, including photocopying and recording, or in any information storage or retrieval system, without permission in writing from the publishers.

Trademark notice: Product or corporate names may be trademarks or registered trademarks, and are used only for identification and explanation without intent to infringe.

Library of Congress Cataloging-in-Publication Data

Sperry, Len.
  How master therapists work : effecting change from the first through the last session and beyond / Len Sperry & Jon Carlson.
    pages cm
  Includes bibliographical references and index.
  1. Psychotherapy—Practice. 2. Psychotherapist and patient—Case studies. 3. Psychotherapists—Training of. I. Carlson, Jon. II. Title.
  RC480.5.S642 2014
  616.89'140068—dc23
  2013021842

ISBN: 978-0-415-81046-3 (hbk)
ISBN: 978-0-415-81047-0 (pbk)
ISBN: 978-0-203-07095-6 (ebk)

Typeset in Goudy
by Apex CoVantage, LLC

The American Psychological Association holds copyright to the transcript excerpted herein from 'Psychotherapy Over Time' copyrighted by APA 2006. The reproduction of the material in this work is granted by permission from APA and the participating volunteer in the demonstration of psychotherapy.

This book is gratefully dedicated to Aimee. The story of how she worked in therapy to change herself will inspire hope, confidence, and courage in those needing help. She is the "Gloria" of psychotherapy of this generation.

CONTENTS

Foreword   xvii
BARRY L. DUNCAN
Preface   xxi

1   Effecting Change: Master Therapists in Action   1

2   Effecting Change: The First Session   19

3   Effecting Change: The Second Session   49

4   Effecting Change: The Centrality of the Case Conceptualizations   74

5   Effecting Change: Incorporating Second Order Change   100

6   Effecting Change: Incorporating First Order Change   128

7   Effecting Change: Incorporating Third Order Change   140

8   Effecting Change: Monitoring, Evaluation, and Termination   156

9   Effecting Change: Becoming a Master Therapist   176

Bibliography   195
Index   197

FOREWORD

*Barry L. Duncan**

There seems to be a prevailing view that to be an accomplished psychotherapist one must be well versed in evidence-based treatments (EBTs) or in those models that have been shown in randomized clinical trials (RCTs) to be efficacious for different "disorders." The idea here is to make psychological interventions dummyproof, where the people—the client and the therapist—are basically irrelevant (Duncan & Reese, 2012). Just plug in the diagnosis, do the prescribed treatment, and voilà, cure or symptom amelioration occurs! This medical view of therapy is perhaps the most empirically vacuous aspect of EBTs because the treatment itself accounts for so little of outcome variance, while the client and the therapist—and their relationship—account for so much more. The fact of the matter is that psychotherapy is decidedly a relational, not medical, endeavor (Duncan, 2010), one that is wholly dependent on the participants and the quality of their interpersonal connection. This is not to say that there is anything wrong with EBTs or incorporating them in the work, but rather it is not the stuff that makes a master therapist.

So what does? First, let me remind the reader about what makes psychotherapy effective. Enter the therapist—not what method or techniques the therapist wields but rather the person of the therapist, who he or she is. Recent investigations reveal that the person of the therapist (called therapist effect) has a significantly greater effect on treatment outcomes than the treatment method and techniques used (Baldwin & Imel, 2013). In fact, therapist effect is five to eight times greater than treatment method.

Therapists vary significantly in their ability to bring about positive outcomes. The big question, of course, is what makes one therapist better than another.

---

*Barry L. Duncan, Psy.D., is a therapist, trainer, and researcher with over 17,000 hours of clinical experience. He is the director of the Heart and Soul Change Project (https://heartandsoulofchange.com). Dr. Duncan has over one-hundred publications, including fifteen books addressing systematic client feedback, consumer rights and involvement, the power of relationships, and a risk/benefit analysis of psychotropic medications. His work in consumer rights and client feedback—the Partner for Change Outcome Management System (PCOMS)—has been implemented across the United States and in twenty countries across the globe. PCOMS is included in SAMHSA's National Registry of Evidence-Based Programs and Practices.

Although we know that some therapists are better than others, there is not a lot of research about what specifically distinguishes the best from the rest. Demographics (gender, ethnicity, discipline, and experience) do not seem to matter much (Beutler et al., 2004), and although a variety of therapist interpersonal variables seem intuitively important, there is not much empirical support for any particular quality or attribute (Baldwin & Imel, 2013). So what does matter? And what distinguishes those who join the ranks of "master therapists?"

Drs. Len Sperry and Jon Carlson address these critical questions in this unique book. *How Master Therapists Work* combines a one-of-a-kind look at an entire course of therapy, an incisive integration of the literature about expert therapists and professional development, and both an inside look at the action as it unfolds by the therapist conducting the therapy (Dr. Carlson) and an outside observer (Dr. Sperry)—commentary by two master therapists. To say that these two renowned individuals bring a world of experience, scholarship, insight, and humanity to life in the pages of this book would not do this book credit. This book offers much more than that. It guides the reader into introspection about not only Dr. Carlson's gifted work with this gifted client, but also about his or her own development as well as a continued reflection about what it means to be a psychotherapist and how one can excel at it.

There is so much to like about this book. First, there is a keen attention to the client, his or her resources, resiliencies, and social contexts, those variables incidental to the treatment model, idiosyncratic to the specific client, and part of the client's life circumstances that aid in recovery despite participation in therapy (Asay & Lambert, 1999)—everything about the client that has nothing to do with us. Although hard to research because of their idiosyncratic nature, these elements are the most powerful of the common factors—the client is the engine of change (Bohart & Tallman, 2010). If we do not recruit these unique client contributions to outcome, we are inclined to fail, and Dr. Carlson does not fail. He exemplifies not only his expert ability to rally client resources to the cause of change but also a strong belief that clients have the innate ability to transcend the unthinkable and become their own best therapist. He shows that as therapists evolve toward mastery, they learn that their best ally for successful psychotherapy is not the books on their shelves touting the latest miracle cure but rather the person in the room with them right now.

Then there is the continued integration of the variable that most accounts for therapist differences, and that tends to separate a master therapist from the rest—the therapeutic alliance. The client's view of the alliance is a robust predictor of therapy outcomes. In a recent meta-analysis, Horvath, Del Re, Fluckinger, and Symonds (2011) examined 201 studies and found the alliance to account for 7.5% of the variance. Putting this into perspective, the amount of change attributable to the alliance is about seven and a half times that of specific treatment method. Dr. Carlson's insightful work and Dr. Sperry's crisp commentary adeptly answer the oft heard question about why some therapists are better than others. It is that tried and true but taken-for-granted old friend, the therapeutic alliance.

There is no mystery here. Therapists who form strong alliances across more clients get better results, period.

While there are many other things that are noteworthy (e.g., the importance of embracing uncertainty, and my favorite way of encouraging positive outcomes—the collaborative monitoring of outcome and the alliance with clients [Duncan, 2012]) and the reader can harvest the nuggets that are most meaningful to their work, the discussion that I enjoyed the most addressed what I consider to be perhaps the most difficult therapist skill to master, namely the ability to keep the session focused not only on client goals but also on making a meaningful difference in the lives of those we serve. Dr. Carlson demonstrates a masterful process of following the client's lead while simultaneously never losing sight of where the client wanted to go. He expertly balanced being empathic to the sometimes overwhelming presentation of topics and concerns with ensuring that these topics and concerns were thematically tied to the end result of making a meaningful difference in the way the client lived and experienced her life. So often, therapy meanders across a myriad of worthwhile topics and legitimate concerns but does not connect the conversation to what the client will actually do in between sessions. The unfortunate result is a therapy that represents an ongoing commentary of the client's life that never leads to any real change.

This does not mean that I agreed with everything, and herein is yet another beautiful contribution of this book. It permits the reader to sit behind the one-way mirror and watch the therapeutic process as it unfolds, allowing an ongoing contemplation of Dr. Carlson's next move and how you would have handled it similarly or differently. Moreover, the reader then can join in the collegial discussion with Drs. Sperry and Carlson, reacting to, agreeing or disagreeing with their case conceptualizations. This is great fun and will inspire your own reflections about the work to emerge.

In sum, this one-of-a-kind comprehensive look at a master at work delivers far more than the latest thoughts and insights from two leading scholars steeped in clinical experience; it effortlessly escorts the reader into his or her own therapy world, encouraging introspection about not only the work but also why we became a therapist to begin with. This book reaffirmed my belief that the odds for change when you combine a resourceful client, a strong alliance, and an authentic therapist who brings him/herself to the show, are worth betting on, certainly cause for hope, and responsible for my unswerving faith in psychotherapy as a healing endeavor.

References

Asay, T. P., & Lambert, M. J. (1999). The empirical case for the common factors in therapy. In M. A. Hubble, B. L. Duncan, & S. D. Miller (Eds.), *The heart and soul of change* (pp. 33–36). Washington, DC: American Psychological Association.

Baldwin, S. A., & Imel. Z. (2013). Therapist effects. In M. J. Lambert (Ed.). *Bergin and Garfield's Handbook of psychotherapy and behavioral change* (6th ed., pp. 258–297). New York, NY: Wiley.

Beutler, L. E., Malik, M., Alimohamed, S., Harwood, M. T., Talebi, H., Noble, S., & Wong, E. (2004). Therapist variables. In M. J. Lambert (Ed.), *Bergin and Garfield's Handbook of psychotherapy and behavioral change* (5th ed., pp. 227–306). New York, NY: Wiley.

Bohart, A., & Tallman, K. (2010). Clients: The neglected common factor. In B. Duncan, S. Miller, B. Wampold, & M. Hubble (Eds.), *The heart and soul of change: Delivering what works* (2nd ed., pp. 83–12). Washington, DC: American Psychological Association.

Duncan, B. (2010). *On becoming a better therapist*. Washington, DC: American Psychological Association.

Duncan, B. (2012). The partners for change outcome management system (PCOMS): The heart and soul of change project. *Canadian Psychology, 53*, 93–104.

Duncan, B. L., & Reese, R. J. (2012). Empirically supported treatments, evidence based treatments, and evidence based practice. In G. Stricker & T. Widiger (Eds.), *Handbook of psychology: Clinical psychology* (2nd ed., pp. 977–1023). Hoboken. NJ: John Wiley.

Horvath, A., Del Re, A. C., Flückiger, C., & Symonds, D. (2011). Alliance in individual psychotherapy. *Psychotherapy, 48*, 9–16.

PREFACE

Over the years, I (L.S.) have had the good fortune to know a number of extraordinary individuals who have made a real difference in the lives of others. These individuals were and are mental health professionals who practiced the art of psychotherapy. They practiced in a way that was considerably different than most other psychotherapists I have taught, supervised, or observed.

For instance, on several occasions I watched Dr. Richard H. Cox conduct a full interview and administer selective psychological tests within the space of an hour or so. These evaluations involved adults or adolescents who had been recently admitted to psychiatric inpatient units at a local hospital. What was most remarkable about these evaluations was that in the 20-minute ride back to his office, he would dictate a full initial evaluation report. This full-scale report included everything from presenting problem to developmental history to test results to case conceptualization and treatment plan. I was awestruck that anyone could integrate all this information from an in-depth interview and testing and then formulate it into a clinically useful report effortlessly in 20 minutes. At that time I was doing a one-year postdoctoral internship at his center, and I had a few years of clinical experiences following completion of my PhD I knew, or thought I knew, something about the practice of psychotherapy and psychological assessment. So, "How did he do it?" was a question I asked myself repeatedly over the course of that postdoctoral year. He was just as awesome in his role as psychotherapist. It seemed like all or most of his clinic clients improved. While I did not have the opportunity to observe his sessions with individuals, I was directly involved with him in conjoint couples therapy. In this conjoint setting, he and I worked therapeutically with a couple. Actually, most of the time he would work therapeutic magic with the couple while I occasionally made comments, usually agreeing with what he said. Most of the time, however, I observed the therapeutic process and the brilliant way that he facilitated that process. Supervision was also remarkable: he would listen as I reported on a case, ask a couple of focused questions, next ask me what I thought, and then help me process the case. In those days, the terms "case formulation" and "case conceptualization" were not part of many clinical discussions nor of supervision, but my mentor was teaching me, by example, the centrality of the case conceptualization in effecting change in therapy.

PREFACE

A few years later, Dr. Barry Blackwell supervised me during my fellowship in behavioral medicine. In the morning, I would do rounds with him on the consultation liaison service in the medical school's teaching hospital. I had already done complete consultations and reports on a given medical patient who was exhibiting psychiatric symptoms. He would then ask me to briefly present the case outside the patient's hospital room. Then we would go into the room and he would interact with the patient in a supportive manner and ask no more than three or four questions. After leaving the room, he would ask if I wanted to add anything more to my report. Then, he would give his conceptualization of the case and his treatment recommendations. So, I would regularly ask myself how he could mine so much information by observation and by asking only a few questions? When I did ask him directly on a couple of occasions, he would respond with "clinical intuition" or "clinical acumen." In the afternoon, in the department's outpatient clinic, he showed himself to be equally effective as a therapist. His formal training had been in behavior therapy which emphasized exposure and desensitization interventions. He practiced an eclectic form of cognitive behavior therapy during the time he supervised me. I was amazed at his "cure" rate with patients with depression and anxiety disorders. I learned how he helped these patients "face" their fears and dreaded past experiences instead of avoiding them. They not only relinquished their symptoms but also replaced their maladaptive patterns of avoidance with more adaptive patterns for dealing with life issues directly and without avoidance. In short, they experienced a transformation and no longer met diagnostic criteria. Today, this strategy continues to be a common way to achieve second order change (transformation).

If space allowed, I could also recount experiences with two others that I consider to be mentors. But, I can comment on the similarities among these. All were easily approachable, centered, and emotionally mature individuals who could very easily and comfortably relate to a wide range of clients or patients. Clinically, they worked quickly, intuitively, effortlessly, and with laser-like precision. Colleagues considered them highly proficient and effective. But, none of these mentors could articulate how exactly they went about conceptualizing cases, or why they said what they said and did what they did in working with their clients or patients. Today, these individuals would be designated as master therapists.

Several times over the past six years, I have viewed the "Psychotherapy Over Time'" DVD therapy series that features Dr. Jon Carlson and Aimee with my psychotherapy trainees. The usual format was to watch and then discuss each of the sessions of this completed six-session therapy. Each round of going through this series was different for trainees and for me. Trainees' responses were relatively similar and if there were differences among them they were minor and depended largely on their level of experience and training. So, interns were more likely to appreciate more of obvious change efforts than practicum students. For me, going through this complete therapy series several times has increased my appreciation not only for Dr. Carlson's expertise but also my recognition of the more subtle change strategies that supported the more obvious changes effected in Aimee.

Each viewing has allowed me to reflect more deeply about the operative psychodynamics and system dynamics impacting Aimee and the session dynamics that influenced therapeutic outcomes. Sometimes, I found myself approaching the viewings with a beginner's mind (Suzuki & Chadwick, 2011), a perspective not influenced by psychotherapy theory and research. This is akin to the way many trainees tend to watch therapy videos. At other times, I approached these viewings from the perspective of the psychotherapy researcher that I am by training. So, in the first instances my perspective was close to that of the beginning trainee, and I could appreciate their amazement at the therapeutic alliance that seemed to effortlessly develop and the major changes effected within Aimee and in her daily life. This way reminded me of observing the master therapists who had mentored me, particularly my wonder and awe at what they were accomplishing given my limited ability at the time to adequately understand and make sense of what I had observed.

In the second instance, however, I was able to systematically replay the sessions while reflecting on different themes across various sessions. It was in this mode that I was able to conceptualize the various operative dynamics and to identify specific strategies for effecting various orders of change. Subsequently, my discussion of this course of therapy with trainees came to life as I could more accurately explain to them various dynamics, themes, interventions, and outcomes. Following one of these discussions, I happened to be talking with Jon Carlson and broached the idea of this book that could provide readers with an understanding, appreciation, and explanation of the many changes effected in this seminal case.

What This Book is About and What It Can Mean to You

The case of Aimee is a seminal and heuristic case. It is seminal in demonstrating how psychotherapy can effect significant changes within a limited number of sessions and can sustain those changes for several years. It is heuristic in that relatively few successful therapy cases have been captured on video. This case is particularly unique in that it also contains a therapeutic conversation between Dr. Carlson and Aimee that took place some seven years after the sessions were taped. In this conversation Aimee talks about the changes she made in therapy and how these changes continue in the present. To the best of our knowledge, there are few, if any, similar cases.

This is a cutting edge book about master therapists. It addresses concerns that are increasingly important for the practice of psychotherapy today. Who are master therapists and how did they develop psychotherapeutic expertise? What do they do? And, most important, how do they go about effecting significant change in their clients?

First and foremost, this is a book about one master therapist's remarkable six-session therapy that changed a client's life, life changes that have been sustained for more than seven years. It is a casebook containing actual transcriptions of much of the therapy process. It also provides succinct, user-friendly summaries of the latest research on master therapists and psychotherapy expertise. Among all other psychotherapy books that we know, it is unique in that it contains two sets of commentaries on transcribed segments of the sessions of a complete and successful therapy.

The first commentary, by a master therapist-psychotherapy researcher, explains how these significant changes were effected from the perspective of psychotherapy research. The second commentary is by the master therapist—Dr. Carlson—who effected these changes. He explains what he was thinking and why he did what he did at key points in the therapy process. The passage of seven-plus years since the sessions were recorded provides Dr. Carlson with a most unique perspective. He can comment on specific segments of a transcribed session knowing whether his specific interventions and the therapeutic process that he fostered had long-term effectiveness or not. In this conversation Aimee reveals that not only have the changes effected in therapy been sustained, but also that she has made even more changes. Additional changes? How could this have happened? In part because she was encouraged in the course of her therapeutic work with Dr. Carlson to become her own therapist. This she did, and she has continued to grow and flourish. For many this may seem to be an extraordinary additional benefit of therapy. But for the master therapists we know, this is an expected outcome of highly effective therapy.

By now it may occur to you that master therapists differ from adequate therapists. That would be an accurate conclusion. Existing research on psychotherapy expertise and our experience with the master therapists that we know confirms this conclusion. This book offers theory and research on psychotherapy expertise, a clinical illustration of a completed, successful therapy, as well as advice and strategies on what it takes to become a more proficient therapist.

So, what specifically can the reader learn from this book? First and foremost, the reader will be directly involved in the therapy process itself, viewing a completed course of therapy with positive clinical outcomes. Trainees rarely, if ever, have the experience of talking with a master therapist about a particular case, much less sitting side-by-side with that therapist in actual therapy sessions with a specific client. Ideally, watching the DVD sessions (available from APA Books) and then reading the chapters of the book with transcriptions and commentary provides the ideal learning situation. However, reading and studying the text are sufficient, and access to the videotaped session is not essential in learning how a completed, successful therapy proceeds from first through the last session and beyond.

Here is a preview of what is to come. Chapter 1 provides a grand tour of the landscape of psychotherapy as it is practiced today. It describes expertise in general and in regard to psychotherapy. It provides a profile of master therapists and how early life experiences and professional work settings have influenced the development of their unique expertise. The text in Chapters 2–8 is centered around this extended case example. It will help you understand all the aspects of the therapeutic process and how all the components of successful therapy fit together: the therapeutic alliance; assessment of a client's change potential; clinician credibility; case conceptualization; interventions that foster first, second, and third order change; monitoring and evaluation; and termination. It sets the stage for better understanding the transcribed therapy segments and the two sets of commentaries. Chapter 9 lays out the necessary developmental tasks and strategies for progressing along the developmental trajectory of the master therapist.

One indicator of where therapists are on this developmental trajectory is their initial evaluation of a potential client like Aimee. She has a long history of neglect, abandonment, and abuse. An important clinical question is: What is her prognosis for therapy, particularly time-limited, brief therapy? Is it guarded or is it very good to excellent? Many therapists might consider the prognosis as guarded, at best. In contrast, other therapists, particularly those with high psychotherapy expertise, would have elicited information, and relied on clinical experience and intuition, to conclude that her prognosis was quite good. That was clearly Dr. Carlson's prognosis of Aimee. He quickly concluded that she would be capable of significant second order change in a six-session therapy. Whether he anticipated that she was capable and willing to make third order change during and beyond the last therapy session is something you'll have to read on to learn. His clinical acumen and intuition were the basis of his optimism and his very carefully modulated way of both supporting Aimee and challenging her to change. Considerable emotional support in the beginning with increasing encouragement and challenge to grow as the sessions evolved was one of Dr. Carlson's strategies for effecting change. Again, this is a preview of what you will discover in subsequent chapters.

In short, this book has been designed to serve as an illustration and exemplar of how highly proficient and effective therapy can be learned and practiced. It provides a high level of understanding and explanation of the various factors and strategies involved in effecting deep, enduring change. As a teaching case, it provides trainees and therapists multiple perspectives for understanding the inner and outer world of a master therapist endeavoring to effect major changes in a traumatized individual—albeit an articulate one—in a very short period of time. The first perspective for understanding and appreciating expert psychotherapy in action involves viewing the case in its entirety (on DVD). The second perspective involves carefully reading and reflecting on the case transcriptions in this book. The third perspective involves carefully reading and considering the explanations from the psychotherapy theory and research literature provided in each chapter that specifically addresses a key feature of the case. Such key features include the role of the therapeutic alliance, the centrality of the case conceptualization, and the importance of the corrective experiences and third order change in effecting long-term, enduring change. The fourth perspective involves reading the double set of commentaries in each chapter on the transcribed sessions and segments. The first commentary "explains" what is happening in the session from the perspective of related psychotherapy theory and research, while the second commentary "explains" the inner world of the therapist as Dr. Carlson shares his reflection on what he was thinking, feeling, and considering during specific transcribed segments. Presumably, as more perspectives are involved, the greater the readers' depth of understanding, appreciation, and explanation.

Our Experience with Master Therapists

For some time, I (L.S.) have been fascinated with psychotherapy expertise. The fascination can be traced to a doctoral seminar in clinical psychology that I took with Kenneth Howard, PhD, in one of my last semesters of PhD studies at Northwestern University. Among the assigned readings in the course were some recently published articles by Ken and his colleague at the University of Chicago, David Orlinsky, PhD. It was in the discussion of these articles that I first learned of the Chicago Northwestern Psychotherapy Project, which later came to be known in the history of psychotherapy research as the Chicago Northwestern Studies. I became fascinated with this research and began what became a lifetime habit of reading widely and then contributing to the psychotherapy literature. Little did I know then that I would become a collaborator with Ken on a number of clinical outcomes projects.

By the mid 1970s, Howard and Orlinsky had founded the Society for Psychotherapy Research. They also began studying the therapist's contribution to therapeutic outcomes, which came to be called the "therapist effect." A classic line in one of their papers summarized this interest in therapist effects. It concluded that successful therapeutic outcomes depended on "the right therapist doing the right thing at the right time for the right patient" (Howard, Orlinsky, & Perilstein, 1976, pp. 525–526).

For much of the 1990s I worked with Ken and Peter Brill, MD, on developing and norming clinical outcome instruments for use in inpatient and outpatient settings. The most important of these was the Compass-OP. In 1996, our book *Treatment Outcomes in Psychotherapy and Psychiatric Interventions* was published (Sperry, Brill, Howard, & Grissom, 1996). In 1997, I edited a special issue on "Treatment Outcomes in Clinical Practice" for *Psychiatric Annals* that showcased more of our recent work on application of the various Compass instruments.

My increasing involvement in core competencies and psychotherapy expertise was a natural outgrowth of Ken's work on outcomes and therapist effects. My involvement was prompted by the Psychiatry Residency Review Committee's decision to require all accredited residency training programs in the United States to incorporate competence in psychotherapy as a learning outcome for all psychiatry residents. My sixteen years on a psychiatry department faculty implementing core competency training provided me with the experience set needed to incorporate them in my current role as director of clinical training in a graduate school setting.

A brief note about my psychotherapeutic experience. My initial psychotherapy experience was in graduate psychology practicum courses beginning in 1966, and later in an internship at Chicago State Hospital—Read Mental Health Center. Over these forty-seven years I have worked with approximately 5,000 patients/clients.

While some of these involved single session evaluation in a medical-psychiatric consultation setting, many involved short-term or long-term therapy. I estimated that I have logged approximately 22,000 hours over the years in individual, group, couples, and family therapy.

I (J.C.) have earned doctoral degrees in counseling and clinical psychology as well as an advanced certificate of psychotherapy. Although I have a solid academic education, I learned most from seeing many diverse clients and then seeking answers for effective treatment protocols. From 1985 through 1993, Len Sperry served as my supervisor and provided me with a deeper appreciation of the psychotherapy process and how to be a more effective therapist.

Over the years, Jeffrey Kottler and I have been working together as partners to explore cutting edge issues in the field, whether related to clinical failures (Kottler & Carlson, 2002), seminal cases (Kottler & Carlson, 2008), creative breakthroughs (Kottler & Carlson, 2009), reciprocal influence in therapeutic relationships (Kottler & Carlson, 2005), spiritual transformations (Kottler & Carlson, 2007), indigenous healing methods (Kottler, Carlson, & Keeney, 2004), lying in therapy (Kottler & Carlson, 2010), practicing social justice (Kottler, Englar-Carlson, & Carlson, 2012), or master therapy (Kottler & Carlson, 2014). In each case, we have been interested in looking at some of the most neglected issues in the field, or at least those that dig a bit deeper into phenomena that are least understood. We have also been huge fans of the power of narratives to illuminate major themes and inspire deeper exploration of some very complex issues.

During the past dozen years, Jeffrey and I have been privileged to interview the world's most famous and prominent psychotherapists and psychotherapy theoreticians. These books have included master therapists such as Albert Ellis, Jay Haley, William Glasser, Judith Jordan, Laura Brown, and more than 100 other notable figures representing every therapeutic approach and style. In addition, I have produced 300 videos in which the field's most accomplished clinicians demonstrate their work in action and then talk about their approaches. Seeing master therapists working with real clients with real problems and being able to critique and question their approaches has had a significant impact on my therapeutic ideas and practice. Through these experiences, I have essentially modeled the innermost experiences of the century's most important contributors to the field of psychotherapy.

I was originally trained in Individual Psychology, or what is known as Adlerian psychology. I never met Alfred Adler, but it seems like I have spent much of my life getting to know him and his ideas. His approach was actually the precursor to what is now known as CBT or cognitive-behavioral therapy. For most of my professional life, I have been a devoted scholar and practitioner of Adlerian psychology in which the idea of service remains at the core (Carlson, Watts, & Maniacci, 2006; Carlson & Maniacci, 2012). This system of understanding human behavior places a strong emphasis on understanding individuals in their social context. Adler believed that all behavior has social meaning, and he equated having a high level of social interest as similar to being mentally healthy.

The German word for social interest is *gemeinschaftsgefuhl* and translates as having a commitment to community welfare as opposed to a life focus on one's own personal concerns or issues. This involves having a positive outlook on life with an interest in furthering the welfare of others. I have lived much of my professional life trying to develop social interest in the world around me. The idea of social interest fits quite nicely with the other major influence on my commitment to service and professional practice, which is the study and practice of Buddhist ideas as they may be integrated into life and work. Buddhism emphasizes showing compassion and realizing that all work is important and can serve society.

Concluding Note

We met in 1972 while in postdoctoral study at the Alfred Adler Institute in Chicago. The in-depth program was unique in that it provided advanced psychodynamic psychotherapy training similar to that found at the psychoanalytic training institutes. We both completed this training and returned to school for additional doctoral degrees in clinical psychology. We have received many awards and recognitions for our professional skills and accomplishments. Over the past forty years, we have remained close friends and colleagues and combined on many scholarly books, journal articles, book chapters, and videos related to the various aspects of psychotherapy. The connection now deepens as another generation, our sons, Jon Sperry and Matt Englar-Carlson, have careers in the same field. Psychotherapy has been central to our lives.

Our experience with master therapists is both personal and collegial. It is personal in that both of us have been peer-nominated by our colleagues with this designation. It is collegial in that we have known a number of master therapists over the years; some who are no longer among us. When we use the phrase "the master therapists we know" throughout this book, we are referring to the many inspirational male and female masters whom we have had and continue to have the pleasure of knowing.

The complete actual footage of the six sessions is available for further study and analysis under the title of *"Psychotherapy Over Time"* from the American Psychological Association. To order *"Psychotherapy Over Time,"* please contact the order department of the American Psychological Association at 800-374-2721 or visit www.apa.org/pubs/videos. We strongly urge that readers deepen their understanding and appreciation of master therapy by watching all six sessions both with and without the therapist's comments.

References

Carlson, J., Watts, R. E., & Maniacci, M. (2006). *Adlerian therapy*. Washington, DC: American Psychological Association Books.

Carlson, J., & Maniacci, M. (2012). *Alfred Adler revisited*. New York, NY: Routledge.

Howard, K., Orlinsky, D., & Perilstein, J. (1976). Contribution of therapists to patients' experiences in psychotherapy: A components of variance model for analyzing process data. *Journal of Consulting and Clinical Psychology, 44*, 520–526.
Kottler, J., & Carlson, J. (2014). *On being a master therapist: Practicing what we preach.* New York, NY: Wiley.
Kottler, J., & Carlson, J. (2002). *Bad therapy: Master therapists share their worst failures.* New York, NY: Routledge.
Kottler, J., & Carlson, J. (2008). *Their finest hour: Master therapists share their greatest success stories*, 2nd ed. Camarthan, UK: Crown House Publishers.
Kottler, J., & Carlson, J. (2005). *The mummy at the dining room table: Eminent therapists reveal their most unusual cases and what they teach us about human behavior.* San Francisco: Jossey Bass.
Kottler, J., & Carlson, J. (2005). *The client who changed me.* New York, NY: Routledge.
Kottler, J., & Carlson, J. (2007). *Moved by the spirit: Discovery and transformation in the lives of leaders.* Atascadero, California: Impact Publishers.
Kottler, J., & Carlson, J. (2009). *Creative breakthroughs: Tales of transformation and astonishment.* New York, NY: Wiley.
Kottler, J., & Carlson, J. (2010). *Duped: Lies and deception in psychotherapy.* New York, NY: Routledge.
Kottler, J., Englar-Carlson, M., & Carlson, J. (2012). *Helping beyond the fifty minute hour.* New York, NY: Routledge
Kottler, J., Carlson, J., & Keeney, B. (2004). *The American shaman: An odyssey of global healing traditions.* New York, NY: Routledge.
Sperry, l., Brill, P., Howard, K., & Grissom, G. (1996). *Treatment outcomes in psychotherapy and psychiatric interventions.* New York, NY: Brunner/Mazel.
Suzuki, S., & Chadwick, D. (2011). *Zen mind, beginner's mind.* Boston, MA: Shambhala.

1
EFFECTING CHANGE: MASTER THERAPISTS IN ACTION

In the past decade, magazine articles and *New York Times* best sellers like *Outliers* (Gladwell, 2008) and *Talent Is Overrated* (Colvin, 2008) have popularized research on expertise across various professions (Ericsson, Charness, Feltovich, & Hoffman, 2006; Ericsson & Lehmann, 1996). This focus on expertise is beginning to affect the profession and practice of psychotherapy. In the past few years, there is increasing interest about expertise and mastery in psychotherapy among therapists, researchers, academics, supervisors, students, and trainees. Commonly asked questions about expertise and mastery in psychotherapy abound: What is a master therapist? How do master therapists work (i.e., perform therapy)? How does one become a master therapist? This book addresses all three questions. This chapter begins the discussion of the first two questions, and Chapter 9 addresses the third question. More specifically, this chapter starts by discussing the context in which psychotherapy is currently practiced, which has sparked an interest in psychotherapy expertise and master therapists. Next, a description and a profile of master therapists are given. Then, the chapter begins the discussion of how master therapists work, continuing in subsequent chapters.

The Context of Psychotherapy Practice Today

Why is there such an interest in psychotherapy expertise and master therapists? One needs some knowledge of the context of psychotherapy practice today to more fully understand and appreciate the answer to this question. The past decade has witnessed a remarkable evolution in psychotherapy research and practice. A number of factors explain this evolution, with accountability being the most important. In the current era of accountability, the practice of psychotherapy has become increasingly focused, clinically effective, cost-effective, monitored, and evidence based. Evidence-based practice (EBP) is defined as "the integration of best research evidence with clinical expertise and patient values" (Institute of Medicine, 2001, p. 147). EBP is broader than the concept of empirically supported treatment (described below) in that it explicitly considers client values and clinical expertise (i.e., using clinical skills and past experience to rapidly identify the client's health status, diagnosis, risks and benefits, and personal values and expectations). Presumably, then, competent and well-informed therapists would develop and maintain enhanced therapeutic alliances; use best practices information; implement treatment tailored to match client diagnoses, need, and preferences; and monitor clinical outcomes (DeLeon, 2003).

This section overviews five elements that reflect current psychotherapy theory, research, and practice, and their evolution: outcomes, treatments, therapeutic alliance, and client and therapist factors. Competency and expertise are key therapist factors.

Outcomes

Therapeutic or treatment outcomes have become the coin of the realm in psychotherapy today. While therapeutic processes remain important, the culture of accountability and the related EBP movement have made treatment outcomes the central consideration in psychotherapy practice. Outcomes refer to the effects or end points of specific interventions or therapeutic processes. Two types of outcomes can be distinguished: immediate or formative outcomes and final or posttreatment outcomes. Outcomes can be assessed in a pretreatment and posttreatment manner or in an ongoing manner (i.e., by monitoring outcomes at each session). Research points to better outcomes when therapists engage in ongoing monitoring than with pre-post assessment or no formal assessment of outcomes (Duncan, 2012; Lambert et al., 2003; Lambert & Shimokawa, 2011).

Treatment

Empirically supported treatments (ESTs) are interventions for which empirical research has provided evidence of their effectiveness. Often, these are manual-based treatments. As health care costs were spiraling upward, clinician practice patterns were portrayed as the basic cause of waste, inefficiency, and escalating costs. As a result, health care systems and managed care plans moved to standardize care and specify guidelines for the provision of that care. The expectation was that clinicians—including psychotherapists—would provide only encounter-based, as opposed to relationship-based, services and be able to demonstrate that these services were evidence based and cost-effective. This was the beginning of what has been called the EST movement in psychotherapy (Reed, McLauglin, & Newman, 2002). While there is controversy about the use of ESTs, particularly those that are manual based, there is a growing consensus that EBP treatments are useful and necessary.

Therapeutic Alliance

The therapeutic relationship remains the single most important variable in psychotherapy outcome research. An early meta-analysis by Lambert (1992) found that specific treatments or techniques accounted for no more than 15% of the variance in therapy outcomes. On the other hand, the therapy relationship and factors common to different therapies accounted for 30% of the variance in therapy outcomes. Therapeutic alliance is a type of therapeutic relationship that encompasses three factors: the therapeutic bond between client and therapist, the agreed-on goals of treatment, and an agreement about methods to achieve that goal or goals. It is described in more detail in Chapter 2. The Lambert meta-analysis and other data became a rallying cry for proponents of the therapeutic relationship against proponents of ESTs. For years, this "either-or" battle raged until an increasing acceptance emerged that both treatments and relationships are operative in treatment outcomes.

Client

However, this "both-and" understanding would soon be found to be shortsighted. Another meta-analysis of the elements accounting for psychotherapy change (Lambert & Barley, 2001) found that the largest element accounting for change (40%) was due to extratherapeutic factors, also referred to as "client resources" or "client." While this finding was essentially the same as previously reported (Lambert, 1992), its significance had been underplayed. The client element includes several factors such as motivation and readiness for change, capacity for establishing and maintaining relationships, access to treatment, social support system, and other nondiagnostic factors. Chapter 2 describes client resources in detail.

Therapist

As useful as the Lambert research (1992) has been in understanding the elements contributing to psychotherapy outcomes, there was no direct consideration of the role of the therapist. It has long been observed that some therapists are much more effective than others (Orlinsky et al., 1999). For years, terms like "master therapist" and "supershrink" have been used to describe the expertise of such therapists. Increasingly, research demonstrates that therapist factors positively affect the client, the therapeutic alliance, and the implementation of treatment interventions, resulting in improved clinical outcomes. This and the remaining chapters of this book continue this discussion of therapist factors, also called the "therapist effect."

There has also been a growing awareness among therapists throughout the world (Orlinsky, Botermans, & Ronnestad, 2001) that psychotherapy outcomes are influenced as much or more by the therapist providing the therapy as by the therapeutic approach. Outcomes research has likewise demonstrated the influence of therapist effects on treatment outcomes (Crits-Christoph et al., 1991; Teyber & McClure, 2000; Wampold, 2001). In commenting on the results of his meta-analysis, Wampold (2001) concluded that "the particular treatment that the therapist delivers does not affect outcomes . . . therapists within treatment account for a large proportion of the variance" (p. 202). In other words, it is the therapist and not the treatment that influences the amount of therapeutic change that occurs. Research also finds that master therapists are better at effecting change than are less proficient therapists (Orlinsky et al., 2001; Orlinsky & Ronnestad, 2005). In short, this interest in expertise and the emphasis on psychotherapy outcomes is reflected in the increasing number of research studies, articles, books, and workshops on master therapists. This book clearly reflects this trend.

In addition to the focus on these five factors is the role of competencies. Competency is the current *zeitgeist* in psychotherapy training. Competency represents a paradigm shift in psychotherapy training, and, not surprisingly, has affected and will continue to affect psychotherapy practice. Requirement standards are beginning to be replaced with competency standards, core competencies are replacing core curriculums, and competency-based licensure is on the horizon. The shift to psychotherapy competency has also become an accreditation standard in psychiatry training programs that now requires that trainees demonstrate competency in three psychotherapy approaches. Training programs in clinical psychology programs have solidly embraced competencies, and marital and family therapy and professional counseling programs are poised to follow suit. Because competencies involve knowledge, skill, and attitudinal components, competency-based education is quite different from how psychotherapy previously had been taught, learned, and evaluated.

Six core psychotherapy competencies have been described: (a) articulate a conceptual framework for psychotherapy practice, (b) develop and maintain an effective therapeutic alliance, (c) develop an integrative case conceptualization and treatment plan based on an integrative assessment, (d) implement tailored interventions, (e) monitor treatment progress and outcomes and plan for termination process, and (f) practice in a culturally sensitive and ethically sensitive manner (Sperry, 2010a, 2010b). In our experience, master therapists demonstrate high levels of these competencies.

Profile of the Master Therapist

The designation "master" refers to one who teaches or practices with a high level of expertise or proficiency. Such expertise reflects mastery in practice that involves "an encompassing, inventive, procedural kind of knowledge that can be modeled impressively for others or used as a basis for supervisory shaping of the practice of others" (Orlinsky, 1999, p. 13). The term "master therapist" is used in the psychotherapy literature to describe therapists who are considered to be "the best of the best" among fellow therapists with regard to psychotherapeutic expertise (Jennings & Skovholt, 1999). Psychotherapeutic expertise can be defined as knowing "what happens moment-by-moment during therapy sessions . . . precision, subtlety, and finesse in therapeutic work . . . ability to guide the development of other therapists" (Orlinsky et al., 1999, p. 211).

Because the study of expertise in psychotherapists is a relatively recent undertaking, there are few profiles of master therapists. Jennings and Skovholt (1999) have proposed a model of expertise for master therapists that specifically addresses three domains of knowledge—cognitive, emotional, and relational— vital to the success or failure of therapists. This model assumes that one must develop expertise in all three areas to reach the level of master therapist. Whereas other expertise models emphasize the cognitive domain, the three-domains model is one of the first therapist expertise models to highlight the role of the emotional or relational domains in the development of expertise. As such, it represents a necessary first step in identifying the characteristics of master therapists and the developmental pathways by which psychotherapists can achieve mastery.

Key Characteristics

Over the past three decades, seminal qualitative research has been undertaken to identify the characteristics and developmental journey of master therapists. Several studies were done in the United States, Canada, Korea, Singapore, and Japan (Jennings & Skovholt, 1999; Jennings, Skovholt, Goh, & Lian, 2013; Skovholt & Jennings, 2004). The initial research project identified nine key personality characteristics (cognitive, emotional, and relational) among the 10 peer-nominated master therapists studied (Jennings & Skovholt, 1999). It found that therapeutic mastery involves considerably more than accumulated experience doing therapy. Rather, mastery involves an ongoing effort in improving skills and competencies, gaining new knowledge, and remaining open to experience and others' feedback. This study provides further support for the notion that relationship skills and therapeutic alliance form the cornerstone for therapeutic excellence. Unfortunately, the study did not compare master therapists with a sample of beginning and lesser experienced therapists.

The following 11 characteristics represent a prototype of the ideal therapist (Jennings & Skovholt, 1999; Jennings et al., 2013). "Each therapist possesses his or her own unique constellation of gifts, characteristics, and skills that need to be cultivated and leveraged in order for that individual to become the best therapist possible" (Jennings et al., p. 237). These studies suggest that master therapists possess many, if not all, of these characteristics.

Master Therapists Are Voracious Learners

Continuous professional development is a hallmark of these therapists. To say they are committed to lifelong learning is an understatement. They are enthusiastic learners who not only want to fully understand their clients but also want to know as much as they can about their craft. So, they continually read new literature in the field, are curious about the history of the field, and stay current with the newest developments, techniques, and studies.

Master Therapists Use Their Accumulated Experiences

These therapists, with a average of 29.5 years of professional experience, draw on their rich experience with similar problems These experiences seem to have increased their depth and competence as persons and psychotherapists. Like others, they have experienced personal and family problems and professional doubts. Unlike some, these therapists have learned to resolve them. Furthermore, they are not afraid to acknowledge these personal experiences and draw from them to better understand and assist their clients.

Master Therapists Value Cognitive Complexity and Ambiguity

These therapists do not simply tolerate complexity and ambiguity; they seek it. They understand that not everything in the human realm follows linear thinking and logic. Rather, they can understand and appreciate the complexity and ambiguity of subjective emotional experiences. From this deep and broadened understanding, they are able to more effectively help their clients. Cognitive complexity is described in detail later in this chapter.

Master Therapists Have Emotional Receptivity

These therapists are emotionally open, self-aware, reflective, nondefensive and seek feedback. This openness includes the capacity to accept any feelings that the client brings up, as well as the capacity to recognize and share their own emotional reactions. Such therapists are likely to engage in their own personal therapy, seek supervision, and involve themselves in peer consultation to receive feedback to increase their awareness of themselves and others. They value being in touch with their feelings, deal with them constructively, and communicate them effectively.

Master Therapists Are Healthy and Nurture Their Own Emotional Well-being

These therapists are emotionally healthy and mature. They strive to act congruently in their personal and professional lives. They view themselves as honest, authentic, and congruent. Like others, they experience emotional distress and subjective discomfort but are able to process their problems and are able to nurture their own emotional and spiritual well-being. They can continue to meet the emotional needs of others without burnout because they have learned how to care for themselves and meet their own needs. As a result, they are excellent at modeling emotional well-being.

Master Therapists Are Aware of How Their Emotional Health Affects Their Work

These therapists are keenly aware of how their own emotional well-being affects others, particularly in the context of psychotherapy. They are able to recognize and use transference and countertransference reactions as a normal process in therapy. They deal with their own countertransference issues by working through them in their own psychotherapy or by seeking consultation with senior colleagues. They are also very aware of personal and professional boundaries and are careful to avoid boundary violations and unnecessary boundary crossings.

Master Therapists Possess Highly Developed Relationship Skills

These therapists have developed the requisite relational skills of listening, responding, negotiating, and caring for others, often from an early age in their family of origin. This means when they formally begin therapy training they have a 10- to 15-year or greater head start over others on developing the relational skills necessary for becoming an effective therapist. In fact, master therapists-to-be often impress clinical faculty and supervisors as "natural-born therapists." These already learned relational skills are then honed and extended over the course of their formal therapy training. Besides using these highly developed skills with clients, these skills are valuable in communicating with family members, colleagues, administrators, and others.

Master Therapists Cultivate Strong Working Alliances

These therapists hold a number of positive beliefs about human nature that help in building strong therapeutic alliances. They firmly believe in the value of developing and maintaining a strong therapeutic alliance. They also believe in their clients' capacity to heal and change and in their clients' right to self-determination. It appears that these beliefs somehow instill hope and activate clients' internal resources and sense of self-efficacy.

Master Therapists Excel in Using Their Exceptional Therapy Skills

These therapists also have the capacity to engage clients fully in the treatment process. Besides providing support and encouragement, they can therapeutically challenge clients when necessary. They are able to carefully and effectively address difficult and painful issues of their clients. Because of their finely honed therapeutic skills, the strength of their character, and a personal power, they can face highly sensitive and troublesome issues with relative ease.

Master Therapists Trust Their Clients

Master therapists were found to implicitly trust that their clients have sufficient internal resources to make positive change. This finding reflects their positive view of human nature and is related to themes that emphasize the importance of relationships, deep acceptance of self, and their intense desire to learn and grow. This new theme has emerged in more recent research (Ronnestad & Skovholt, 2013)

Master Therapists Are Culturally Competent

The most recent research on master therapists has underscored the importance of therapists knowing about the cultural background and possessing the requisite cultural competencies to assist clients in effecting change in their lives. These studies demonstrate how master therapists used their cultural knowledge and awareness, conceptual framework, understanding of cultural barriers, and culturally sensitive interventions—or referral for such interventions—to provide services to culturally diverse populations (Ronnestad & Skovholt, 2013).

Early Life Experiences

What about the early personal lives of master therapists? Intensive interviews with these therapists revealed some common themes (Ronnestad & Skovholt, 2013; Skovholt & Jennings, 2004). First, most were attuned to human relations from an early age, as was their understanding of themselves and others. Some grew up in demanding, achievement-oriented families and received conditional love from their parents. These experiences were viewed as influencing their initial "selection of a theoretical orientation, definition of work role, choice of therapeutic style and focus, attitudes toward colleagues, hardship experiences, and ways of coping in practice" (Ronnestad & Skovholt, 2013, pp. 129–130).

While many had experienced significant distress and suffering, it was not overwhelming. Their response to this distress was not to distance themselves from human relations in early life. Nor did it lead to career choices in which they distanced themselves from others. Such distancing is not uncommon in those who gravitate toward science, mathematics, engineering, computer science, or other high-tech careers. Instead, master therapists gravitated toward psychotherapy, a high-touch career.

The research interviews also found that master therapists took on or were given the family role of helper for others. Their early life experiences seemed to have encouraged the development of a caring attitude, helping skills, and a relatively high degree of psychological resiliency that they carried forward into their adult lives. Furthermore, their experience of early suffering appears to have made it easier for them to relate to the suffering of clients. In fact, these master therapists appear to have been less frightened than those with other developmental histories. In short, these therapists considered human suffering to be a positive part of a deep and meaningful life.

> Overall, the early developmental years seemed to provide a laboratory for intensive leaning about human life and early therapist development.

A form of significant but not overwhelming stress was present. The person took on the role of helper or at least acute observer of human behavior, and there was an approach that involved immersion in human feelings rather than distancing and cutoff. Such an early laboratory has a balance between support and challenge within the arena of understanding others and helping others. A good support/challenge balance is one way of conceptualizing optimal conditions for growth (Skovholt & Jennings, 2004, p. 129).

Cognitive Complexity, Metacommunication, and Self-Reflection

It was already noted that cognitive complexity is a central element in the expertise literature (Ericsson & Lehmann, 1996) and a key characteristic of master therapists (Jennings & Skovholt, 1999). Because of its importance in how master therapists work, particularly in how they identify patterns and conceptualize cases, this section describes cognitive complexity and related factors of metacommunication, self-reflection, and self-awareness in more detail.

Cognitive complexity has been defined as "the ability to absorb, integrate and make use of multiple perspectives" (Granello, 2010, p. 92). It tends to be domain specific, which means an individual may be able to think more complexly about some topics than about others. Experts across various domains can be distinguished from novices in the way they deconstruct problems and in the types of information they consider in problem solving (Ericsson & Lehmann. 1996). For example, experts in music, chess, and physics remember more and perform better than novices largely because they can "chunk" their specialized knowledge into meaningful patterns. They also easily differentiate relevant from irrelevant information in contrast to novices, who tend to base their problem-solving approaches on concrete, immaterial details (Chi, Glaser, & Farr, 1988; Jennings, Hanson, Skovholt, & Grier, 2005). Experts also differ by the organization and structure of their knowledge, depth of their problem formulations, quality of their mental models, efficiency of their problem-solving procedures, perception of patterns in their realm of expertise, automaticity and speed of their task performance, their superior memory for domain-specific information, and their ability to engage in metacognition about task performance (Jennings et al., 2005).

Metacognition is a central component of cognitive complexity and is important in promoting expertise. Metacognition refers to thinking about one's thoughts, including what one knows, what one is doing, and one's cognitive and affective state (Owen & Lindley, 2010).

Like cognitive complexity, metacognition is vital to the development of expertise in psychotherapy. Unlike master therapists, trainees and beginning therapists develop inadequate conceptual maps of client issues, leading them to premature, and often inaccurate, problem formulations and ill-advised advice (Jennings et al., 2013). Conversely, the ability to recognize complex patterns and develop high-quality case conceptualizations reflects high levels of cognitive complexity and metacognition. We have noted that the quality and ease with which trainees and beginning therapists are able to identify maladaptive patterns and conceptualize cases are related to the complexity of their thinking and capacity for metacommunication.

Continuous self-reflection and self-awareness also are critical to optimal therapeutic relationships and professional development (Ronnestad & Skovholt, 2013; Skovholt & Jennings, 2004). Research on master therapists demonstrates the importance of these factors that involve therapists' understanding of their own emotional needs and understanding of unfinished business, knowing the boundaries of their competence, viewing themselves as change agents, using their power in therapeutic settings, and recognizing their own capacity for relationships (Jennings et al., 2013). Training in and the practice of self-reflection provide a useful strategy for increasing both cognitive complexity and metacommunication. Chapter 9 further discusses self-reflection and other strategies for becoming a more proficient therapist.

Influence of Situational Factors on Therapist Development

So far, all of the findings presented on master therapists and psychotherapist development have reflected qualitative studies (Skovholt & Jennings, 2004). By contrast, considerable quantitative data have been, and continue to be, collected on therapist development as part of the Society for Psychotherapy Research/Collaborative Research Network (SCR/CRN) studies (Orlinsky & Ronnestad, 2005). The first of these studies of 5000 therapists worldwide is reported in Orlinsky and Ronnestad's book, *How Psychotherapists Develop: A Study of Therapeutic Work and Professional Growth* (2005). Currently, the data set now includes some 11,000 therapists. This first study identifies the factors that are involved in either promoting or retarding the development of a psychotherapist. Because it considers situational factors in the therapist's work setting, the SCR/CRN study nicely complements the qualitative research on psychotherapist development that does not consider the influence of situational factors.

Three dimensions of work involvement experiences by therapists were identified in the SCR/CRN study: healing involvement, stressful involvement, and controlling involvement (Orlinsky & Ronnestad, 2005). Healing involvement and stressful involvement were found to underlie all therapists' experience of their therapeutic work. Quantitative data were collected and analyzed for 5000 therapists worldwide and reported in Orlinsky and Ronnestad (2005). It was found that all therapists concurrently experienced some level of healing involvement and some level of stressful involvement.

Healing involvement is defined by indicators of the therapist's sense of current skillfulness in their work; minimal difficulties in practice; reliance on constructive coping strategies when difficulties occur; sense of being personally invested in genuine, affirmative, and receptive relationships with clients; experiencing a feeling of "flow" in therapy sessions; and an overall sense of therapeutic efficacy. Stressful involvement is defined by indicators of multiple difficulties in work practice. In contrast to healing involvement factors, stress involvement factors were primarily situational in nature. These included high caseload, little or no support or satisfaction, and stressful work settings like an agency or a hospital with no involvement in private practice. It also included using therapeutically unconstructive coping strategies such as blaming or avoidance or experiencing in-session feelings of boredom and anxiety. Stressful involvements were found to be greater for the therapist who experienced little or no support in their primary work setting and seemed to be trapped in a cycle of demoralization.

Four practice patterns reflected the extent of healing and stressful involvements experienced by therapists. The greater majority of therapists—over 50%—were in settings characterized by high healing involvement and low stressful involvement. Some 10% of therapists were in work situations characterized by low healing involvement and high stressful involvement. The SCR/CRN study provides convincing evidence that situational factors can either promote psychotherapist growth or foster stagnation.

How Master Therapists Work

At this point, there is not yet definitive research on exactly how master therapists effect deep and lasting change in clients. However, there has been increasing theoretical speculation as well as some qualitative and quantitative research directed at identifying the manner in which master therapists function in contrast to less expert therapists. As early as 1980, Marvin Goldfried, PhD, identified four principles of change and ways in which highly effectively therapists function (Goldfried, 1980). Some 42 years later, based on his and others' research, he remains convinced that these four principles are the defining indicators of how master therapists work (Goldfried, 2012). These four indicators are (a) enhance the therapeutic alliance, (b) enhance positive expectations and client motivation, (c) increase client awareness, and (d) facilitate corrective experiences. Based on observation of the master therapists that we know, we would add two additional indicators: (e) identify patterns and focus treatment and (f) facilitate first, second, and third order change. This section describes all six indicators.

Enhance the Therapeutic Alliance

The therapeutic alliance is the bond between the client and therapist as well as a mutual agreement on the goals of therapy and the methods of achieving them. Effective therapy is associated with a productive therapeutic alliance in which the clients trust that their therapist is competent and interested in their well-being. Therapeutic alliances vary from client to client, such that the therapist may rather easily develop a bond with a motivated client or may exert considerable effort and clinical skills in developing and maintaining an effective alliance with an unmotivated or defiant client. The therapist's competence and experience in enhancing the therapeutic alliance are reflected in the outcomes of therapy as effective therapy is associated with a productive therapeutic alliance. Enhancing the therapeutic alliance not only fosters client involvement in therapy but also encourages the client's willingness to engage in the oftentimes difficult and painful process of change (Goldfried, 2012). Chapter 2 further describes and illustrates the critical importance of the therapeutic alliance.

Enhance Positive Expectations and Client Motivation

Clients entering therapy need a reasonable expectation that therapy can help them and have some motivation for change if therapy is to work. Both are essential prerequisites for therapeutic change to occur. Several factors can increase or decrease both of these factors. Talking to a friend who has experienced therapeutic change or reading about the effectiveness of therapy for panic attacks, for example, can increase both expectation and motivation. Thereafter, if one experiences a symptom like panic attacks or worry, that individual is more likely to be motivated to change than if an acting-out adolescent is sent to therapy by his parents. When the expectation and motivation are low, the therapist's immediate task is to enhance or increase both of these essential prerequisites for change (Goldfried, 2012). Not surprisingly, the master therapists we know excel at this task. Whether they use motivational interviewing or other interventions to increase a client's motivation and readiness for change and the expectation that therapy will be effective, these therapists also increase their clinician credibility in the process.

Increase Client Awareness

Another prerequisite for therapeutic change is increasing clients' awareness. Irrespective of the therapeutic orientation, awareness is needed for change to be effected. Granted, the kind and degree of awareness may differ depending on the client personality and the nature of the presenting problem.

> Some clients may be unaware of how their thinking is influencing their feelings, others may be unaware of how their emotional reaction results in behavior, and still others how their behavior negatively impacts on others. Thus, individuals who are unaware of their anger, and also their tendency to withdraw when angry be unaware of how this emotion-action links adversely affects their relationships with others (Goldfried, 2012, p. 20).

Increasing client awareness involves several therapeutic considerations such as time, frequency, and nature of the thoughts, feelings, and behaviors. A clear and accurate case conceptualization can identify the operative dynamics and determinants of the case and provide the therapist with the basis for assisting clients to become more aware of the factors influencing their life.

Facilitate Corrective Experiences

Often, deep and enduring change requires more than insight or simple behavior change. It can and often requires a corrective experience. Corrective experiences are those in which the individual experiences an event or a relationship in a different and unexpected way. They are not just ordinary, helpful events in therapy but usually events that disconfirm past negative experiences and have a profound effect (Castonguay & Hill, 2012). Corrective experiences represent "second order change" and play a central role in the transformative processes of various psychotherapy approaches. For such transformation to occur, clients must "take the risk of behaving differently, often in the presence of some skepticism and apprehension. By experiencing a positive outcome, thinking (e.g., expectations that something bad with happen) and emotion (e.g., anxiety) will start to change as well" (Goldfried, 2012, pp. 20–21). One clear indicator that a corrective emotional, cognitive, or relational experience has occurred is "when clients report a between-session experience with the tone of surprise in their voice—either because they behaved in a way that was different for them or because of the unexpected positive consequences that followed what they did. At other times, the (corrective experience) may result from ongoing interaction with a supportive and affirming therapist" (Goldfried, 2012, p. 21). Master therapists we know are able to easily facilitate corrective experiences. Chapter 3 further describes and illustrates the critical importance of the corrective experiences in effecting therapeutic change.

Identify Patterns and Focus Treatment

A pattern is a succinct description of a client's characteristic way of perceiving, thinking, and responding (Sperry, 2010b). Patterns can be adaptive or maladaptive. An adaptive pattern reflects a personality style that is flexible, appropriate, and effective and is reflective of personal and interpersonal competence. In contrast, a maladaptive pattern tends to be inflexible, ineffective, and inappropriate and typically causes symptoms, impairment in personal and relational functioning, and chronic dissatisfaction. Expert researchers have identified pattern recognition as a useful marker in distinguishing experts from novices (Chi et al., 1988). They note that experts are consistently able to identify larger, more complex, and more meaningful patterns in their chosen domain than are novices. They tend to accomplish this quickly, accurately, and effortlessly. In the domain of psychotherapy, this translates to mean that master therapists are able to identify maladaptive patterns in clients more quickly, accurately, and effortlessly than do trainees. This capacity for complex pattern recognition is not surprising given the thousands of hours and extensive experience needed to develop this expertise (Ericsson et al., 2006).

Patterns are the heart of case conceptualizations for master therapists. An accurate and focused case conceptualization is a prerequisite for planning, guiding, and effecting change (Sperry & Sperry, 2012). For many therapists, conceptualizing a case may take one or two sessions and is based on eliciting and reviewing considerable case information. In contrast, master therapists typically conceptualize cases early during their initial evaluation interview and base it on recognition of patterns. They test out this conceptualization as they continue their inquiry and modify it, if necessary. Accordingly, the conceptualization process is quick and intuitive, while for the trainee and beginning therapist the process tends to be much slower and more deliberate (Sperry & Sperry, 2012).

Treatment focus provides directionality to treatment and aims at replacing a maladaptive pattern with a more adaptive pattern (Sperry, 2010b). It also serves as a stabilizing force in maintaining a focus on change. The capacity to track a treatment focus is associated with positive treatment outcomes. Not surprisingly, master therapists excel at establishing and maintaining a productive treatment focus. Chapter 4 further describes and illustrates the case conceptualization process. It emphasizes the critical importance of pattern recognition and treatment focus.

Facilitate First, Second, and Third Order Change

There are a number of strategies available for dealing with life concerns. These include career counseling, crisis counseling, personal counseling, coaching, case management, and psychotherapy. Presumably, psychotherapy is a primary strategy that is designed to effect deep and enduring change. To fully appreciate the impact of psychotherapy, it is useful to conceptualize change and the change process in terms of orders of change. Three orders of change have been identified (Good & Beitman, 2006). In first order change, clients are assisted in making small changes, reducing symptoms, or achieving stability. Generally speaking, career counseling, crisis counseling, personal counseling, coaching, and case management can assist a client in achieving either symptom relief or resolution of a current life problem. They effect stability but not transformation of the personality. In second order change, clients are assisted in changing a maladaptive pattern to a more adaptive pattern. This order of change is transformative (Fraser & Solovey, 2007). In third order change, clients change patterns on their own without the assistance of a therapist. In essence, clients become their own therapists. Deep, lasting change is not possible with first order change. Rather, such change is the domain of second and third order change. Whether they are familiar with language of the orders of change, the master therapists we know are experts in effecting all three orders of change.

Dr. Carlson's Commentary

"Mastery is not a function of genius or talent but a function of time and intense focus applied to a particular field of knowledge" (Greene, 2012, p. 269).

I have been engaged in counseling and psychotherapy for more than 45 years. This field has become my passion, calling, and life's task. I have studied by reading books and journals, attending classes and workshops, participating in professional activities, and watching masters work. I have also written books and articles, conducted research, edited journals and books, created many training videos, and received many awards and recognitions. I have been immersed in the field of psychotherapy.

I have never considered what I do to be work. I am so passionate about this field that I spend parts of everyday engaged in some aspect of psychotherapy. I don't want the reader to think that it is the only thing that I do but it is a part of most of what I do. My wife, Laura, and I have been married for 45 years and have five grown children and five grandchildren. We are close to our families and very engaged with our dogs, Huxley and Harper. We have many friends and a wide range of interests including going to movies and plays, spending time at our cabin in northern Wisconsin, all kinds of sports and outdoor activities, and reading widely including fiction and mysteries. We love new experiences and cultures and have been fortunate enough to have traveled extensively.

I have worked as a school counselor, school psychologist, university professor, author, editor, and film producer and even spent four seasons as the head coach of a university cross country team. All of my work experiences involved helping people to grow and change. Each of the work and life experiences added to the depth of who I am as a person.

I have earned doctorates in counseling and clinical psychology and boards in couple and family work. I also received a certificate of psychotherapy which allows me to be a psychoanalyst. I have written about and received advanced training in such topics as parenting, working with children and teens, international psychology, meditation and Eastern religions, spirituality, sports, hypnosis, couples, families, sex therapy, culture, and social justice.

I have had the good fortunate to have had many mentors and teachers. Some of my teachers and mentors were in my formal training, but I learned so much more from informal training. I learned through modeling others by watching hundreds of counseling sessions. Some of these were live, while others were audio and videotaped sessions. Dr. Sperry provided me with formal supervision for eight years including one year of a postdoctoral internship.

To be a master therapist is a journey that is different for each of us. It must be a passion. It involves a lot of work and practice. I have over 60,000 clinical hours of psychotherapy practice. It also requires the ability to take feedback and use it to grow. Robert Greene (2012) sees the path to mastery as involving a long and diverse apprenticeship. I hope that through my experiences and training you can see the variety of activities that went into building my version of master therapy. The formal trainings, the informal experiences, and the balanced life are needed to provide high-quality therapy to others. I deeply resonate with the many characteristics highlighted in this chapter and have unconsciously discovered them without the benefit of a single guide or map. I wish I would have had this type of guidance as I struggled through many years wondering what I was doing and if I was really any good at therapy. There was some interesting research that was done a few years ago in which psychotherapists were asked to rank themselves against all others therapists and almost all ranked themselves above average. Psychotherapists regularly overestimate their influence and effectiveness compared with external ratings and client ratings.

Concluding Comment

This chapter began with three questions: What is a master therapist? How do master therapists work (i.e., perform therapy)? and How does one become a master therapist? The second section of the chapter addressed the first question about the profile and characteristics of master therapists. The master therapist studies reported in this chapter provide a useful profile of these extraordinarily effective therapists. Basically, master therapists possess most of the following characteristics. They are voracious learners; draw extensively from accumulated experience; value cognitive complexity; are emotionally receptive and nondefensive; are mentally healthy and mature individuals who attend to their own emotional well-being; are aware of how their emotional health affects work quality; possess strong relationship skills and are experts at using those skills in therapy; trust their clients; are culturally competent; and believe that the foundation for therapeutic change is a strong therapeutic alliance. Finally, they trained and worked in settings that facilitated healing involvement and minimized stressful involvement.

The third section of this chapter addressed the second question about how master therapists work. We provided six ways in which master therapists work that differentiates them from less proficient therapists. Basically, master therapists enhance the therapeutic alliance, enhance positive expectations and client motivation, increase client awareness, facilitate corrective experiences, identify patterns and focus treatment, and then facilitate first, second, and third order change. Chapter 5 further describes and illustrates the critical importance of second order change and the process of effecting deep and enduring change. Chapter 6 describes and illustrates the role of first order change, while Chapter 7 emphasizes the role of third order change in effecting change within therapy as well as additional change post-therapy. The third question is taken up in Chapter 9.

References

Castonguay, L., & Hill. C. (Eds.). *Transformation in psychotherapy: Corrective experiences across cognitive-behavioral, humanistic, and psychodynamics approaches*. Washington, DC: American Psychological Association.

Chi, M., Glaser, R., &. Farr, M. (Eds.). (1988). *The nature of expertise*. Hillsdale, NJ: Erlbaum.

Colvin, G. (2008). *Talent is overrated: What really separates world-class performers from everybody else*. New York, NY: Portfolio.

Crits-Christoph, P., Baranackie, K., Kurcias, J., Beck, A. T., Carroll, K., Perry, K., et al. (1991). Meta-analysis of therapist effects in psychotherapy outcome studies. *Psychotherapy Research, 1*, 81–91.

DeLeon, P. H. (2003). Remembering our fundamental societal mission. *Public Service Psychology, 28*, 13.

Duncan, B. (2012). The partners for change outcome management system (PCOMS): The heart and soul of change project. *Canadian Psychology, 53*, 93–104.

Ericsson, K. A., Charness, N., Feltovich, P., & Hoffman, R. (Eds.). (2006). *The Cambridge handbook of expertise and expert performance*. New York, NY: Cambridge University Press.

Ericsson, K. A., & Lehmann. A. C, (1996). Expert and exceptional performance: Evidence of maximal adaptation to task constraints. *Annual Review of Psychology, 47*, 273–305.

Fraser, J., & Solovey, A. (2007). *Second-order change in psychotherapy: The golden thread that unifies effective treatments*. Washington, DC: American Psychological Association.

Gladwell, M. (2008). *Outliers: The story of success*. New York, NY: Little, Brown.

Goldfried, M. (1980). Toward the delineation of therapeutic change principles. *American Psychologist, 35*, 991–999.

Goldfried, M. (2012). The corrective experiences: A core principle for therapeutic change. In L. Castonguay & C. Hill (Eds.), *Transformation in psychotherapy: Corrective experiences across cognitive-behavioral, humanistic, and psychodynamic approaches* (pp. 13–29). Washington, DC: American Psychological Association.

Good, G., & Beitman, B. (2006). *Counseling and psychotherapy essentials: Integrating theories, skills, and practices*. New York, NY: Norton.

Granello, D. H. (2010). Cognitive complexity among practicing counselors: How thinking changes with experience. *Journal of Counseling and Development, 88*, 92–100.

Greene, R. (2012). *Mastery*. New York, NY: Viking

Institute of Medicine. (2001). *Crossing the quality chasm: A new health system for the 21st century*. Washington, DC: Author.

Jennings, L., Hansen, M., Skovholt, T., & Grier, T. (2005). Searching for mastery. *Journal of Mental Health Counseling, 27*, 19–31.

Jennings, L., & Skovholt, T. M. (1999), The cognitive, emotional, and relational characteristics of master therapists. *Journal of Counseling Psychology, 46*, 3–11.

Jennings, L., Skovholt, T., Goh, M., & Lian, P. (2013). Master therapists: Exploitations of expertise. In M. Ronnestad & T. Skovholt (Eds.), *The developing practitioner: Growth and stagnation of therapists and counselors* (pp. 213–246). New York, NY: Routledge.

Lambert, M. (1992). Psychotherapy outcome research: Implications for integrative and eclectic therapists. In J. Norcross & M. Goldfried (Eds.), *Handbook of psychotherapy* (pp. 94–129). New York, NY: Basic Books.

Lambert, M. J., & Barley, D. E. (2001). Research summary on the therapeutic relationship and psychotherapy outcome. *Psychotherapy: Theory/Research/Practice/Training, 38*, 357–361.

Lambert, M. J., & Shimokawa, K. (2011). Collecting client feedback. *Psychotherapy, 48*, 72–79.

Lambert, M., Whipple, J., Smart, D., Vermeersch, D., Nielsen, S., & Hawkins, E. (2003). Is it time for clinicians to routinely track patient outcomes? A meta-analysis. *Clinical Psychology: Science and Practice, 10*, 288–301.

Orlinsky, D. E. (1999). The master therapist: Ideal character or clinical fiction? Comments and questions on Jennings and Skovholt's "The cognitive, emotional, and relational characteristics of master therapists." *Journal of Counseling Psychology, 46*, 12–15.

Orlinsky, D. E., Botermans, J. F., & Ronnestad, M. H. (2001). Toward an empirically grounded model of psychotherapy training: Four thousand therapists rate influences on their development. *Australian Psychologist, 36*, 1–10.

Orlinsky, D., & Ronnestad, M. (2005). *How psychotherapists develop: A study of therapeutic work and professional growth*. Washington, DC: American Psychological Association.

Orlinsky, D. E., Ronnestad, M. H., Ambuehl, H., Willutzki, U., Botersman, J., Cierpka, M., et al. (1999). Psychotherapists' assessments of their development at different career levels. *Psychotherapy, 36*, 203–215.

Owen, J., & Lindley, L. D. (2010). Therapists' cognitive complexity: Review of theoretical models and development of an integrated approach for training. *Training and Education in Professional Psychology, 4*, 128–137.

Reed, G. M., McLaughlin, C., & Newman, R. (2002). American Psychological Association policy in context: The development and evaluation of guidelines for professional practice. *American Psychologist, 57*, 1041–1047.

Ronnestad, M., & Skovholt, T. M. (2013). *The developing practitioner: Growth and stagnation of therapists and counselors*. New York, NY: Routledge.

Skovholt, T. M., & Jennings, L. (2004). *Master therapists: Exploring expertise in therapy and counseling*. Boston, MA: Allyn & Bacon.

Sperry, L. (2010a). *Highly effective therapy: Developing essential clinical competencies in counseling and psychotherapy*. New York, NY: Routledge.

Sperry, L. (2010b). *Core competencies in counseling and psychotherapy: Becoming a highly competent and effective therapist*. New York, NY: Routledge.

Sperry, L., & Sperry, J. (2012). *Case conceptualization: Mastering this competency with ease and confidence*. New York, NY: Routledge.

Teyber, E., & McClure, E. (2000). Therapist variables. In C. R. Snyder & R. E. Ingrain (Eds.), *Handbook of psychological change* (pp. 62–87). New York, NY: Wiley.

Wampold, B. (2001). *The great psychotherapy debate: Models, methods, findings*. Mahwah, NJ: Lawrence Erlbaum Associates.

2
EFFECTING CHANGE: THE FIRST SESSION

For clients, the first session is a map and foretaste of the course of therapy. It may be a good and encouraging experience or just the opposite. For trainees and beginning therapists, the first session is often the most structured part of the therapy process. Typically, it is structured in its format, focus, and expectations: the therapist asks specific questions and the client answers. This inquiry is typically followed by establishing a diagnosis and then planning treatment. For the master therapists we know, the first session is the most important of all the sessions. They are less likely to follow a structured format. Instead, they are likely to focus on developing a deep understanding—including a provisional case conceptualization—and a deep connection with the client.

There are five key tasks that master therapists endeavor to accomplish in this important session: (a) establish a productive therapeutic alliance; (b) specify a provisional case conceptualization; (c) perform an initial assessment and identify client concerns, resources, and deficits; (d) establish clinician credibility; and (e) effect some initial change. This chapter describes four of these tasks. Because of the centrality of the case conceptualization in effective psychotherapy, the task of specifying a case conceptualization is the focus of Chapter 4 as is the case conceptualization of Aimee. In this chapter, background information on Aimee is provided. Then, a full transcription of Session 1 follows, which illustrates how Dr. Carlson effortlessly accomplishes these essential tasks. This is followed by two commentaries.

Therapeutic Alliance

Effective therapy typically begins with the establishment of a productive or effective therapeutic relationship, also called a therapeutic alliance. The therapeutic alliance can have a profound effect on treatment process and outcomes. Research consistently demonstrates that the therapeutic relationship is the best predictor of therapeutic outcome (Horvath & Symonds, 1991; Orlinsky, Ronnestad, & Willutzi, 2004). The therapeutic alliance is essential in both effecting change and reducing the likelihood of premature termination (Sperry, 2010a).

Establishing a Productive Therapeutic Alliance

The therapeutic alliance begins with the first contact between client and therapist and continues until the last contact. Although initial interactions are especially important, as first impressions usually are, the development of the therapeutic alliance is intertwined with all aspects of the treatment process and evolves and changes over time. An effective therapeutic alliance may develop as quickly as the first session but must be firmly in place by the third session if treatment is to be successful (Orlinsky et al., 2004; Sperry, Brill, Howard, & Grissom, 1996). Needless to say, every client–therapist contact, either positive or negative, influences the development and maintenance of the therapist alliance.

A clinically useful view of the therapeutic alliance is that it involves three factors: bond, goals, and treatment approach and focus (Bordin, 1979). Important to the formation of a strong therapeutic bond is that clients feel understood, safe, and hopeful. Such a bond fosters the likelihood that clients will take the risk of disclosing painful affects and intimate details of their lives. They must also take the risk of thinking, feeling, and acting in more adaptive and healthier ways. Only in a safe, trustworthy, and nurturing environment—the bond—is this risk-taking likely to occur.

Besides the therapeutic bond, clinicians need to attend to mutually agreed-on therapeutic goals and to intervention methods. This entails a recognition of the client's explanatory model and expectations for treatment goals and focus and the way treatment will be provided (Sperry, 2010b; Sperry, Carlson, & Kjos, 2003). Such expectations are influenced by cultural factors and norms. Since there may be the unspoken expectation that family members be included in the treatment process, highly effective clinicians will inquire about such expectations. Similarly, there may be "silent expectations" about the type of approach used. Sometimes, the silent expectation is that healing requires some measure of touch or contact. Some clients prefer action-oriented approaches over strictly talk-oriented approaches. In short, an effective therapeutic alliance involves a "meeting of hearts" and a "meeting of minds" between clinician and client (Sperry, 2010a, 2010b).

Therapist and Therapeutic Alliance

Clinical lore holds that therapists who embody the core conditions of effective treatment—empathy, respect, and acceptance (Rogers, 1961)—and who demonstrate active listening and responding, facilitate the development of an effective alliance. In such a relationship, clients will feel accepted, supported, and valued, and believe that their therapist cares about them and is worthy of their trust. As a result, they become hopeful and confident that treatment will be successful.

Research has validated some of the clinical lore of the therapist's contribution to the alliance but does not support Rogers' claim that the three core conditions are the necessary *and* sufficient conditions for therapeutic change

(Norcross, 2002). However, there is increasing support for the premise that specific therapist attributes and skill sets are positively related to an effective therapeutic alliance (Orlinsky et al., 2004). Therapists in an effective alliance present in a warm and friendly manner and are confident and experienced. They are interested in and respectful toward the client, and they relate with honesty, trustworthiness, and openness. During treatment, they remain alert and flexible and provide a safe environment in which clients can discuss their issues. They are supportive, use active and reflective listening, affirm the client's experience, and demonstrate an empathic understanding of each client's situation. Furthermore, they attend to the client's experiences and facilitate the expression of affect, to enable a deep exploration of concerns. They provide accurate interpretations of the client's behavior and are active in treatment and draw attention to past therapeutic successes (Ackerman & Hillensroth, 2003; Orlinsky, Grawe, & Parks, 1994).

In short, the development of a good therapeutic alliance is essential for the success of psychotherapy regardless of the approach. The therapist's ability to incorporate the client's needs, expectations, and abilities into a therapeutic plan is essential in building the alliance (Sperry, 2010b). Because the therapist and client often judge the quality of the alliance differently, active monitoring of the alliance throughout therapy is needed. Responding nondefensively to a client's hostility or negativity is critical to establishing and maintaining a strong alliance. Finally, the client's evaluation of the quality of the alliance is a better predictor of outcome than the therapist's own evaluation (Horvath, Del Re, Flückiger, & Symonds, 2011).

Maintaining a Productive Therapeutic Alliance

Maintaining an effective therapeutic relationship is an equally critical therapeutic challenge for therapists as developing a productive therapeutic alliance. It, too, requires a specific set of competencies and skills. Needless to say, therapist competency and capability in dealing with these challenges and impasses are essential to the competent practice of psychotherapy.

Just as there are "treatment-promoting factors," there are also "treatment-interfering factors." Treatment-interfering factors, also called impasses, are factors that arise within and between sessions that impede the progress of therapy. Treatment-interfering factors can involve the client, therapist, client–therapist relationship, and treatment process. Specific interfering factors are: resistance and ambivalence, alliance ruptures, and transference–countertransference enactments (Sperry, 2010b).

In our experience, master therapists are experts in developing and maintaining productive therapeutic alliances. While trainees and less proficient therapists may be able to achieve productive alliances with some clients, master therapists are more likely to consistently achieve productive alliances with many clients.

Clinician Credibility

Clinician credibility is a complex phenomenon that involves all of the preceding therapist attributes. It is defined as the client's perception that the therapist is trustworthy and effective (Sue & Zane, 1987). The first element is trustworthiness. A therapist is considered trustworthy if he is caring, respectful, accepting, and is sensitive to the client's needs and expectations and instills faith, confidence, and hope in the client. The second element is a perceived sense of therapist effectiveness and interpersonal influence (i.e., the use of expertise and power to foster self-awareness and constructive change). Clients recognize such influence when therapists show they are competent, have a clear sense of direction, give structure to the sessions, and empower and affirm clients by encouraging and fostering client change in sessions and between sessions. Credibility must be achieved in the early sessions for the client to remain in treatment long enough to gain therapeutic benefit. Clinician credibility is particularly important in the treatment of culturally diverse clients (Paniagua, 2005). In short, when a client perceives a therapist is trustworthy and effective and then believes that the therapist and the proposed therapeutic process can and will make a difference in his or her life, the therapist has achieved clinician credibility.

Client Resources and Deficits

Client resources, also called extratherapeutic factors, are client factors or contextual factors that contribute to therapeutic change irrespective of the client's participation in therapy (Lambert, 1992). These factors include client strengths and talents, psychological resilience, self-control, intelligence, power, success in school or work, motivation and readiness for change, self-efficacy (belief in one's ability to bring about change), a secure or relatively secure attachment with at least one individual, a past history of success in making a lifestyle change such as smoking cessation, an inherent capacity for growth, self-confidence, having a best friend while growing up, and the capacity to connect with and use social support. These resources and strengths are referred to as "protective factors" in the case conceptualization described in Chapter 4.

Self-control may be the client resource that most impacts therapy. In fact, many consider self-control and intelligence to be the two "personal qualities that predict 'positive outcomes' in life" (Baumeister & Tierney, 2011, p. 1). Self-control is the capacity to change one's behaviors and inhibit impulses. Those with high self-control tend to accomplish more, are less impulsive and procrastinating, and are more successful in life. In contrast, those with low self-control tend to accomplish less, are more impulsive and procrastinating, and are less successful in life (Baumeister & Tierney, 2011).

Contextual factors include access to effective treatment and therapists, supportive family members, a network of supportive friends, and chance events that influence the change process. The more therapists can accommodate such client resources in their planning and implementing treatment, the better are the therapeutic alliance and treatment outcomes.

Client deficits refer to dispositions and circumstances that have stunted psychological growth, limited the development of resiliency and/or self-control, or resulted in an insecure attachment (Sperry, 2010b). Examples of client deficits include an abusive family history, particularly sexual abuse; abandonment experiences; early experiences of loss; overly critical or demanding parents or caregivers; history of early psychiatric diagnoses and treatment; history of substance or behavioral addictions; multiple foster care placements; and the like. The more therapists can accommodate such client resources and deficits into their planning and implementing treatment, the better are the therapeutic alliance and treatment outcomes.

Profiling Client Resources and Deficits

Trainees typically find it difficult to make predictions about how specific clients will respond in therapy (i.e., prognosis). A helpful way to think about prognosis is to consider clients' resources and deficits and their likely impact on the course and outcomes of therapy. But without a framework in which to conceptualize the impact of these factors in a particular client's life, this advice is often not clinically useful. For this reason, I provide trainees with profiles of four different clients (Sperry, 2010b; Sperry & Sperry, 2012). These profiles compare six client resources and *protective factors as well as* deficits across a continuum from the highest level of client functioning and prognosis (Profile I) to the lowest level of client functioning and prognosis (Profile V).

For example, imagine you are doing consecutive evaluations of four female clients. They are similar in age, education, and level of acculturation. They all complain of "feeling sad" following the breakup of an intimate relationship; beyond these similarities are differences.

Profile I: This client meets criteria for a situational, stress diagnosis, such as Adjustment Disorder with Depressed Mood. There is no indication of a personality disorder, although some avoidant and dependent features are noted. Previously, she has been successful in maintaining intimate relationships and in maintaining a job. She reports having lost 25 pounds two years ago with diet and exercise and has maintained her weight since. Her level of resilience and self-control appears to be high with readiness for change at the action stage and a high level of self-efficacy.

Profile II: This client meets criteria for Major Depressive Disorder: Single Episode and has some Avoidant Personality traits. She reports being reasonably successful in intimate relationships and in her career. Her level of resilience and self-control are moderately high, as is her self-efficacy with readiness for change at the preparation stage.

Profile III: This client meets criteria for Depressive Disorder NOS and for Avoidant Personality Disorder with obsessive–compulsive traits. She reports early emotional neglect and physical abuse with her parents but was raised by a nurturing relative. Her levels of resilience and self-control are moderately high, as is her self-efficacy with readiness for change at the preparation stage. She has worked consistently over the past seven years to support her children but has had difficulty maintaining intimate relationships.

Profile IV: This client meets criteria for Major Depressive Disorder: Recurrent and for Avoidant Personality and Obsessive–Compulsive Personality Disorder. She reports difficulty in maintaining intimate relationships and has had three jobs in the past two years. She has attempted to live independently but still resides with her mother. Her levels of resilience, self-control, and self-efficacy are in the lower range, while her readiness for change is at the contemplative stage.

Profile V: This client meets criteria for Major Depressive Disorder: Recurrent and Post Traumatic Stress Disorder, as well as Borderline Personality Disorder and Obsessive–Compulsive Personality Disorder. Her physician has recommended that she lose 50 pounds and stop smoking, yet she has repeatedly failed the lifestyle change programs prescribed her. She has not been successful at either work or relationships and has been on disability for the past four years. Her levels of resilience, self-control, and self-efficacy appear to be very low with readiness at the precontemplative stage.

The prognosis for Profile I clients is excellent. Given their high self-control, self-efficacy, and previous success in life and in weight loss, these clients are quite likely to respond quickly and effectively to therapeutic support. On the other hand, the prognosis for Profile IV clients is guarded to poor given their lack of success in life and failures in personal change efforts, such as weight loss and smoking cessation. Profile III clients tend to have early neglect and/or abuse histories like Profiles IV and V clients, but they have a better prognosis because of their moderate to high levels of self-control and self-efficacy and their successes in life and in previous personal change efforts. Prognosis for therapeutic change is generally good for Profile II clients. It can be fair to good for Profile III clients if a productive therapeutic alliance is developed and their maladaptive pattern is shifted to a more adaptive pattern. Clients with Profile V may well be better candidates for case management rather than psychotherapy as the primary intervention. Table 2.1 summarizes these profiles.

Effecting Change in the First Session

Clients who are new to therapy often come to their first session hoping to get relief from chronic and troubling symptoms, to deal with pressing life problems, or both. Clients who have been in therapy before may have similar expectations or quite different expectations. For both types of clients, the first session is crucial in determining whether they will bond—or not—with the therapist, and whether they will continue—or not—in this therapy. Assuming that the client's treatment expectations have been elicited, the therapist has two options: endeavor to address one or more of these expectations during the first session, or return to them later in the course of treatment. Many, if not most, therapists tend to choose

Table 2.1. Profiles of Client Resources/Protective Factors and Deficits

Client Resources and Deficits	I	II	III	IV	V
Chronic major symptom disorders(s)	– – –	– – +	– + +	– + +	+ + +
Severe personality disorder(s)	– – –	– – –	– – +	– + +	+ + +
Early neglect and/or abuse	– – –	– – –	– + +	+ + +	+ + +
No/low job and relationship success	– – –	– – –	– – +	– + +	+ + +
No/low success in change efforts(s)	– – –	– – –	– – +	– + +	+ + +
No/low readiness and self-efficacy	– – –	– – –	– – +	– + +	+ + +
No/low self-control and resiliency	– – –	– – –	– – +	– + +	+ + +

Key: +, present; –, absent; – +, partial.

the second option. The consequence of not dealing with such client concerns in the first session is that there might not be a second session. By contrast, the master therapists we know are more likely to choose the first option. In other words, they believe that it is essential for some change to be effected during the first session. Besides fostering the therapeutic alliance and increasing the likelihood that the client will continue in treatment, such early change efforts increase clinician credibility.

For clients who come expecting some kind of emotional first aid, master therapists will likely offer some measure of help for the troubling symptom or life problem. For clients who been previously involved in less than successful therapies, the master therapists we know will also attempt to effect change in the first session. For example, an effective change strategy is to do something novel in the first session, such as a paradoxical suggestion. This strategy can be particularly useful with personality-disordered clients (Cummings & Cummings, 2013).

Case of Aimee

Aimee is a 30-year-old single mother of two boys, aged 12 and 11. She's currently employed as a limousine driver and attends graduate school part-time. Her stated reason for seeking therapy was to learn to deal with anger and resentment toward her mother. She describes herself as passive and hides her anger and resentment but manifested these feelings "by beating myself up, running myself ragged," which means she continually focuses on meeting the needs of others and not relaxing or enjoying life. Aimee is very careful and circumspect in talking with her mother, fearful she will hurt her mother's feelings. Essentially, Aimee was abandoned by her mother as a child and raised by her maternal grandmother. She indicated that she was and is very close to her grandmother and remains much closer to her father than to her mother.

She also reported that her ex-husband had been verbally and physically abusive to her and that he is being released from prison soon. In anticipation of his release, she worries for her safety and that of her children. Aimee reports that she remains very close to her father but quite emotionally distant from her mother. On the intake form, she stated, "I have very angry feelings about her." No current medical problems are reported, although she does note having somewhat severe headaches, anxiety, depression, trouble with sleeping, and bad dreams. On a brief inventory, the *Kern Lifestyle Scale*, she scored high on the areas of needing to please and being a victim. She reports that her greatest worry is that she is lonely.

If DSM diagnoses were to be given, they would be Unspecified Depressive Disorder with mixed features, as well as Dependent Personality Disorder and Obsessive–Compulsive traits. On the Global Assessment of Functioning scale, she would be assessed as 62 now, with her highest functioning at 68 in the past year.

Dr. Carlson's treatment goals were to (a) empower her and have her view herself in a more positive way, (b) have her realize that she has the resources that are necessary to live a happier and a more satisfying life, (c) help her to be more confident and independent and (d) to take better care of herself. These treatment goals directly reflect a more adaptive pattern of caring for others and caring for herself. In the process of achieving these four goals, she effectively dismantled her maladaptive behavior of caring for others but not caring for herself. Several intervention strategies were seamlessly combined to achieve this new pattern and four treatment goals.

Transcription of Session 1

Because of its singular importance in setting the frame for the rest of the sessions, the transcription of the first session is presented in its entirety.

DR. CARLSON: Aimee, is that how you pronounce your name?
AIMEE: Yes.
DR. CARLSON: I'm glad that you're willing to come and to participate. Aimee what's, is that an unusual name?
AIMEE: French...
DR. CARLSON: It's a French name, and is that your background, French?
AIMEE: Yes, it's French and Swedish.
DR. CARLSON: Aaah OK.
AIMEE: It means friend.

EFFECTING CHANGE: THE FIRST SESSION

DR. CARLSON: Oh, it means friend.

AIMEE: Yes.

DR. CARLSON: If you're coming here and you have a purpose for coming here, what would you like to see change in our time together?

AIMEE: Umm . . . I really need to learn to deal with a lot of anger and resentment feelings I have about my mother.

DR. CARLSON: Mhmm . . . so we have anger, resentment and you think it's toward you mother?

AIMEE: Well, yes, but it's not . . . I don't, it's in here [*pointing to her chest*]. I don't show it, but I feel it. You know, I get very angry alone. I'm very passive, so I don't show anybody the anger, but I have a lot of deep resentment towards my mother and so I manifest it in other ways by beating myself up, running myself ragged.

DR. CARLSON: I see, so beating yourself up and doing too much?

AIMEE: Yes, yes . . . not relaxing, never having the time to sit down and enjoy the day.

DR. CARLSON: If you had the time, could you enjoy the day?

AIMEE: I don't know, I'd probably find something to do rather than sit there [*laughs*]. That seems to be the case.

DR. CARLSON: Was work a big part of your upbringing?

AIMEE: Yes, my dad was really hard worker. He was a musician in a band, he was a drummer, and so the first couple years of my life were spent on the road with a band, but, umm, it was a hard work to set the band up and take it down at the end of the night and during the daytime and then during the daytime he would work on the railroad so I don't think the man ever slept, I don't remember seeing him sleeping or resting so maybe where that comes in . . . I don't know.

DR. CARLSON: In some ways he's been like a role model for you. And, you got along better with him than your mother.

AIMEE: Yes, definitely. I'm very close to my father; I'm the only child to him. I have a half sister when my mother remarried but my dad is . . . I'm all he has, also he's not married again so he's very close to me, we have a very close relationship.

DR. CARLSON: And what does close mean?

AIMEE: I take care of him . . . you know, he doesn't have a wife. I don't feel like I have to, but I do.

DR. CARLSON: Does he live near you, your dad?

AIMEE: Right down the street.

DR. CARLSON: Right down the street, OK. So you live close by and how long has that been?

AIMEE: That I live close by? Just a month now . . . I just moved out there but I did live near him before and I moved away for awhile, but it just made me homesick sort of so I'm back.

DR. CARLSON: And then you said you had this resentment toward your mom.

AIMEE: I lived with my mom when they got a divorce and my mother was kind've not around a lot and I felt a little abandoned and I felt angry inside from that, I guess, angry at her for not paying attention to me I guess, but I don't . . . I'm friendly with her now. I never tell her that. And it's funny because sometimes she'll mention that, but I tell her no don't feel guilty when inside I inside I kind of feel guilty because I'm resentful . . . so, it's funny how that works.

DR. CARLSON: So your mom feels guilty for what she did, you feel angry for what she did, but you can't really talk about it with one another?

AIMEE: No, I feel like if I tell her how I feel that I'm going to hurt her feelings.

DR. CARLSON: Even though that's the way she feels?

AIMEE: Mhmm . . . I don't want to hurt her feelings, I feel like if I tell her I really am angry, I really do resent you, you know, to a degree . . . I can't do that . . . So, I kind've walk around with these feelings inside me that have never really come out.

DR. CARLSON: Any idea why that might be? I guess, would that be being honest with your feelings?

AIMEE: Yeah, I guess it would be but I have a hard time expressing how I feel to people, well unless it's something good, because I don't want to hurt anyone's feelings so I'm very nice even at the expense of myself . . . I'm a very passive person.

DR. CARLSON: Nice, but it sounds like you're not honest?

AIMEE: No [*says while laughing*].

DR. CARLSON: And how does that work in relationships?

AIMEE: It doesn't [*laughing*] . . . No, I don't really have many relationships that last. I really don't have too many relationships, I'm kind of a loner.

DR. CARLSON: So, that would be a lot like your dad?

AIMEE: Mhmm, yeah.

DR. CARLSON: I see and how about your mom?

AIMEE: She's very social. I'm very social but um as far as adhering to a relationship . . . I'm a chauffeur, I talk to many people, conversing is a part of my job, but to make a relationship, to build a relationship is very hard for me.

DR. CARLSON: And what does hard mean?

AIMEE: Difficult letting people in, difficult letting them see a different side of me other than what I want them to see . . . you know the friendly, happy me.

EFFECTING CHANGE: THE FIRST SESSION

DR. CARLSON: And that's the thing that you learned from your mom?

AIMEE: Yeah, probably . . . She's a very outgoing, very charismatic person.

DR. CARLSON: But you learned this idea that it's important to be what somebody wants you to be other than to be yourself?

AIMEE: Yes, probably. I'm not ashamed of who I am, but I just don't want anybody to know that I have these bad sides too . . . I guess everybody is sort of like that in a way.

DR. CARLSON: But the bad side, for you, is that you don't want to hurt anyone's feelings?

AIMEE: Yeah, I have resentment and anger toward a family member, and I feel sort of guilty for that because I feel like I should be an obedient child . . . and I was a very obedient child growing up. I was good all the time I still am like that, I never disappointed my parents and to disappoint my parents makes me feel really bad . . . it makes me feel very bad about myself so I sort of over-achieve in order to gain . . . I mean I know they love me but there's no room for failure, but I'm always doing and doing to try please everybody else.

DR. CARLSON: No wonder you don't relax . . .

AIMEE: No, I don't.

DR. CARLSON: There's no time. Do you think this is the way you'll be forever?

AIMEE: I hope not.

DR. CARLSON: How would you like to be?

AIMEE: I would like to be able to sit down and not think about the day, what needs to be done. I mean everybody . . . you can't really automatically shut your mind off of the different things you're thinking about and worrying about . . . anticipating, but just sort of serenity inside, that would be nice, just to sit down and enjoy the day.

DR. CARLSON: But I'm wondering how much time a day you have?

AIMEE: Not much.

DR. CARLSON: I mean you work, you're going to school, and you're taking care of your father . . .

AIMEE: My kids too . . .

DR. CARLSON: Two children you're taking care of . . .

AIMEE: And my grandmother . . .

DR. CARLSON: And your grandmother?

AIMEE: Yeah, my grandmother, she's 80 now. She'll be 80 in a couple weeks and so I take care of her also. I go over and clean her house and you know just visit her, she's very lonely.

DR. CARLSON: This would be your dad's mother?

AIMEE: My mother's mother.

DR. CARLSON: Oh, your mother's mother.

AIMEE: Yeah, she actually raised me; she's like my mother because my mother was gone a lot.

DR. CARLSON: So, she's really not like your mother but . . .

AIMEE: She is my mom.

DR. CARLSON: She is your mother . . .

AIMEE: In a sense, I take care of my parents. So, I liked the company of her too, it's not burdensome, I don't go over there and think I gotta clean her house again, it's sort of time with her.

DR. CARLSON: But being a single mom . . . you are a single mom?

AIMEE: Yeah.

DR. CARLSON: And what does that word you used "serenity" . . . how does that fit in?

AIMEE: I don't know. I'd like to fit it in somehow, some way, you know, because right now it really wears me down and I also have problems sleeping and I'm very tired when I go to bed at night. I lay in bed and start thinking about what I have to do and so the process starts all over again and it just doesn't seem like I have time to just take five and, you know, just watch TV, and lay around.

DR. CARLSON: So, getting to sleep would be a problem?

AIMEE: Oh yeah, definitely it is. I have a really hard time sleeping through the night, going to sleep, finally getting to sleep, and I wake up pretty early even if I go to bed really late . . . I wake up really early, I'm just . . . as soon as the sun comes up.

DR. CARLSON: So, it's not enough that you have so many things to do, but then you don't charge your battery in the evening when you could sleep.

AIMEE: Well, sometimes I do, it depends, umm . . . If I drink some beer before I go to bed, which is not a good idea, but it helps, it does . . . it helps me to shut off.

DR. CARLSON: So, the best solution you've come up with, so far, is drinking beer.

AIMEE: Yes, drinking beer. I don't think that's the best solution but my best. I don't do it every night but some day when I really need the sleep . . .

DR. CARLSON: And I guess if you drink the beer you can't really do anything else?

AIMEE: No, I just drink the beer and it makes me tired and thus I fall asleep. It gets me into a relaxed state where I don't think about what tomorrow has to offer and what's going on, so . . .

DR. CARLSON: So, with the help of beer you're able to be more like what you would like to be like?

AIMEE: Yes, mhmm.

DR. CARLSON: Mhmm, have you found any other ways to get there?

AIMEE: Uh yes a massage . . . I got a massage not too long ago and that seemed to help . . . Music, music helps me to relax. I'm uh really into music.

DR. CARLSON: Yeah, you said your dad was a drummer.

AIMEE: Yeah, so I have a lot of music at my house, so I do listen to music and that helps me to relax but a lot of the times I'm listening to the music and I'm doing those things too, I'm not just sitting there listening to it . . . I'm listening to it and doing the dishes or mopping the floor . . . so I'm still doing.

DR. CARLSON: And when you say music, what kind've music do you like?

AIMEE: Everything, jazz, classical . . . everything, I could listen to anything.

DR. CARLSON: And do you play or sing?

AIMEE: I play the drums.

DR. CARLSON: So like your dad?

AIMEE: Mhmm.

DR. CARLSON: And did you ever take it to the level of . . .

AIMEE: I, you know, I probably would have if I didn't pursue a family and you know it's just I saw how it worked with myself and my family and being in a rock band in the 70s and trying to raise a family was a little too much for my family to deal with so I just chose to raise my children and I still play once in a while, but to be in a band it's really demanding if you want to be good at it you have to practice a lot and I'm sure my neighbors wouldn't enjoy that either.

DR. CARLSON: So again, you're always thinking of others. Thinking of the family, thinking of the neighbors, thinking of . . .

AIMEE: Mhmm, yeah, always.

DR. CARLSON: But there's somebody we're not thinking about?

AIMEE: No, no, I don't know why. I need to start thinking about myself because I feel like I don't know who I am anymore. I'm running so much that I never took time to learn who I am as a person, to figure out who I am as a person. I became a mother at sixteen, I was married out of high school I . . . it was just a rat race so I never really stopped to think what I really want or like, I just do . . . I don't stop to think of who I am as a person.

DR. CARLSON: I don't know who I am, so I do everything, because I do everything, I'm so tired to figure out who I am.

AIMEE: Yes, that sounds like a good song.

DR. CARLSON: Yeah, only you would think of that . . . it sounds like the song you're writing.

AIMEE: Yeah, definitely.

DR. CARLSON: Now did your dad ever get off that race since he was so busy?

AIMEE: Yeah, well, the band finally broke up and now he's a truck driver and it suits him because he doesn't like to be around a lot of people so he's driving and he's by himself and he sees people here and there and so he doesn't have to deal with the public and he's very eccentric and he's an artist so he's very unconventional even in his 50s. He's anti-establishment and he's really kind of hard to get along with at times because you just can't go over to his house and sit down; he's got to tell you about his views and then he wants you to adhere to what his opinion is. . . . he's very charged, emotionally charged all the time.

DR. CARLSON: So if you always do what other people want you to do, do you take on these far out views like that?

AIMEE: No, well I don't always agree with him, I just sit there and listen rather than argue because he's become more distant as far as political and different realms from me so he points that out a lot and tells me my faults about being the person I am, but I just let him talk, I don't ever argue with him because arguing with him is not, it just doesn't seem to accomplish anything, to me, I just feel like what's the point?

DR. CARLSON: So that would be the same way that you deal with your mom too?

AIMEE: Yeah.

DR. CARLSON: I see, and it sounds though it's not safe, you don't believe, to tell your mom things even though your mom tells you that that's the way it is for her . . .

AIMEE: Yeah, I don't know why . . .

DR. CARLSON: And it's safe for you to be around your dad, but your dad judges and criticizes you.

AIMEE: Oh yeah, he's very hard on me.

DR. CARLSON: This is a puzzle. How does that work?

AIMEE: It works by me just carrying the weight of it all, I don't really do anything either way, I listen to what my father has to say, all the while thinking he's crazy but I'll never tell him that and when my mother tells me she feels guilty or you know I'm sorry I did these things, I just tell her oh don't worry about it, that's water under the bridge, when really feel like you know what I'm really mad about what you did so I always go away walking out the door feeling like I haven't really accomplished anything in this engagement between two people talking.

DR. CARLSON: It sounds like it's only an engagement between one person . . .

AIMEE: Yeah.

DR. CARLSON: Because no one is representing you.
AIMEE: Yeah.
DR. CARLSON: And yet, you feel more comfortable with your dad who's criticizing you.
AIMEE: Well, because my father umm . . . he did really pay attention to me a lot. He treated me like a princess, he spoiled me. As far as . . . well he was hard on me, but he always played with me, he was like the number one dad, you know . . . so . . .
DR. CARLSON: When he wasn't on the road or working . . .
AIMEE: Oh, well by this time, when the marriage broke up, so did the band it kind of all fell apart there, so my father just had a regular job, so I saw him on the weekends, so all the time I was with him was spent with me, and I was the only child so I got all the attention . . .
DR. CARLSON: I see.
AIMEE: So, I really enjoyed that time.
DR. CARLSON: And how old were you when they separated?
AIMEE: Four.
DR. CARLSON: Four, OK. So, that was quite a bit of time you had, weekends with dad.
AIMEE: Mhmm, yeah.
DR. CARLSON: And then, you were with your grandmother during the week?
AIMEE: Yeah, most of the time . . . my mom worked for a little while and did other things so a lot of the times I was at her house, at my grandmother's house, and I would stay there for days, sometimes weeks.
DR. CARLSON: You know, when you started to talk about that your face changed a little bit, did you notice that?
AIMEE: No [*laughs*].
DR. CARLSON: Like you like had a different feeling was going on when you thought about that.
AIMEE: Yeah, well, it hurt a lot because I felt like a burden to my grandmother because my mom would be gone and she wasn't really . . . she was out doing whatever, you know getting drunk and high and umm . . .
DR. CARLSON: Oh, so she wasn't out working?
AIMEE: Well, she was working, but she would keep . . . I stayed there for days and she would never come to get me and I would wait for her thinking when is she gonna come and I'd stand by the window and . . . I had other . . . my aunts and uncles they still lived in that house. She has seven kids so there were some that still were living in the house and they'd say well where is she? When's her mom gonna come home? When is she gonna come pick her up? And, so I'd feel like, gosh, I'm a real burden here and

here she is with all these kids still but she never made me feel that way she was always very loving, she really inspired me, she was a beautiful person, she was a great person. So, I don't know, I felt that way, I felt like I don't belong here, I'm just dropped off here.

DR. CARLSON: And sometimes our mind kind of plays tricks on us, at times like that, and you try to come up with some belief about why our mom isn't around, doesn't want to be with us. What did you come up with?

AIMEE: That she just didn't want to be bothered with me, it seemed that way. I mean even the time that we were together; she didn't really interact with me too much. She's kind of like a self-centered person. Even until this day she's like that . . . like alright I'll call her and tell her well why don't you . . . she'll want to come over and talk . . . it's all, you know, everything is about her . . . I'll even pose the problem, I'm really stressed out with the kids you know they're talking back, Tyler is in trouble at school . . . and instead she comes over and talks about everything in her life and never asks me one thing about how I feel so I just let her go on and on about, you know, all this, and my financial troubles and blah blah blah and then she leaves and I was like oh I might as well have just talked to myself. So, she's still like that, I don't know, I can't say that . . . maybe that isn't a fault. I just feel like, you know, she's not very effective as far as being a comfort person in my life.

DR. CARLSON: And it seems that part of your belief is that if I am perfect or if I overachieve and do things right then maybe she'll like me?

AIMEE: Yeah, yeah, definitely, and of course, my little sister, my half-sister, she's 19, and she's really bad in school and she's, you know, she's the exact opposite from me. She's not intellectual, she's kind of materialistic and, you know, and so now my mother has been kind of doting on me to her, you know, because she's not doing anything she wants her to do so she says, why can't she be more like Aimee . . .

DR. CARLSON: I see . . .

AIMEE: But, I don't want her to be more like me because me isn't fun, not to me, but to everyone else.

DR. CARLSON: And you learned, too, that it's better to laugh rather than cry?

AIMEE: Yeah.

DR. CARLSON: Because you'd be crying a lot?

AIMEE: Oh yeah. Sometime that happens, I'll finally just get to the point where it gets so bad that I'd have to go in my room and break down and cry, for an hour I'll just cry and it would feel really good after I come out of there . . . but uh . . . I'd like to deal with it in a more healthy way . . . but . . .

DR. CARLSON: So crying tends to help?

AIMEE: Yeah.

DR. CARLSON: And the pain, though, is that the people I love don't love me?

AIMEE: I know that she loves me. She tells me that she loves me, but just isn't a mother-figure, you know, she comes over my house and she gets drunk, and she wants to get drunk with me, she wants to go out and party, she's not like my mom, she's more like my friend and I want her to like be my mom. I mean, like, she is now in her 50s and you would think she would wanna be my mom now, but she like wants to go out and get wild . . . she's wild . . . she's wilder than . . . I'm 30 now she kind of embarrasses me when we go out because she gets wild, like . . . you know . . .

DR. CARLSON: So, she's really like the child still?

AIMEE: Yeah, and so was my father. My father is the same way . . . um but on a different way . . . he's very responsible, but, you know, he goes to work . . . but he gets the same way, loud, kind of like a kid. He's still charged emotionally about this and that, you know . . . and he hates anything that's mainstream. It's kind've like being a teenager, he's got sort of that teenager attitude still.

DR. CARLSON: You seem to have a pretty good handle, or insight, onto what's going on.

AIMEE: Well, that comes from growing up being the parent; I was kind of like the parent all my life that was my responsibility.

DR. CARLSON: What do you need to know to get unstuck from it? I mean because you really have a good knowledge . . . you can report.

AIMEE: I don't know. It seems like I know what to do.

DR. CARLSON: I see.

AIMEE: I've always known what to do; I'm very efficient and insightful . . .

DR. CARLSON: It sounds like that.

AIMEE: But for some reason I found this "niche" that's like protecting me from whatever . . . going out on a limb, I guess.

DR. CARLSON: And what's the advantage of that?

AIMEE: I don't know, there isn't really an advantage of that . . .

DR. CARLSON: Well, there must be.

AIMEE: . . . other than taking the risk of hurting somebody else's feelings maybe.

DR. CARLSON: So, I'd rather not live than possibly hurting somebody's feelings?

AIMEE: I guess so . . . I guess I'm going to have to hurt some feelings . . . but just thinking about it . . .

DR. CARLSON: Well, I don't know if you're going to have to hurt somebody's feelings.
AIMEE: That's the way I view it.
DR. CARLSON: That's your view?
AIMEE: Yeah.
DR. CARLSON: Now, you said that . . . you know you're not in a relationship now, but you have kids?
AIMEE: Mhmm.
DR. CARLSON: So you were in a relationship?
AIMEE: Oh yeah . . . umm . . . he was my first sweetheart and I ended up marrying him and I thought I was just madly in love.
DR. CARLSON: And that was, then, earlier you said though?
AIMEE: Oh yeah, I was . . . umm 18 when I got married, but I had my kids before I was 18. My parents wouldn't consent . . .
DR. CARLSON: I see.
AIMEE: And rightly so, he wasn't the perfect catch for me that's for sure.
DR. CARLSON: So you had kids?
AIMEE: Uh huh . . .
DR. CARLSON: Before you were 18 and then you got married at 18 because then you could do it without their permission?
AIMEE: Yeah.
DR. CARLSON: I see.
AIMEE: And uh . . . it didn't last long once I got married. I was with him for six years, but once I got married I left him after a year . . . so . . .
DR. CARLSON: How did that happen? I mean how did you . . .
AIMEE: It's very strange.
DR. CARLSON: Did that make him happy that you left?
AIMEE: Oh, no!
DR. CARLSON: OK, so that would be a time that that you did something that you knew would hurt somebody's feelings
AIMEE: I did, but it was strange . . . you know I think it was because I was abused . . . he physically abused me, since I was . . . I was a child when I met him, I was 14 so I was a child myself and uh the physical abuse and the emotional abuse that he put me through made me sort of numb . . . and one day it was the strangest thing because I really loved him and I thought I was so in love with him and I thought I was gonna spend the rest of my life with him . . . one day I just got up and I left, I went to my dad's and that was it . . . and I knew that I would be protected by my father because my father . . . he was afraid of my dad, so I knew if I ran to my father and went to live with him he wouldn't be around . . . I didn't have to live in fear . . . but it was

strange because I didn't feel . . . I didn't mourn the break-up of the marriage or anything, it was like I just woke up from a dream and said I don't love you anymore and just left. And he proceeded to stalk me for six years . . . calling, calling the phone company. It was crazy . . . for six years he did that.

DR. CARLSON: So, you must've really had to keep your resolve?

AIMEE: Mhmm, yeah.

DR. CARLSON: Did you ever go back?

AIMEE: No. I never even thought about it. In fact, it was strange because, you know, I was married to this man, but then talking to him over the phone. I was thinking well how the heck did I ever end up with this guy? You know, because he's nothing like me so, you know, I don't know I was just a child . . . I was attracted to the "bad boy" image, the rebellion against my parents, society

DR. CARLSON: Would you like another explanation?

AIMEE: OK.

DR. CARLSON: Could it be that the attractiveness with him is that he's a lot like your mom?

AIMEE: Yeah, he is.

DR. CARLSON: They're both kind of self-centered, do what they want?

AIMEE: Mhmm.

DR. CARLSON: Don't have a lot of concern for others?

AIMEE: Yes, definitely.

DR. CARLSON: And sometimes we're attracted to people with whom we have unfinished business.

AIMEE: That sounds true because I end up in relationships with people just like that all the time and then I end up feeling like you know I'm not getting anything out of this it's just me, me, me . . . giving and giving, you know, I'm giving to these people and I'm not receiving anything so I'll put up with it for a while because I pity them because that . . . that's what happens once they feel like they're losing me then they act like oh, well you can't leave me and then I'd feel sorry for them and I'll drag it on for a little while, but not six years, and never marriage again, I just finally get fed up after a while and say I'm not getting anything out of this, goodbye. But uh . . . it always ends pretty bitter and like they're really . . . they hate me for ending it, when I'm always thinking well what did you expect . . . so uh . . . I don't have too many . . .

DR. CARLSON: They hate you for not doing what they want you to do?

AIMEE: Yeah, mhmm . . . because I did, I did do what they wanted until finally I've had enough. So, I don't have too many friendly ex-boyfriends unfortunately.

DR. CARLSON: And the way that you stay friendly with your mom, though, is by losing yourself?

AIMEE: Yeah . . . just agreeing with her, listening to her, not intervening on what she's telling me.

DR. CARLSON: You know, the theory on this is that you really need to resolve that unfinished business.

AIMEE: I know that I do because I can feel . . .

DR. CARLSON: You heard that theory too?

AIMEE: Oh yeah, but I also felt like . . . I can feel it inside of me like . . . I won't be a whole person, I won't be able to grow myself until I get over this hump, but this thing is making me run in place, I know it is, I can feel it.

DR. CARLSON: I see. But you've had some taste of it though and it sounds like the consequences of it are that you lose the relationship with that person?

AIMEE: Yeah.

DR. CARLSON: Which is probably . . . you didn't have a relationship anyway.

AIMEE: Yeah, exactly. But, you know, I don't know if I would be so dismayed if I didn't have a relationship with my mother . . . I don't think she would do that, I don't think she would disown me if I told her how I felt, but it wouldn't be that great of a loss because I'm not that close to her . . . I don't talk to her that much, I like see her on the holidays and I talk to her maybe once every two or three weeks.

DR. CARLSON: So you're talking yourself right now into doing this?

AIMEE: I don't know maybe. I don't know.

DR. CARLSON: So, if you were to . . . is your mom live . . . how far away?

AIMEE: Probably like 25 minutes away.

DR. CARLSON: Oh, so like a half hour . . . pretty close.

AIMEE: Yeah, she doesn't live that far.

DR. CARLSON: So if you were to call your mom up and say let's go out for lunch . . . ?

AIMEE: I don't know that would be really hard for me to do because I'd be thinking about how I'm gonna say it, and I've tried to do it a few times, actually, and I always think . . . I go in with the best intentions OK I'm gonna tell her how I feel and then I never do. I always chicken-out at the end.

DR. CARLSON: I see, so you haven't . . . you've worked yourself up and you really never delivered the goods.

AIMEE: No. I always chicken-out at the last minute or I find an excuse, oh well looks like the roast is done, I better go check it, you know. I'm always finding a way not to do what I intended to do.

DR. CARLSON: And in your rehearsals, what have you wanted to say?

AIMEE: Umm, gently tell her that, you know, yeah your right I did feel kind of disowned, abandoned . . . ummm, the thing is I don't want to blame her for my problems like the person . . . what goes on in my life isn't because of what she did, I don't believe that, but I feel like that's what she's gonna think . . . oh well you've got into this abusive relationship, you're a single mom and all these things it must be my fault. That's what I think she's going to . . . how she's going to react so . . .

DR. CARLSON: You're probably right; it'll be all about her.

AIMEE: Yeah, so, ummm . . .

DR. CARLSON: What would happen if you did it a little differently and said mom I feel sad that I don't have a mother and I wish I had one?

AIMEE: I don't know that seems really harsh to me; see if that were my kids telling me that I would probably really be upset because I get my feelings hurt really easy.

DR. CARLSON: Would you be upset enough to do something different?

AIMEE: Well yeah, definitely.

DR. CARLSON: Well, that's part of giving feedback.

AIMEE: OK.

DR. CARLSON: And when you love somebody and you get feedback that doesn't fit your idea of a person. In other words, if I'm a good mom, my kids will respect me as a mom, and if they say they don't you'd probably want to change that.

AIMEE: Mhmm . . . OK.

DR. CARLSON: I'm wondering if your mom might respond if you were to say I feel sad that I don't have a mom and I wish I did . . . And she'll probably say what do you mean I'm your mom and you'd say well I mean that . . . And we have a two-way conversation.

AIMEE: It's funny that you mentioned that because my aunt . . . um like I said, there's seven kids in the family so I'm kind of close . . . we're really diffused family, everybody is in each other's business and . . .

DR. CARLSON: So, there are seven kids in the family and your mother's family . . .

AIMEE: My mother is the oldest girl.

DR. CARLSON: I see, but it's almost a family that you're the youngest girl.

AIMEE: Exactly, because my grandmother raised me.

DR. CARLSON: Right.

AIMEE: And my youngest aunt, she was nine years old when I was born. So, we're like sisters and she told me that she called my mother up one time, I forget what happened, but my mom was being irresponsible . . . so my aunt called her up and was saying why don't you just be her mother for once so she did tell her that, but it didn't come from me . . . so that felt good when she said that, but it didn't come from me and it didn't change anything either.

DR. CARLSON: Well, the part that would change is that if you were to say what I'm suggesting is that it would change; it would change the way you are with her, that you would be honest. It might not change her response, but this would be a way to be honest without having to attack her.

AIMEE: Yeah, I was really struggling with what I was going to tell her because I'm thinking uh well mom I really love you and I do respect you, but I resent you at the same time . . . so I really didn't know how to go about telling her, you know, it was just really hard for me, even to initiate that.

DR. CARLSON: Could you say that, what I said about I feel sad that I don't have a mom and I wish that I did?

AIMEE: Yeah.

DR. CARLSON: How would that to sound if you were to do that right now? [*asks client to enact it*]

AIMEE: "I feel sad that I don't have a mother and I really wish that you could be my mother . . . "

DR. CARLSON: Mhmm . . . that's wonderful. How hard was that?

AIMEE: That was really hard.

DR. CARLSON: But, do you see that it sends two messages?

AIMEE: Yeah.

DR. CARLSON: One . . . that this is true and on the other hand I wish it wasn't.

AIMEE: Yeah.

DR. CARLSON: Is it possible for you to learn how to send both the messages?

AIMEE: Yeah, I need to do that, I mean not only with my mother, but people I encounter in my everyday life. I am too nice.

DR. CARLSON: But let's just do one step at a time . . .

AIMEE: Yeah.

DR. CARLSON: I mean, I think change is a journey of a thousand miles, right?

AIMEE: Oh, yes, definitely.

DR. CARLSON: One step at a time.

AIMEE: Yeah.

DR. CARLSON: You think that's too big of a step?

AIMEE: Starting with my mom? Or . . .

DR. CARLSON: Yes.

AIMEE: No, actually . . .

DR. CARLSON: And it seems like that if you could work at being honest and learn that . . . honest doesn't mean you're being negative, it means being honest and usually there's pluses and minuses about all situations and learning how to be that way I bet it would change many of your relationships.

AIMEE: Oh, I'm sure it will . . . um because they're all kind of based on me passively accepting who they are, but they don't accept who I am.

DR. CARLSON: Yeah, it's like you don't show up, it's not representing yourself and you picked some pretty tough cookies, by the way.

AIMEE: Yeah, I do. That's no joke, that's for sure.

DR. CARLSON: I mean you pick people who are pretty self-centered.

AIMEE: Yeah, it seems to fall into place like that every time. They all end up being the same person, but in a different form, you know, but the same personality type.

DR. CARLSON: You know, and there's people out there who don't love you, it sounds like, at least that's what you believe they've abandoned you, they leave you, they . . .

AIMEE: I know that my mother loves me, but . . .

DR. CARLSON: OK, and there's people like your grandmother, then there's other people like your aunt who seem like they know you pretty well?

AIMEE: Yeah, they do.

DR. CARLSON: They kind of get you.

AIMEE: Yeah, they do, but I don't . . . I just . . . my mother . . . I always feel like she loves me, but she loves herself more than her children and that's kind of like . . . to me as a mother, I feel like how could she be that way, you know, because my kids are always first in my life. It's not about me, it's about them and it was never like that for her. She never had that instinctual drive to protect or feed or nurture and so . . .

DR. CARLSON: Yeah, it sounds like her mother did it for her.

AIMEE: Yeah, my grandmother is like the Aunt Bea of the neighborhood, you know. She feeds everyone, her door's always open, and all the kids in the neighborhood were fed, my grandma fed them.

DR. CARLSON: It sound like there's some things that your mom has that you'd like to be able to have?

AIMEE: Yeah, definitely, the ability to be selfish once in a while; to say, well I'm not gonna do what you wanna do I'm gonna do this, but . . .

DR. CARLSON: Yes, that's exactly right. I mean it sounds like she's really a dud as a mom?

AIMEE: Yeah, yeah.

DR. CARLSON: I don't know if that's a real technical word, dud, but it seems like she didn't do a very good job at being a mother.

AIMEE: Yeah.

DR. CARLSON: And you do an overly good job at being a mother.

AIMEE: Yeah.

DR. CARLSON: You not only mother your children, but you mother parents and grandparents.

AIMEE: I'm very umm . . . I let my kids . . . I do too much for my kids.

DR. CARLSON: I see, you're overfunctioning as a parent.

AIMEE: Yeah, I'm always fixing them meals, I clean . . . making sure they're clean, I'm just kind of OCD about it. I mean they're gonna be teenagers they can fix their own breakfast, but I still do it for them.

DR. CARLSON: Did you know that's what happens if you grew up with a parent who underfunctions that that's what you learn?

AIMEE: No I didn't.

DR. CARLSON: And since you know what you don't want to be, you do exactly the opposite. You do too much.

AIMEE: Yeah, I always thought that too. I always thought, I'm not going to be they type of mother my mom was, but then I see myself talk and I tell them to turn the music down.

DR. CARLSON: What happened was you're not being the kind of mother your mother was, but you're not also being the person your mother was too . . . where she cared too much about herself and you care too little about yourself.

AIMEE: I know and I think my kids really need to learn responsibility.

DR. CARLSON: Right.

AIMEE: And they have ways . . . I'm a very intuitive person . . . they have ways to try and manipulate me.

DR. CARLSON: Right.

AIMEE: Instead of just doing the tasks and I'll say alright you can do this. Somehow they find a way to um . . . I can't say they manipulate me but they just do, they try to find a way to get things to go in their favor.

DR. CARLSON: Mhmm.

AIMEE: I don't think they think mentally they're trying to get one over on me, they just . . . that's what they're used to.

DR. CARLSON: And you don't like to rock the boat?

AIMEE: No. Well, I do now. They have laundry day that they're doing . . .

DR. CARLSON: Wow!

AIMEE: So, I'm starting to do it, but I should've done it earlier. But it's better late than never.

DR. CARLSON: Yes, if you have to err with kids, overlove in the beginning.

AIMEE: I don't want them to be 18 or 19 years old still living at my house, you know, partying and doing what they want, and not going to school, and not doing anything productive.

DR. CARLSON: Well, there probably won't be room by the time the rest of your relatives move out.
AIMEE: I know definitely.
DR. CARLSON: OK.
AIMEE: I really enjoy taking care of my grandmother, though, because I felt like she did that for me, I don't mind it.
DR. CARLSON: Right, it's love.
AIMEE: She feels guilty, too, about it, and it's like she always tell me oh you don't have to do this.
DR. CARLSON: She's a good giver of love and has a hard time receiving it.
AIMEE: Oh yeah, definitely.
DR. CARLSON: You know anyone else like that?
AIMEE: Yeah, me, exactly.
DR. CARLSON: And we'll have to talk about receiving love when we talk in the future. We're near the end of our time.
AIMEE: OK.
DR. CARLSON: Any final questions you might have?
AIMEE: No, well how long does it take to actually begin to start to practice on people?
DR. CARLSON: Well, we'll know better next week to see how the conversation goes with your mom.
AIMEE: Yeah, that's a challenge.
DR. CARLSON: OK you remember how you're going to say it?
AIMEE: Mhmm.
DR. CARLSON: How are you going to say it again?
AIMEE: I'm gonna say . . . I'm gonna say it a little bit different than you did.
DR. CARLSON: OK.
AIMEE: But I'm going to definitely tell her that I need her to . . . I'd really like you to be my mother now and I don't care about what's happened in the past, I just want you to be my mother now and be a grandmother to your grandchildren.
DR. CARLSON: Mhmm.
AIMEE: And it would be sad if you wouldn't wanna accept that role. Would that be a good thing to say?
DR. CARLSON: It's important that you say something, that would be your first step.
AIMEE: She's not a very good grandmother either, she's kind of the same way.
DR. CARLSON: But no one gives their feedback to the contrary.
AIMEE: No, but it's funny because I'll pick up my kids there and it's like a party house, you know . . . and I'm like what's going on here? My kids are eating candy and it's like three in the morning.

> DR. CARLSON: Well, it gives you an example of what you went through.
> AIMEE: Yeah.
> DR. CARLSON: OK, we'll talk again next week. Thank you.
> AIMEE: OK, thank you.

Commentary

Four markers of an effective first session have been described in this chapter. They are to (a) establish a productive therapeutic alliance, (b) perform an initial assessment and identify client concerns, resources, and deficits, (c) establish clinician credibility, and (d) effect some initial change. This commentary addresses each marker in this session.

There is little doubt that the beginnings of a productive therapeutic alliance were developed in this first meeting. Evident are its three components: a bond characterized by trust and caring, mutual agreement on treatment goals, and mutual agreement on treatment focus. In addition, Dr. Carlson developed a provisional case conceptualization. Central to it is her core maladaptive pattern of meeting others' needs while ignoring her own needs, and her secondary pattern of perfectionism. This conceptualization is described in detail in Chapter 4.

Dr. Carlson expertly identified Aimee's concerns and her resources and deficits in his initial assessment. Besides presenting concerns that she described on the information sheet that she filled out before the session, Dr. Carlson clarified these presenting concerns and elicited additional ones, as well as developmental, social, cultural, and history information. He also elicited and clarified her expectations of therapy. In this session, it is clear that despite considerable parental neglect and emotional abandonment by her mother, Aimee managed to establish some degree of attachment to her maternal grandmother. She is intelligent and verbally articulate and completed a bachelor's degree and was admitted to graduate studies. Despite longstanding physical and emotional abuse from an ex-husband, she was able to leave and divorce him. As a single parent, she is deeply committed to caring for her children and works to support them. Dr. Carlson elicited this information and skillfully accommodated his therapy to her resources and deficits.

It is not uncommon for trainees to consider Aimee's prognosis as poor to guarded. Inevitably, they point to her early life history of neglect and abuse and her longstanding physical abuse from her ex-husband as justifications for their prognosis. While they considered her neglect/abuse history as a major deficit, they typically fail to consider the many resources she brings to therapy. Not the least of these resources is her success at leaving that abusive relationship and never returning, a significant positive prognostic indicator that Dr. Carlson appears to have considered in his determination that she was a good candidate for brief, time-limited therapy.

In terms of the four profiles, Aimee appears to be closest to Profile III. She definitely has deficits but also has the kind of client resources that, if they can be activated and encouraged by the therapist, can significantly impact the therapeutic process and outcomes. As it turns out, a master therapist like Dr. Carlson might well achieve positive therapeutic outcomes in a six-session therapy with a Profile III client. But that does not mean that trainees or less proficient therapists would be able to achieve similar outcomes in brief therapy. More likely, it might take 5 to 10 times the number of sessions for another therapist even with expert supervision. The reason for this is the "therapist effect" described in Chapter 1.

With regard to clinician credibility, it is likely to have begun before the first session and then increased as therapy progressed. Prior to their first meeting, Aimee is likely to have had some knowledge of Dr. Carlson's reputation as a highly regarded therapist. As the first session unfolds, there are several indications that she experiences him as understanding, respectful, accepting, caring, and knowledgeable. It appeared that she left this session hopeful and expectant that her situation would improve. This is confirmed at the beginning of the next session when she indicates that she had felt considerably better after their first meeting and was intrigued by what he had said. All of these are indicators of a high level of clinician credibility.

Finally, with regard to effecting change in the first session, Dr. Carlson did effect a measure of change. Aimee presented with both a symptom, insomnia, and a life problem, inability to confront her mother. Aimee had been drinking beer to induce sleep, and Dr. Carlson helped her identify healthier alternatives. He also helped her frame a gently assertive way of responding to her mother. Subsequent sessions bore out that both of these first session change efforts were effective.

Dr. Carlson's Commentary

As I began the session with Aimee, I was excited to be putting my work out for others to see. I wanted to do well because I served as the host for all the other videos in the American Psychological Association Video Series. I was confident because I do this every day and told myself this was just another day. I had Aimee fill out some forms, and as I read through them, I was concerned about her husband getting out of prison and tried to imagine her fear as a single mom. I was impressed by her courage, intelligence (obvious from reading her answers on the forms), insight, and ability to communicate. My initial reaction from reading the forms left me worried about post-traumatic stress disorder, alcohol problems, and issues with her mother.

As the session continued, I found her easy to talk with, which is always an important sign for me. I follow a rough outline in gathering information. I am trying to understand her issues and what is going on in her world that I might be able to help her with sufficiently that she will want to return. Essentially, I want to give her hope and maybe a new way to see her life and problems and perhaps even something that she can do differently.

I listen carefully using empathy, respect, and caring and let her know that I am attempting to understand her in the way she wants to be known. This type of connection builds an alliance with Aimee. I busily form a conceptualization of Aimee's problems as I assess her concerns, assets, resources, and defenses. I am especially focused in on what is going right and what strengths she will be able to call on to create a more satisfying life. By focusing on her strengths, she can tell that I like her and that I believe in her. Therapists are trained in diagnosing and treating mental illness or problems and see focusing on flaws, mistakes, and problems as the necessary focus of therapy. Too often therapists focus too much on what is wrong, which discourages clients and makes them less optimistic about themselves and the psychotherapy process. Therapists too often focus on psychopathology and deficits, and so have a hard time even identifying strengths or what is going well for the client.

My years of experience allow me to lead the session in a warm and friendly manner at a slow and deliberate pace. I believe that my calmness (facilitated by a 40-year meditation practice) influences Aimee and she believes that I have seen this situation before and have the wisdom needed to help her create a better life. If Aimee feels a strong alliance with me, she will feel safe enough and hopeful enough to want to talk about issues that previously were seen as intimate, painful, or taboo.

In working with Aimee, I became aware of her dependent personality traits and realized that I needed to help her while facilitating her independence. Aimee has a hard time believing that she is able and can manage her own life. My responses to her are respectful and usually questioning, which subtly keeps her in the driver's seat of the session and her life.

I was also concerned that Aimee was a pleaser and seemed to care more about others at the expense of herself. I initially wondered whether Aimee would be able to be honest in her responses to me or would merely tell me what she thought I wanted to hear. She seemed to take good care of her children, father, and grandmother but did not seem aware of how poorly she treated herself. Right from the opening exchange, I tried to help Aimee feel special, important, and significant in my eyes by asking her about her name.

I began the session by asking Aimee what she would like to change. The focus of each session was to be on action and her role of needing to be responsible.

An early confrontation or observation that she is not honest and that this does not work in relationships lets her know this will be a session that focuses on action. This led to addressing her unsatisfying relationship with her mother. As I indicated earlier, it was important to effect some change in this first session and speaking up to her mother was selected.

Throughout this initial session I asked Aimee questions that she could answer as well as helped her to pinpoint the myriad of problems that plagued her. She discussed issues such as her lack of sleep, alcohol use, early pregnancies and marriage, poor self-care, not being honest with others or herself, staying too busy and stressed, her relationships with parents (primary love objects), the burden of relationships, hiding her feelings, and her overfunctioning with her sons.

Overall, this was a productive first session in which Aimee left feeling hopeful and believing that her life could change. I was active in the session and helped Aimee to disclose many of the issues that she needs to address. Despite the "heavy" nature of the confrontations or corrective experiences, she was able to understand how her decisions limit her happiness and satisfaction.

Concluding Comment

This chapter described five essential tasks that master therapists typically achieve in the first session: establishing a productive therapeutic alliance; performing an initial assessment and identifying client concerns, resources, and deficits; specifying a provisional case conceptualization; establishing clinician credibility; and effecting some initial change. The transcription of the first session between Aimee and Dr. Carlson and the two commentaries suggest that all five of these tasks were accomplished in their first session.

References

Ackerman, S., & Hillensroth, M. (2003). A review of therapist characteristics and techniques positively impacting the therapeutic alliance. *Clinical Psychology Review, 23*, 1–33.

Baumeister, R., & Tierney, J. (2011). *Willpower: Rediscovering the greatest human strength.* New York, NY: Penguin.

Bordin, E. (1979). The generalizability of the psychoanalytic concept of the working alliance. *Psychotherapy: Theory, Research and Practice, 16*, 252–260.

Cummings, N., & Cummings, J. (2013). *Refocused psychotherapy as the first line intervention in behavioral health.* New York, NY: Routledge.

Horvath, A., Del Re, A. C., Flückiger, C., & Symonds, D. (2011). Alliance in individual psychotherapy. *Psychotherapy, 48*, 9–16.

Horvath, A., & Symonds, B. (1991). Relationship between working alliance and outcome in psychotherapy: A metaanalysis. *Journal of Counseling Psychology, 38,* 139–149.

Lambert, M. (1992). Psychotherapy outcome research: Implications for integrative and eclectic therapists. In J. Norcross & M. Goldfried (Eds.), *Handbook of psychotherapy* (pp. 94–129). New York, NY: Basic Books.

Norcross, J. (2002). Empirically supported therapy relationship. In J. Norcross (Ed.), *Psychotherapy relationships that work: Therapist contributions and responsiveness to patients* (pp. 3–16). New York, NY: Oxford University Press.

Orlinsky, D., Grawe, K., & Parks, B. (1994). Process and outcome in psychotherapy. In A. Bergin & S. Garfield (Eds.), *Handbook of psychotherapy and behavior change* (4th ed., pp. 270–376). New York, NY: Wiley.

Orlinsky, D., Ronnestad, M. & Willutzi, U. (2004). Fifty years of psychotherapy process-outcome research: Continuity and change. In M. Lambert (Ed.), *Bergin and Garfield's handbook of psychotherapy and behavior change* (5th ed., pp. 307–389). New York, NY: Wiley.

Paniagua, F. (2005). *Assessing and treating culturally diverse clients: A practical guide* (3rd ed.). Thousand Oaks, CA: Sage.

Rogers, C. (1961). *On becoming a person.* Boston, MA: Houghton-Mifflin.

Sperry, L. (2010a). *Highly effective therapy: Developing essential clinical skills in counseling and psychotherapy.* New York, NY: Routledge.

Sperry, L. (2010b). *Core competencies in counseling and psychotherapy: Becoming a highly competent and effective therapist.* New York, NY: Routledge.

Sperry, L., Brill, P., Howard, K., & Grissom, G. (1996). *Treatment outcomes in psychotherapy and psychiatric interventions.* New York, NY: Brunner/Mazel.

Sperry, L., Carlson, J., & Kjos, D. (2003). *Becoming an effective therapist.* Boston, MA: Allyn & Bacon.

Sue, D., & Zane, N. (1987). The role of culture and cultural technique in psychotherapy: A critique and reformulation. *American Psychologist, 59,* 533–540.

3
EFFECTING CHANGE: THE SECOND SESSION

One of the most tangible markers of an effective first session is that the client returns for a second session. As noted in Chapter 2, a key marker of highly effective therapy is that some change has occurred in the client within and following the first session. Dr. Carlson began to develop a strong therapeutic alliance in the first session. By doing this and by demonstrating his understanding of Aimee's basic maladaptive pattern, his level of clinician credibility increased. In Session 2, it will become evident that not only does the therapeutic alliance continue to develop but also that Dr. Carlson expands his case conceptualization. As the pattern identification process continues, Aimee's secondary pattern of perfectionistic striving and self-criticalness becomes more evident. This pattern complements the client's basic maladaptive pattern of meeting the needs of others while ignoring her own needs. This dual pattern is summarized in Dr. Carlson's response to Aimee: "You were a high achiever to please your parents." Chapter 4 details this expanded case conceptualization, which is all-important in setting the direction for the therapeutic process in the remaining sessions.

This chapter emphasizes the role that corrective experiences play in successful therapy. It may well be that corrective experiences were the necessary and sufficient conditions for successful outcomes in Aimee's therapy. In any event, this chapter begins with a description of corrective experiences and its types. Then, it discusses research on the factors and therapist skills needed to effect corrective experiences. This is followed by a transcription of Session 2 in its entirety. Two commentaries round out the chapter.

Corrective Experiences

The treatment strategy of corrective experience is based on the assumption that insight alone is insufficient to effect a change in a client behavior. As the legendary Freida Fromm-Reichmann is credited with saying, what clients need is a corrective experience, not insight (Levenson, 1995). There is increasing evidence that true change is more likely to occur when insight is followed—or even preceded—with a corrective experience. Since 2007, a group of psychotherapy researchers have been meeting to articulate theory and research on corrective experiences. They view corrective experiences as one of the central dynamics of change in psychotherapy. While historically, corrective experience has been associated with the psychodynamic tradition, many now consider it a broad, trans-theoretical construct. This research group defines corrective experiences as "ones in which a person comes to understand or experience affectively an event or relationship in a different and unexpected way" (Castonguay & Hill, 2012, p. 5). Such "events are not just typical helpful events in therapy, but . . . they are surprising or disconfirming of past experiences and often have a profound effect" (Castonguay & Hill, 2012, p. 6).

As such, corrective experiences play a central role in the transformative processes of various psychotherapy approaches ranging from the psychoanalytic, to the humanistic-experiential, and to the cognitive behavioral. Despite their crucial role in therapy, relatively little research and theoretical attention has been directed at such corrective experiences. This is particularly the case in clarifying the nature of corrective experiences, identifying the therapeutic mechanisms that foster them, and specifying their consequences for positive outcomes. Fortunately, this is beginning to change as the rest of this section demonstrates.

Types of Corrective Experiences

Corrective experience can be of four types: emotional, relational, cognitive, and/or behavioral. Typically, these corrective experiences revise self-other schemas across all types (Constantino & Westra, 2012). Of the four types of corrective experiences, therapists tend to be more familiar with "corrective emotional experiences," which involve reexposing a client, under more favorable circumstances, to emotional situations that he or she could not handle in the past (Alexander & French, 1946). However, based on a quick review of several introductory counseling and psychotherapy texts, it is quite likely that most trainees and practicing therapists do not even know about it. The reason: corrective experiences are mentioned in only one such introductory text (Good & Beitman, 2006) and in only a handful of the many theories of counseling and psychotherapy texts.

Alexander and French (1946) first defined corrective emotional experiences as "reexperiencing the old, unsettled conflict but with a new ending" (p. 338). They pointed out that by behaving differently than the client's significant other, "the therapist has an opportunity to help the patient both to see intellectually and to feel the irrationality of his emotional reactions . . . When one link (the parental response) in this interpersonal relationship is changed through the medium of the therapist, the patient's reaction becomes pointless" (Alexander & French, p. 67). Historically, corrective emotional experience referred specifically to the positive effects of experiencing the discrepancy between how clients expected a therapist to react to them regarding an important life issue or event (e.g., critical) and how the therapist actually responded to them about an issue or event (e.g., supportive). Today, corrective experience has a more general meaning. It refers to any aspects of the therapeutic process that allow clients to experience an unexpected form of relational interaction than can help in healing a previously maladaptive pattern (Beitman & Yue, 1999).

Therapists can use one or both of these understandings of the corrective emotional experience in therapy (i.e., they can foster a corrective experience by actively processing clients' specific relational expectations or, in a more general way, they can foster a caring, positive therapeutic alliance). The value of this more general understanding should not be underestimated. Experiencing a therapist's caring, empathy, concern, and unconditional acceptance may be the first and most important corrective emotional experiences in the lives of many clients. This experience can continue to occur throughout the therapeutic process as practitioners respond to them in a manner that is respectful, accepting, and caring—often the opposite of their own parents or parental figures. Furthermore, corrective emotional experiences can occur outside therapy as clients begin discovering that, because of their corrective experiences with their practitioners, others respond to them differently than in the past. In short, the genuine relationship between clients and therapists, and its constancy, often serves as an ongoing corrective emotional experience that can generalize to other relationships.

Corrective Relational Experiences

In the context of the therapeutic alliance, the client "has the opportunity to actively try out new behaviors in therapy, to see how they feel, and to notice how the therapist responds. This information then shapes the client's interpersonal schemata of what can be expected from self and others" (Alexander & French, 1946, p. 41). This statement was based on the authors' clinical observations. Is there research that supports this observation and what conditions and therapist skills are needed to foster corrective experiences? Some research has already been reported and more studies are under way.

Based on a review of their own and others' research, it is postulated that three general skills are required to effect corrective relational experiences (Constantino & Westra, 2012). First, the therapist must provide a sufficiently favorable therapeutic alliance in which the client can tolerate previous emotional and relational experiences. Second, the therapist must be able to respond to the client in a manner that is different and unexpected from how others have responded to the client. Third, when the client encounters unexpected experiences "the therapist must tread lightly while paying constant attention to the clients' anxieties, responses, and powerful pulls to revert to what is familiar, as well as to the climate of the therapeutic alliance" (p. 125).

A seminal qualitative research study of corrective relational experiences seems to bear out Constantino and Westra's observation on these three skills. In this study, of the factors that foster corrective experiences in psychotherapy, the corrective emotional experiences of 12 clients, all therapists-in-training, were analyzed (Knox, Hess, Hill, Burkard, & Cool-Lyon, 2012). Based on their analyses, several conclusions were reached. First, both client and therapist needed to be actively involved in the therapeutic process. The client "had to be willing to examine their thoughts and feelings, and also to assert themselves or their emotions. In essence they had to be willing to stay fully engaged in the work of therapy, even when doing so was difficult or uncomfortable" (Knox et al., 2012, p. 206). Their willingness to remain engaged reflected the strength of the therapeutic alliance, because, without the therapist providing a nurturing space, it would have been less likely for them to experience the level of vulnerability needed for healing and growth.

Therapists who fostered corrective relational experiences were found to provide sufficient empathy and acceptance and a safe and compassionate space and were fully present to their clients as they grappled with their therapeutic issues. Presumably, because of these factors and that clients experienced their therapists as neither critical nor judgmental, these corrective, tranformational experiences were able to be manifest. As a result, they responded quite differently than did the clients' significant others from the past. In such a healing space, clients could begin to challenge their assumptions about the futility or pain of entering into close relationships with others (Knox et al., 2012).

The results were remarkable.

"All noted welcomed transformations within themselves, and most also experienced improvement in their therapy relationship, in their relations with others in their work with their own clients.... (T)heir lives were changed in the here and now of the therapy relationship and they began to productively alter their long-standing relational patterns. Their now broader and more flexible relational schemas likely also contributed to their ability to engage with others more healthily, allowing them to resolve rather than repeat earlier problematic behavior patterns" (Knox et al., 2012, pp. 206–207).

 Transcription of Session 2

The entirety of Session 2 is presented here followed by two commentaries.

> DR. CARLSON: Hi Aimee, it's good to see you again. It's been one week since we talked.
>
> AIMEE: Yeah.
>
> DR. CARLSON: And I had you fill out a sheet, before we began, with three questions and one is what's been different, the second one is what's improved, and three is what do you want to talk about tonight? So let's go to the first one, you said what's been different, you said you were beginning to understand why you made some of the choices that you've made in the past ...

AIMEE: Well...
DR. CARLSON: What's that about?
AIMEE: Like last week, what you were talking about my mother, how I choose mates, I sort of started to analyze that after I left here. I was... it was so weird because everything... every single guy I've chosen had the same characteristics, characteristic traits as my mother.
DR. CARLSON: What were the ones that jumped out? Some of the ones that...
AIMEE: Of boyfriends or traits?
DR. CARLSON: Yeah, the traits.
AIMEE: OK, umm... selfishness, kind of umm... self-centered... a lot of me statement from all those people.
DR. CARLSON: Oh.
AIMEE: What they want instead of what I wanted. Also, a lot of dramatics...
DR. CARLSON: Oh, really?
AIMEE: It seemed like when losing me was a threat to them, they pulled out these tricks of oh I'm gonna kill myself, I don't know how I'd live without you, and I'm a very loving person and caring so I would feel like oh I better not tell them to get lost just yet, so...
DR. CARLSON: You said that last week that you'd kind of stick with them for a while until things calmed down a little and then end it.
AIMEE: Until they did something that would really make me upset and then it was easy. It was the only way to iron that out.
DR. CARLSON: So, one of the things you're seeing is that pattern. Were there any other patterns that you noticed?
AIMEE: Uh... it seemed like the more I gave to these people the less they, you know, kind of retracted from me. It seemed like if I acted disinterested, which I never really did, but you know just had more going on than usual in my life, they would... they would seem to be more infatuated with me and that's kind of how my mother is. You know, the more I try to be around her the less she's interested in a relationship... so...
DR. CARLSON: Well, that's interesting. So, like the more you distance, the more they pursue?
AIMEE: Yes, definitely.
DR. CARLSON: But you're more of a pursuer?
AIMEE: Umm... not at first, but when I start to like somebody and actually let them into my little shell then yes, then I am the pursuer.
DR. CARLSON: OK, so, it sounds like you've been doing quite a bit of thinking this week.
AIMEE: Oh, yes.

DR. CARLSON: OK, and one of the things that we've talked about you doing was to talk to your mother, were you able to do that?

AIMEE: Uhh . . . I tried. I tried and umm I haven't done it yet. I hate to tell you that because I am a people pleaser and I tried every effort to come in here and tell you yes I did that, but unfortunately . . .

DR. CARLSON: Well, good. Honesty is a good thing too.

AIMEE: Yeah. Well, I need to be honest with her, right?

DR. CARLSON: Well, that's good that you can be honest here as well.

AIMEE: I . . . every time I thought about it, I wanted to do something else . . . like, well the toilet needs to be scrubbed or something . . .

DR. CARLSON: I see.

AIMEE: I always found something hideous that was better than telling my mother that. So, umm . . .

DR. CARLSON: I thought it was going to be pretty difficult, but was that where you thought you wanted to start?

AIMEE: Yeah, and umm I have this week to try to do it again.

DR. CARLSON: Well, you know, when people try to do it, that's when they think about it, but yet they don't do it. Is this a week you could do it?

AIMEE: Yes, but like that last week was kind of hectic for me. Uh, she had gone out of town a couple of days. I didn't want to tell her on the phone. I only saw her once and it was brief for like five or ten minutes at my grandmother's house and everybody was celebrating my grandmother's birthday so I kind of didn't want to . . .

DR. CARLSON: That was not a good time.

AIMEE: No. So, conveniently it wasn't a good time for me so I'm hoping that maybe that, you know, sometime this week I can make time.

DR. CARLSON: This is good; I'm hoping that maybe sometime . . . uh, I'm not betting on it.

AIMEE: Well . . .

DR. CARLSON: How can you help me to be more confident in you because it's your choice?

AIMEE: Well, this week I will. I will go there or she will come to my house. She was going to be at my house actually on Saturday, so . . .

DR. CARLSON: And what is it again that you're going to say?

AIMEE: I think I'm going to tell her.

DR. CARLSON: I think I'm going to tell her?

AIMEE: Well, I was thinking about what we were going to say and what I was going to, and I kind of like refined it once again.

DR. CARLSON: OK, so it isn't like you didn't think about it this week.

AIMEE: No, I thought a lot about it. It's been on my mind everyday actually . . .

DR. CARLSON: OK.
AIMEE: So, I believe this time I'm going to tell her that I didn't have a mother . . . well, you tell me what you think . . . I didn't have a mother when I was young, but I would like to have one now.
DR. CARLSON: Well, that sounds beautiful! That's beautiful!
AIMEE: That way I don't . . . it's not so harsh.
DR. CARLSON: Yeah.
AIMEE: I don't know.
DR. CARLSON: And it's right off of what she had said too. I mean, she had said that she wasn't much of a mother when she was younger . . .
AIMEE: Yeah.
DR. CARLSON: And then you bailed her out.
AIMEE: Yes, so . . . would that be . . .
DR. CARLSON: Oh, I think it's wonderful! That's worth the wait . . .
AIMEE: It's kind of putting the guilt off of her, but it's still telling her how I feel.
DR. CARLSON: And it's still a request the focus isn't on where we are, but where we're going to go.
AIMEE: Mhmm. Definitely.
DR. CARLSON: Wow.
AIMEE: So that's what I . . . I've thought a lot about it.
DR. CARLSON: That's good.
AIMEE: I've actually thought about going over there a few times like I said I've always found other activities that I normally would hate to do.
DR. CARLSON: Well, let's see what happens this week and we don't want to make a step too big.
AIMEE: Mhmm.
DR. CARLSON: And it sounds like you were really working at it this week.
AIMEE: Oh, yeah.
DR. CARLSON: And if you were to do it this week, is there a day that's better than any other day that you would be more likely to not be working?
AIMEE: I think Saturday is going to be a good day; work right now is kind of slow for me so I'm kind of enjoying a little mini vacation. I've been home a lot during the daytime; she works during the day, but Saturday I'm having a party for my son so I think that day is going to be a good time because . . . well she's going to come help me set it up and everything so they won't be around really they'll probably be doing their own thing with their friends.
DR. CARLSON: So, you'd do this before the party?
AIMEE: Yeah, but I don't think . . . I think it would set it off alright.
DR. CARLSON: Especially the way that you said it; it sounds so . . . it actually sounds loving.

AIMEE: Yeah.

DR. CARLSON: And it gets your point across too.

AIMEE: Yeah, definitely. So that way I'm not stewing over it through the whole party because I'm protecting myself there because I know if I didn't tell her I'd be thinking about it through the whole party . . . well she's here now . . . because that's what happened when I saw her at my grandmother's, I saw her and I was like well she's here now. But so it kind of put a damper on things for me and I don't want that to happen like the last time around.

DR. CARLSON: OK. Alright, now you said you've improved your state of mind and you feel more at ease this week.

AIMEE: Yeah, I've been pretty relaxed actually. I don't know, I just feel like I haven't been on the turnstile of running around.

DR. CARLSON: Mhmm.

AIMEE: And of finding things to do that much . . . I've kind of relaxed a little bit, I mean I'm still up and running, but I don't know, I feel this peace inside myself.

DR. CARLSON: Does that happen at other times in your life? Is that peace something that comes and goes?

AIMEE: It comes when I have a relationship that's working at the time . . .

DR. CARLSON: Uh huh . . .

AIMEE: But that's not that often.

DR. CARLSON: Would that mean you are in a relationship that's working?

AIMEE: No, I'm not. I'm by myself . . . single.

DR. CARLSON: So, this is the same sort of feeling, but at a different time?

AIMEE: Yeah, and maybe I was relying on having that feeling through other people. I don't know, you know, being in a relationship, having that stability instead of on my own. Because when I was single in the past . . . I was single for a really long time after I got the divorce and it wasn't until about five or six years ago that I had a series of relationships . . . one after the other . . . and I don't know why that happened but umm whenever I was in a relationship and it was going well then I felt the way I'm feeling now. I didn't have to think about, you know, what I'm going to do.

DR. CARLSON: How do you think you created it this time? It's generally something we want to attribute to something else, but these feelings really have to come from within you, it's something that you have to do.

AIMEE: You know, I don't know. I think a lot of it has to do with I'm thinking about the mom situation and I'm kind of like . . . I've talked to my friends, a couple of friends about it. Whereas I've never kind of talked about it before, I always kind of kept it inside and it felt good to talk about it and

I felt really guilty to tell them well I don't hate my mom, but I really resent her. So, I think that by talking about it and them accepting . . . that's alright to resent your mom, that's OK to do that . . . that I felt a little better about myself that I wasn't this evil person.

DR. CARLSON: Do you think that's similar to when you have a boyfriend and you are sharing your thoughts and feelings to them?

AIMEE: Yeah, but I don't ever really recall telling them . . .

DR. CARLSON: Well, not necessarily that thought or feeling, but any thought or feeling where you are attempting to talk or . . .

AIMEE: Yes, definitely. For some reason, I can't really tell my family how I feel. I feel like I'm going to hurt somebody's feelings so . . .

DR. CARLSON: OK, well let's not lose track of what you've done here though, and I'm wondering if it isn't two things. One is when you talk about how you feel to others or when you plan to do something about a problem that you start to feel better inside?

AIMEE: Yeah, you're probably right there. I didn't think about that. I thought about how maybe it was just the fact that I was talking about it but . . .

DR. CARLSON: But you've created that, not other people. No one sprinkled pixie dust on you . . .

AIMEE: Yeah.

DR. CARLSON: And it's something if you can figure out what brings that good feeling; you could have more of that peace that you have.

AIMEE: Yeah, I think you're right because once I start, now that I know which direction I'm going into, it kind of feels good and I don't feel like I'm spinning my wheels as much I feel like I have a goal and I'm kind of working towards that and before I was sort of trying to get by.

DR. CARLSON: OK that's . . . that can be very . . .

AIMEE: Just trying to maintain sanity sometimes.

DR. CARLSON: Well, about a minute ago you said 'I can't talk to my family . . .'

AIMEE: No.

DR. CARLSON: Could I have you change what you said and to say 'I can't talk to my family *yet*'?

AIMEE: OK, I can't talk to my family *yet*.

DR. CARLSON: That's a little different feeling . . .

AIMEE: Mhmm.

DR. CARLSON: That goes along with that because we're not going to . . . that'll come in time.

AIMEE: Yes, I . . . like I said I have a few good friends. I don't have many friends; I have a very busy life, but the ones that I do I can tell them things that I can't tell my family which is weird because my family and I we're a very close meshed family, lots of . . . everybody is in everybody's business and all so . . . when it comes to matters of the heart I just kind of like clam up. I can't really tell them like well your drinking makes me mad or . . . you know, I have several alcoholics in my family.

DR. CARLSON: You said, I can't tell them?

AIMEE: I can't tell them how I feel.

DR. CARLSON: I can't tell them . . .

AIMEE: Yet.

DR. CARLSON: Yet, OK.

AIMEE: How I feel. So, I bottle that in and that gets me angry and it bogs me down, you know, to think about the situations in my family that I can't control, but I'd like to at least, you know, acknowledge . . .

DR. CARLSON: Ahh.

AIMEE: Instead of ignoring it . . . because that's what I'm doing now, I'm ignoring.

DR. CARLSON: Alright, right now you are, but that's something we can work towards.

AIMEE: Yeah.

DR. CARLSON: And we're going to start with your mom this Saturday?

AIMEE: Yeah, definitely.

DR. CARLSON: And sometimes it's just priming the pump a little to get it started because it's something that you could do with friends, so it's not something that you have to . . . like it's not like learning a foreign language where you have to start all over. It's something you have to know how to do in this situation so now you've got to learn how to do it in this situation

AIMEE: Well, I sort of, kind of, you're right, I kind of practiced it out or gave it a test run through telling my friends about it.

DR. CARLSON: I was thinking the same thing.

AIMEE: Yeah, so it was like hey . . .

DR. CARLSON: So this was really a pretty good week for you?

AIMEE: Yeah, I'm feeling great.

DR. CARLSON: I mean, you did it with friends.

AIMEE: Yeah.

DR. CARLSON: And you thought about how to say it differently even though you didn't do what . . .

AIMEE: I've actually been tired too, I went to sleep the last couple of nights when I should have instead of, you know, stayed up reading until three in the morning.

DR. CARLSON: And no beer or?

AIMEE: No, no.

DR. CARLSON: Wow.
AIMEE: So, I felt good.
DR. CARLSON: Some balance is happening here, isn't it?
AIMEE: Yeah, definitely.
DR. CARLSON: Wow. It's nice to see you smile with what you've created too.
AIMEE: Yeah, I never even realized I was smiling.
DR. CARLSON: Uhuh . . . it was a different kind of smile. It was a smile like of satisfaction.
AIMEE: Yeah.
DR. CARLSON: And you've done this, and you feel better, and you're sleeping better. Yeah, good work. Now down here, on the sheet you said that you wanted to talk about issues related to school.
AIMEE: That too . . . umm for some reason, I don't have a lot of confidence in my ability to go ahead with my schooling. I don't know why that is because I excel as a student I have a very high GPA and I have very high marks on very difficult assignments, but I just don't have any confidence in myself. Like, there's times when I've turned in papers and I sat there and thought about it and I wanted to call the professor up and say oh that was garbage, uhh ignore that one, I've got another one here. And I don't know, it's hard for me to uhh . . .
DR. CARLSON: And what happened to that paper?
AIMEE: I got an A and I actually, this one in particular, I keep thinking about. I went on a limb and a lot of interpretation of a masterpiece, *Moby Dick*, and my professor at the time was this guy that was very brilliant and I was kind of uhh, I don't know what's the word I am looking for, I was kind of scared about . . . intimidated. I thought uh he's not gonna want to hear this bunch of garbage. So he was out of town, this happened years ago, in undergrad, when I was an undergrad, I slid it under the door, then I was thinking about trying to get it out from underneath the door. So, when I, after I got it back I got an A on it and he said I should turn it in for a PhD dissertation. I was blown away.
DR. CARLSON: Wow!
AIMEE: And out of all the times he's read the book, studied it, and he's never heard that interpretation, and I was like wooh, I didn't even realize it. I thought it was a bunch of you know . . .
DR. CARLSON: Wow. So, this feeling of lack of confidence doesn't really seem to be stemming from your performance?
AIMEE: No, it doesn't matter how hard I work, I always think I'm not going to make it, I'm always worried I'm not gonna make the cut and then I get straight As. So, I worry myself over nothing, but I don't know why I do

that and I always feel like I'd like to go on to higher education, but I feel like I can't do that, you know, I was . . . I'm lucky I'm even in grad school, that's what I tell myself.

DR. CARLSON: Oh, so that's interesting. So the part that you would like to change is?

AIMEE: I just wish that I could feel confident in what I do.

DR. CARLSON: And if you felt confident in what you do, how would I know that? What would you do?

AIMEE: I don't know. I just feel like I'd probably pursue a higher education than getting master's, I would like to.

DR. CARLSON: So, one thing that would let you know that you are confident is going on and getting a doctorate degree?

AIMEE: Perhaps, but also I want to be a writer, not . . . that's not what I want to do for a living, but I want to write a couple of books and I have always written. I've written a couple of screenplays.

DR. CARLSON: Oh, wow.

AIMEE: And um . . . I love to write, but then I never show anybody what I write, except a few people or assignments that I've had to do in school and everybody always praises me for my writing and says I have talent, but I always feel like ehh this is a bunch of . . . I tell myself that this really sucks, I don't know why I do that. But other people always tell me it's great so . . . and it isn't about what other people say, it's about me, it's something . . .

DR. CARLSON: How do you feel when you get the paper back and you get an A on it? Do you feel any differently?

AIMEE: No. Well, not really I'm kind of hard on myself. I always think well this is an A, but I see this mistake here and it could've been better. I'm just not . . . I don't know I'm very hard on myself about everything . . . I . . . instead of thinking about all that I've accomplished, in spite all of the setbacks in my life, being a single mom and doing what I've done, I think like oh well I could've done this. There's always room for improvement and I never just sit down and say . . . people tell me wow I'm amazed by what you've done and I just don't give myself credit for any of those things.

DR. CARLSON: Yeah.

AIMEE: I don't know why I'm like that, I just . . . part of me is kind of like um . . . my dad was always really hard on me about working and work ethic, slacking off . . . so I don't feel like . . . just in praise is kind of slacking off to me, I just feel like OK well don't get vain and just keep going, you know, that's the way I feel. So, I need to pat myself on the back, but I just don't know how. I just keep going . . .

DR. CARLSON: Yeah.

EFFECTING CHANGE: THE SECOND SESSION

AIMEE: Instead of, you know, basking in the fact that I've succeeded so far.

DR. CARLSON: And it sounds like this ritual that you have is pretty successful for you.

AIMEE: Yeah.

DR. CARLSON: When you write a paper and you agonize and then you get . . .

AIMEE: It seems like the ones that I stress over the most I do better on. Like, if I think it's great and I don't really put too much effort into it.

DR. CARLSON: And do you get upset about being upset?

AIMEE: Yeah, yeah I do.

DR. CARLSON: What would you say if I said that's perfectly normal what you do?

AIMEE: I don't know I've never met anybody that's like me. Maybe they just don't share that with me. I'm sure there are other people out there that feel that way, but I just feel like I'm the only one.

DR. CARLSON: Right. One of the things that I used to do some coaching in, maybe this could be helpful information, but the person who is always very calm and confident usually doesn't perform very well.

AIMEE: I didn't know that.

DR. CARLSON: The person who has a lot of anxiety and worries and isn't sure about something is usually the one who performs the best. The one who performs the absolute worst is the one who is so worried they can never even do the paper.

AIMEE: OK.

DR. CARLSON: But you do the paper. It doesn't seem to stop you from doing it . . .

AIMEE: No.

DR. CARLSON: It's finally being able to say this is finished and that's the sign of someone who does maximum performance.

AIMEE: Yeah, I have to finish every task. I'm very . . . I can't leave anything unfinished.

DR. CARLSON: So, would it be possible for you to say, when you get worried next time that this is really OK? This is the way people who achieve well . . . it's normal.

AIMEE: Well, that would sound a lot better than me saying oh why am I even trying . . . the things I tell myself you know . . .

DR. CARLSON: There are several books and studies on this that you can read and it has to do with levels of anxiety and peak performance . . . and so it sounds like you're getting down on yourself for something that's normal and when you get down on yourself then it makes it worse than it really is.

AIMEE: Yeah, it does. Yeah, and it seems like I work the best under pressure.

DR. CARLSON: Mhmm.

AIMEE: You know . . .

DR. CARLSON: So, that's your style?

AIMEE: Yeah, mhmm . . . in anything I do, you know, my job I drive . . . so there's a lot of pressure there and it seems like the harder it is to get to a place ho-hum, you know, I drive better, I don't know. I just I have a purpose and I feel a little more responsible.

DR. CARLSON: So, that's something else you know about yourself, that you work better on deadlines and under pressure.

AIMEE: Yes, definitely. I got to have a place or time to be there and everything . . . so.

DR. CARLSON: So, the performance you get nervous and worried and then you get good results. You enjoy things more, perform better when there is pressure. What else do you know about how you do things?

AIMEE: Uh, everything has to be finished and has to be perfect, but I take pride in my work, I don't turn in anything that's really bad, unless maybe there's somehow I misunderstood the criteria or something.

DR. CARLSON: Uh huh, yeah, which is pretty normal . . . so it sounds like you have a lot of pride in what you do?

AIMEE: Yeah, definitely.

DR. CARLSON: That sounds a lot like your dad with his music?

AIMEE: Yes, yes, and uh that's how it is with me and my writing also. I can kind of . . . I'm my own critic, but when I'm writing and it's great . . . it's . . . it feels good not to think about it. Like, oh, well I could've done this differently or I need to change this around. Instead it's just perfect the way it is and that feels good, but it doesn't happen like that all the time, you know, I have to hit and miss a lot.

DR. CARLSON: Well, how many masterpieces does anybody write?

AIMEE: Yeah, exactly.

DR. CARLSON: I think there are one, maybe two, good stories in each of us.

AIMEE: Oh, exactly.

DR. CARLSON: Mhmm . . . so those are some goals that for some people might be lofty with, but for you they sound like they're pretty reasonable . . .

AIMEE: Yeah.

DR. CARLSON: . . . To write your own book or two?

AIMEE: In my spare time, I don't want to be like some Hemmingway or something; I just want to write a book about my life someday. Not yet, I'm still living it, hopefully I'm at least half-way there.

DR. CARLSON: And then you said you were a high achiever?

AIMEE: Yeah.

DR. CARLSON: In high school, you told me last week that you wanted to please your parents, and then you did well in college and you're doing well in graduate school and . . .

AIMEE: Too well, I mean as an undergrad, I had a class and it was a 100 level class, but I was in my senior year and I needed this class to fulfill my requirement and it was really intense and I didn't and I was going through all these other, I mean 400 level lit courses and everything so . . . I kind of got slumped up and I got bogged down and I got a D on it and it was devastating to me. I mean, I felt like killing myself after that happened. I thought about it some of the people in my classes . . . I don't know how they were still there. You know, and it was the first time I got a D in college for 4 or 5 years . . .

DR. CARLSON: Wow.

AIMEE: I mean, I should have looked at it like that way . . . like, look at how far you've gone with really great grades. I got three As and a D. . . . so you know . . .

DR. CARLSON: Two hundred As and a D.

AIMEE: Yeah. Well yeah for the semester yeah of course . . . but I could . . . Yeah, and then there's people that were in my classes with me that would have been happy with a D.

DR. CARLSON: With a D . . .

AIMEE: So, I don't know if I should've of looked it at that way . . . I've been thinking a lot about this.

DR. CARLSON: Well, I don't know if you should've, but it sounds like you felt better if you did?

AIMEE: Yeah, definitely, instead of oh this is it, you know. This is the end, I've failed and I can't fail . . . I'm very hard failing . . . failing tests, failing driving, failing my family, failing my father, you know, it's just the way . . . I don't want to fail, so I try extra hard not to.

DR. CARLSON: So, that's a source of extra motivation.

AIMEE: Mhmm . . . yes definitely.

DR. CARLSON: And at least, in these situations, it sounds like it helps you to achieve . . .

AIMEE: Yes.

DR. CARLSON: And it's going to help you, I mean, I guess if you get all As all the way through, you're probably going to get in a doctoral program, if you want to do that . . . I mean that's usually how you get it.

AIMEE: Yeah, well I, like I said I say ah well you know I'm not going to be able to make the cut or ah I keep telling myself.

DR. CARLSON: That's the high performer in you; kind of working yourself up to try harder. They call that inferiority feelings at times, and these inferiority feelings are things that for many people become catalysts. If you didn't have those, you probably wouldn't do anything.

AIMEE: I remember in fifth grade I had to try out for something and I admit I was kind of the "nerd" type. I wasn't part of the in-crowd and so I had one good friend that was it. So, we had this show, it was kind of like a talent show, you know, it was the last grade before junior high and the fifth graders were supposed had this really special show to put on for the town and school and uh, I tried out for the lead and it took every ounce of courage for me to get up in front of everybody and all my classmates and get up and dance and sing and the teachers were like blown away by my performance and I always wanted to be a performer, but I don't feel that I'd be good enough to do that and I got the lead and all the other girl were making fun of me and stuff kind of out of jealousy I don't know, but I got the lead and I never thought in a million years I would get it, I just did it because I felt like I had to do it. Like, if I didn't I would feel like I failed . . . myself so . . .

DR. CARLSON: So there's a lot of drive that you have . . .

AIMEE: Oh yeah.

DR. CARLSON: But it's in a lot of areas. I mean it's in the arts, it's in writing, and uh you talked about playing music last week.

AIMEE: Yeah, I sing, I play the drums, I write, I can't draw though, but hey we can't win em' all right?

DR. CARLSON: Yeah, that's what they have illustrators there for.

AIMEE: I love to dance, too. I'm a good dancer.

DR. CARLSON: Wow.

AIMEE: So . . .

DR. CARLSON: So, do you know what you just did there, by the way?

AIMEE: No.

DR. CARLSON: You showed confidence.

AIMEE: Yeah, well I can now. Well, now that I'm older, I feel that I am good at these things so . . .

DR. CARLSON: Twenty minutes ago you weren't.

AIMEE: Well, in fifth grade, I never . . . I always put on little shows for my family and friends and stuff, but never . . .

DR. CARLSON: But, you questioned your confidence just a few minutes ago . . .

AIMEE: Oh about . . .

DR. CARLSON: And you talked so confidently when you talked about the things that you could do. So, there's sort of kind of sometimes yes and sometimes no.

AIMEE: With my writing, I feel like I don't know if everything is going to be a masterpiece, but I got to write something that isn't profound enough to show people I know. You know, I don't want them to be like this is great, you know, but it really stinks. So, I waited until I had some type of inspiration and that seems like that's when it happens. You know, I write a lot then I get this idea and it comes to me and it feels right and I don't have to think about it, it just happens so that's when my best work happens.

DR. CARLSON: And you think you're different from anybody else?

AIMEE: I don't know, I guess so. I feel like I'm different.

DR. CARLSON: I think this is another one of those situations that most writers that I know write lots of things before they find something that they know is good. You know, you see them throwing all the paper away and starting all over again.

AIMEE: Definitely, I do a lot of that.

DR. CARLSON: It sounds like you're pretty normal. You know, one of the things that it sounds like you like to do, not like to do but you do pretty easily is describe yourself as though there's something wrong with you.

AIMEE: Yeah, I do that a lot.

DR. CARLSON: The things that you're describing to me seem pretty normal. I mean taking or writing several things before you find something that's good or getting really worked up about a paper.

AIMEE: Yeah, well to me I feel isolated, especially when that's happening. You know, like this is happening to me, you know I can't really turn to anybody else.

DR. CARLSON: Does it help any when I give you feedback that what you're doing is really OK?

AIMEE: Yeah, it does.

DR. CARLSON: Because I got the idea before that you were pretty private when you were growing up.

AIMEE: Well...

DR. CARLSON: You know, your mom was gone and your dad was sort of gone and your grandma had these seven other kids to be taking care of and you had this large family . . . you didn't get a lot of feedback.

AIMEE: No, I didn't get . . . well, that's how I think I expressed . . . I got my attention through like singing and dancing . . . like putting on shows for my family because I demanded attention.

DR. CARLSON: It sounds like you had to?

AIMEE: Yeah, I did, but you know so it was all like oh well isn't that cute and all that stuff, but then I got older and I couldn't do that in the real world . . . just start singing and dancing out there . . . so . . .

DR. CARLSON: Well, you didn't have a lot of guidance.

AIMEE: No.

DR. CARLSON: I mean, maybe you could've if you would've had some guidance?

AIMEE: Yeah

DR. CARLSON: But I got this feeling, like just now I hear you talking negatively about yourself about things that are really pretty normal.

AIMEE: Yeah, well, like I said, I don't feel they're normal because well I didn't really . . .

DR. CARLSON: I understand that we don't think that they're normal . . .

AIMEE: No.

DR. CARLSON: And then you think that you feel that way?

AIMEE: Yeah.

DR. CARLSON: I think it comes from the thought.

AIMEE: Yeah, I think it does.

DR. CARLSON: That would be something that might be helpful or for you to work on . . . to give yourself permission to write a lot of crummy things before you get into something you like or to be nervous about a paper that you wrote.

AIMEE: Yeah . . .

DR. CARLSON: Could you picture yourself doing that?

AIMEE: Yes, I could. I think I'm going to need to because at some point in my life, I'm going to have to just learn to do things on the basis of doing instead of thinking about, you know, what other people think or I'm different or oh this isn't good . . . just do instead of think about those things, you know.

DR. CARLSON: And are you pushing yourself so much for fear of what other people think? Or, I almost got a bit of it from there, for what you think?

AIMEE: For me, yeah.

DR. CARLSON: And that's really important because I wouldn't want you to give up your own standards.

AIMEE: Yeah, who was it that said you're your worst critic or something? Yeah, so.

DR. CARLSON: Yeah, well . . .

AIMEE: That's how I feel.

DR. CARLSON: Mhmm . . . they were talking right to you.

AIMEE: Yeah, they were that's for sure.

DR. CARLSON: Yeah, I could see where for school some of it is just when you do very well, but you just don't feel very good when you do it.

AIMEE: Well, uhh, I just feel like well everybody always encourages me, well you should go on and I'm the first generation college student of my family . . .

DR. CARLSON: Really? Wow.

AIMEE: Yeah.

DR. CARLSON: And you're already in graduate school?

AIMEE: Yeah, so I don't know why I feel like, you know why not make it even better than that and do more and challenge myself . . .

DR. CARLSON: It sounds like you're in no-where's land. I mean, there's no one else to guide you . . . you don't have a brother or sister or parent to follow.

AIMEE: No, in fact, my family umm . . . well they encourage me to go to school, but they're all like hey school's over now come on when are you going to get your degree and do what you have to do?

DR. CARLSON: So, they say two things?

AIMEE: Yeah.

DR. CARLSON: Because they don't understand?

AIMEE: Yeah, but I value learning. I've always been that way, even as a kid I would always read for enjoyment. I wasn't like . . . a lot of other kids didn't like to read and I enjoyed learning about everything and I still do. So, I feel like I don't want to stop learning, I don't . . . I mean I know that if I get a job and I have a career it's not gonna keep me from or stop me from learning. I want to challenge my mind, I want to, I want to use it, instead of this is . . . well alright this is . . . instead of settling for just that. I think there's no limit to what a person could do if they . . . if they're that type of person. I don't think that's for everybody though.

DR. CARLSON: So, where do you think you get the guidance that you need? I mean, would it be helpful to try to find a mentor or somebody who you respect who's where you think you want to be?

AIMEE: Definitely, right now I don't know where I get it from . . . I'm not a religious person, I'm a spiritual person, but I'm . . . I toy with that a lot too . . . I don't know where I want to be as far as that is, but I just kind of like have to rely on myself as my mentor for now because I really don't have anybody else.

DR. CARLSON: Yeah, well that might be something to talk about, too, in terms of how to find someone who could mentor you in some of these areas.

AIMEE: I don't even know how to go about doing that, I have no idea.

DR. CARLSON: Right, well maybe it's something that you haven't thought a whole lot about?

AIMEE: And then, also, I want to get involved with things at school . . . groups, clubs, what have you, but I feel like . . . nobody is like me . . . so I'm kind of reclusive and I have my own life and I come to class . . . I participate in class, but like as far as any social activities outside of the class I don't do . . . I want to, but I feel like eh, I'm not like them. I don't know why because I'm sure like a lot of people, you know, are nontraditional students just like me, but I feel like they just don't know what it's like.

DR. CARLSON: And so you say those things to yourself and you act as if they're true. I mean, sort of like those things we were talking about before about being nervous . . .

AIMEE: Mhmm.

DR. CARLSON: And that's a bad thing as opposed to a normal thing and you say this as if this is true and you don't challenge it. My guess is probably that you're like a lot of the students?

AIMEE: Oh yeah.

DR. CARLSON: You know, like you said, nontraditional students.

AIMEE: Yeah, but when I . . . I feel like I don't connect with a lot of the people, but I mean I'm sure that I . . . if I opened up a little more I would connect with a lot of the people . . . you know, I just kind of like . . .

DR. CARLSON: Mmhm . . . so opening up is a work-in-progress for you right?

AIMEE: Yeah, definitely.

DR. CARLSON: And you started to do it with your friends and now you're going to do it with your mom. You think in time this is something you could do with other students?

AIMEE: Yeah, I prob . . . definitely because I think I need that too because right now it's hard for me to find people like me, you know, when I go places socially because I'm kind of an intellectual and like I meet a lot of people that, you know, I don't think they're dumb or anything, but they're just not into the things like reading or the things that I like to do so I never make a connection with men or friends; it just doesn't happen.

DR. CARLSON: So you could see how some point in time it's going to be important to find some friends who have similar . . .

AIMEE: Yeah, I mean it would be a lot better to meet up with friends, like here at school or wherever, you know that have the same interest as you than as opposed to someone that you have to like because you know they're fun a little bit, but they have no idea what you're talking about as far as music or you know writing is concerned . . .

DR. CARLSON: Mhmm.

AIMEE: So, um . . . the Internet has helped me though the Internet is a great tool to find people that like to do things that you do, but you know they just live in England or somewhere far away so it's kind of . . .

DR. CARLSON: Yeah, you know they're out there, it's just they're not around the corner.

AIMEE: No, that's for sure.

DR. CARLSON: That's where your relatives are, just around the corner. It's really nice to see how excited you're getting about this or how easy it is for you, or at least it appears to me how easy it is to talk.

AIMEE: Yeah.

DR. CARLSON: And you describe having, you know, maybe a difficult time talking with people, but it looks like it's pretty natural for you here.

AIMEE: Well, I could talk to people, but it . . . I always, like I said, it's like the surface person I think I mentioned that last week it's not who I really am and I need to be OK with who I am, you know and say hey what's wrong with me instead of this façade . . . I don't know when I'm ever going to.

DR. CARLSON: Well, it sounds like you're doing that . . . I remember that you said that you did it with two of your close friends this week.

AIMEE: Yeah.

DR. CARLSON: I mean it sounds like you're working on that. I don't know if you want to bare your soul to everybody.

AIMEE: No, I don't. Yeah, hi nice to meet you, I'm a recovering . . . [*laughing*] no, I don't want to do that.

DR. CARLSON: That sort of a thing, but maybe some of that is figuring out when to share and when to keep it superficial.

AIMEE: Yeah, but I'm superficial with everybody . . . see and that's where it goes wrong.

DR. CARLSON: That's another one of those statements that's not true.

AIMEE: Well, I mean that . . .

DR. CARLSON: Superficial with people so far, but I've started with my friends, this Saturday I'm going to talk to my mom.

AIMEE: Yes.

DR. CARLSON: See, that's where you get to be that critic of yourself that doesn't give yourself credit for the progress you're making.

AIMEE: Mhmm. Well, definitely the whole time I was driving here I was thinking well I didn't do it, aww darn, I didn't do it, what have I achieved this week.

DR. CARLSON: But hopefully you saw what you did do. I mean, you were here and then you actually talked to some other people you'd never talked with before and you actually came up with a better way to say it . . . I mean so the next step would be to do it.

AIMEE: Mhmm. Yeah, but I wasn't thinking that way on my way in my car . . . I was thinking oh I failed, that's what I was thinking, I failed to do what I wanted to do . . .

DR. CARLSON: *So far* . . . you have to keep on adding those *so far*'s and *yet*. OK, so this week we got a couple of things; you're going to talk to mom like we talked about . . .

AIMEE: OK.

DR. CARLSON: It would be nice if you give yourself permission to do some of these normal things. You know, like if you write a story and there's nothing there and you throw it away and you go oh well maybe the next one.

AIMEE: Yeah, that's hard for me to do, but . . .

DR. CARLSON: Oh well, now we know it's normal . . . and then you talked about feeling good and you talked about what you did to feel good this week which was sharing with other people, talking with other people and then taking action. It will be interesting to see this week whether you talk and take action if that feeling you talked about is still there.

AIMEE: Yeah, you know it's strange I've always been kind of a melancholy person, not kind of a depressed person, just kind of melancholy kind where my happiness wasn't that happy . . . it was an elation, it was like OK yeah this is great and now I feel like lately I've been happy instead of melancholy.

DR. CARLSON: Oh, wow. So, we're taking the governor off of things.

AIMEE: Yeah.

DR. CARLSON: Well, that's wonderful when you can feel that shift, too.

AIMEE: Yeah, definitely.

DR. CARLSON: Well, I'll look forward to hearing what happens this week.

AIMEE: Definitely.

Commentary

It may well be that the corrective experience that Aimee experienced as the result of her life giving relationship with Dr. Carlson was sufficient to explain the successful outcomes of her six-session therapy. From the vantage point of this second session, it seems that Aimee is beginning to change her self-other schemas (i.e., core beliefs about herself and others). Whether the corrective experience within therapy will generalize to a corrective relational experience with her mother is yet to be seen.

In this current session, as well as the first session, Dr. Carlson demonstrated all three of therapeutic skills necessary for fostering corrective experiences (Constantino & Westra, 2012). First, he has developed a nurturing therapeutic alliance. Next, he responded to Aimee with respect, caring, and concern, which was considerably different than the manner in which Aimee experienced her mother or father. Most important, he tread lightly and paid constant attention to Aimee's anxieties, responses, and the powerful pulls to revert to her maladaptive pattern of pleasing and capitulating to her mother's criticalness, demands, and neglect.

Many therapists may be sufficiently skillful to develop an effective therapeutic alliance, which is the first skill. However, it can be argued that the capacity to use the remaining two skills is lacking in therapies in which corrective experiences are not achieved. The result is that little substantive, enduring change is effected. Like many of the master therapists we know, Dr. Carlson seems extraordinarily adept at all three skills.

Dr. Carlson's Commentary

I was pleased that Aimee returned to therapy and that she found our previous meeting so useful and helpful. Although I thought things went well, I am never really sure exactly what the client takes away from a session. Frequently, I know that what stands out for them is not what I was hoping they would value. I am reasonably sure from Aimee's responses in the second meeting that she and I were in sync—meaning we were clearly understanding each other and working on the same issues. I see this as goal alignment and collaboration. The treatment alliance seemed secure and it was possible to facilitate more corrective experiences in future sessions. These interventions helped Aimee to assess her negative and limiting self-talk and to begin to write a new and more positive narrative of her life.

More effective interventions were made in this session that helped to make the therapy process worthwhile for Aimee. These interventions were more targeted to her basic needs of belonging in a more positive fashion. When I conduct therapy, it is important to "catch the client being good" or doing healthy behavior or having healthy thoughts or appropriate emotions. I also do a lot of positive reframing, which allows the clients to see themselves or a situation in a positive light. Looking for these positive signs and sharing them with the client is very important. Aimee responded very well to this, and she could feel that I cared for her and saw her as able and in the process of becoming healthy. People are attracted to those who see them in a positive light as it reminds them of supportive people in their lives like grandparents who thought everything they did was wonderful.

I began Session 2 by going over Aimee's response to the three questions I have my clients answer before each session. These questions gave her a chance to think about what has changed since our last session and what she wants to talk about at this one. The forms imply that she has an important role in these sessions and that I value her thoughts and opinions. These questions also allow me to get some feedback regarding treatment compliance, improvements, and the issues that are concerning her right now today. It is important to deal with a client's presenting problems and concerns in order for the treatment to have a positive valence for the client.

I was very impressed at the beginning of the session with Aimee's describing the pattern that she saw in her relationships, specifically that she chose partners that allowed her to address unfinished business with her mother. She could easily understand that if she could resolve these issues with her mother then she could choose healthier partners who might be capable of an equal and loving relationship.

Throughout this session I worked at making sure that Aimee could see the many positive things she does and has been doing. She began this session feeling like a failure for not talking with her mother as she agreed to in the initial session and failing to see the many positive steps she had taken. I worked at giving her credit for the many positive things that she does without taking away some of her negative assessments. Therapists need to stay focused and aware of the movement clients are making toward their stated goals.

These corrective experiences created awareness, insight, and served to empower her. She is too hard on herself. She needed help learning to "keep score" differently. I frequently normalized Aimee's behavior to help her to see her thoughts, feelings, and actions as similar to those of others in her situation. Showing similarities between her behavior and that of her parent's allowed her to understand just how deeply she was influenced by her parents or primary love objects. Sometimes I need to make this clearer by saying that we all learn the curriculum from the schools we attend even if we understand that a different school had a better or more desirable program. At times I was able to even put positive labels onto things that she did and had labeled as negative or inferior. Aimee's negative self-talk has to be challenged and changed as it is very powerful and serves to limit what she can become.

Throughout our work together, I was able to work in the moment and to help her understand that she experienced events in a manner different than mine. This immediacy of response from the therapist helps Aimee to experience something in the here and now, which makes for meaningful learning.

Concluding Comment

This chapter has emphasized corrective experiences, which are events that challenge one's fears or expectations and lead to new outcomes. They are often facilitated by a skilled therapist as a breakthrough in the client's efforts to engage in new behaviors, adopt more healthy ways of relating to others, develop a more positive view of self, or feel previously unacceptable feelings (Heatherington, Constantino, Angus, Friedlander, & Messer, 2012). The transcription of Session 2 reveals that the therapeutic alliance and clinician credibility have increased. Both of these factors tend to foster the likelihood of corrective experiences occurring. It also highlights Aimee's secondary pattern of perfectionistic striving and self-criticalness.

References

Alexander, F., & French, T. (1946). *Psychoanalytic therapy: Principles and applications*. New York, NY: Ronald Press.

Beitman, B., & Yue, D. (1999). *Learning psychotherapy*. New York, NY: Norton.

Castonguay, L., & Hill, C. (2010). The corrective experience: A core principle for therapeutic change. In L. Castonguay & C. Hill (Eds.), *Transformation in psychotherapy: Corrective experiences across cognitive-behavioral, humanistic, and psychodynamics approaches* (pp. 3–10). Washington, DC: American Psychological Association.

Constantino, M., & Westra, H. (2012). An expectancy-based approach to facilitating corrective experiences in psychotherapy. In L. Castonguay & C. Hill (Eds.), *Transformation in psychotherapy: Corrective experiences across cognitive-behavioral, humanistic, and psychodynamics approaches* (pp. 121–139). Washington, DC: American Psychological Association.

Good, G., & Beitman, B. (2006). *Counseling and psychotherapy essentials: Integrating theories, skills, and practices*. New York, NY: Norton.

Heatherington, L., Constantino, M. J., Angus, L., Friedlander, M., & Messer, S. (2012). Client's perspectives on corrective experiences in psychotherapy. In L. G. Castonguay & C. E. Hill (Eds.), *Transformation in psychotherapy: Corrective experiences across cognitive behavioral, humanistic, and psychodynamic approaches* (pp. 161–190). Washington, DC: American Psychological Association.

Knox, S., Hess, S., Hill, C., Burkard, A., & Cool-Lyon, R. (2012). Corrective relational experiences: Client perspectives. In L. Castonguay & C. Hill (Eds.), *Transformation in psychotherapy: Corrective experiences across cognitive-behavioral, humanistic, and psychodynamics approaches* (pp. 191–213). Washington, DC: American Psychological Association.

Levenson, H. (1995). *Time-limited dynamic psychotherapy: A guide to clinical practice*. New York, NY: Basic Books.

4
EFFECTING CHANGE: THE CENTRALITY OF THE CASE CONCEPTUALIZATIONS

Case conceptualization is a method and strategy for obtaining and organizing information about a client, understanding and explaining maladaptive patterns, focusing treatment, anticipating challenges and roadblocks, and preparing for termination (Sperry & Sperry, 2012). Clinically useful case conceptualizations provide therapists with a coherent treatment strategy for planning and focusing treatment interventions to increase the likelihood of effecting change (Eells, 2007; 2010). Of all the psychotherapy competencies, case conceptualizations are undoubtedly the most important.

As the subtitle of the chapter implies, case conceptualization is central to effecting change. Average therapists are usually able to conceptualize or formulate a case after completing their initial evaluation interview and reviewing pertinent diagnostic information. After the interview, these therapists review all available information, including that elicited in the interview, and then consider treatment goals and interventions. For therapists-in-training, this process is likely to take even longer and may require input from a supervisor.

On the other hand, master therapists typically conceptualize cases quickly and early *during* their initial evaluation interview. They test out this formulation as they continue their inquiry and modify it if necessary. For the master therapists, the case conceptualization process tends to be quick and intuitive, while for the average therapist the process is slower and more deliberate (Eells, Lombart, Kendjelic, Turner, & Lucas, 2005). As pointed out in Chapter 1, there are various reasons for this difference, including master therapists' high level of cognitive complexity and a highly developed capacity for metacognition and self-reflection. Fortunately, effective supervision, self-reflection, and "deliberate practice" (see Chapter 9) can greatly facilitate the development of this essential competency. So, too, can observing and modeling highly proficient therapists.

This chapter provides an overview of the general process of developing a focused and effective case conceptualization. It begins with a brief description of the components of a case conceptualization, followed by the criteria for evaluating them and the centrality of pattern. Next, a conceptualization of the case of Aimee follows. Then, the reader can "observe" the process of how Dr. Carlson formulated the case. It begins with segments of Session 1, which illustrate how, through a directed inquiry, he begins to formulate the case. His case commentary illustrates his thinking process in conceptualizing this case.

The Four Components of an Effective Case Conceptualization

The capacity to more fully assess and then conceptualize intrapersonal, interpersonal, and contextual dynamics is a key factor in effecting change. As noted in Chapter 2, a case conceptualization has four components: diagnostic, clinical, cultural, and treatment formulations. The capacity to accurately specify these case conceptualization components is essential in identifying and implementing a more adaptive pattern, which is the heart of effecting therapeutic change. This section describes these four components.

Diagnostic Formulation

The diagnostic formulation is a descriptive appraisal of the client's presentation and precipitants and reflects the client's pattern. It answers the "What happened?" question. It is a phenomenological description as well as a cross-sectional assessment of the client's unique situation and pattern.

Presentation

"Presentation" refers to the client's characteristic response to precipitants. Presentation, also called the presenting problem, includes the type and severity of symptoms, personal and relational functioning or impairment, and its history and course. It also includes medical and *Diagnostic and Statistical Manual of Mental Disorders* (DSM-5; published by the American Psychiatric Association 2013) diagnoses.

Precipitant

"Precipitants" refer to the triggers or stressors that activate the pattern resulting in the presenting problem or concern. Another way of saying this is that precipitants are antecedent conditions that coincide with the onset of symptoms, distressing thoughts, or maladaptive behaviors. A precipitant can be identified by considering the factors present at the onset and first manifestation of the problem or concern: where did it occur, at what time, who was there, what was said and done, what happened next, and so on.

Pattern

A "pattern" is a succinct description of a client's characteristic way of perceiving, thinking, and responding. It links the client's presentation with the precipitant and makes sense of the situation. Patterns are driven by the client's predispositions and reflect the client's perpetuants. A pattern can be adaptive or maladaptive. An adaptive pattern reflects a personality style that is flexible, appropriate, and effective and is reflective of personal and interpersonal competence. In contrast, a maladaptive pattern tends to be inflexible, ineffective, and inappropriate and causes symptoms, impairment in personal and relational functioning, and chronic dissatisfaction (Sperry & Sperry, 2012).

A pattern may be situation specific or longitudinal. A situation-specific maladaptive pattern is an explanation that is unique to the current situation only. On the other hand, a longitudinal pattern is an explanation that is common to the current as well as to previous situations. In other words, it reflects a lifelong pattern that can provide a reasonable explanation or set of reasons for the client's situation (Sperry, 2005, 2010; Sperry, Blackwell, Gudeman, & Faulkner, 1992).

Clinical Formulation

The clinical formulation provides an explanation of the client's pattern. It answers the "why" question (i.e., "Why did it happen?" question). Essentially, the clinical formulation is an appraisal of the client's predispositions and perpetuants and offers and provides an explanation for the client's pattern and presenting problem (Sperry, 2010). The clinical formulation is the central component in a case conceptualization that links the diagnostic and treatment formulations.

Predisposition

"Predisposition," also called the etiological or predisposing factors, are all possible factors that account for and explain the client's pattern. The predisposition is derived largely from the developmental, social, and health histories that provide clues about likely predisposing factors and reflect the client's biological, psychological, and social vulnerabilities. Biological vulnerabilities include medical history, current health status, medications, and substance use. It also includes treatment history such as a personal or family history of suicide and substance abuse or dependence. Psychological vulnerabilities include intrapsychic or intrapersonal, interpersonal, and other psychological factors, including intelligence and personality dynamics such as personality style, maladaptive beliefs and schemas, automatic thoughts, intermediate beliefs, resilience, self-concept, self-control, and character structure. It also includes all behavioral deficits and excesses and self-management, problem-solving, communication, relational, negotiation, and conflict-resolution skills. Social vulnerabilities include family dynamics, such as parental and sibling characteristics, interaction styles, family secrets, educational achievement, religious training, sexual experiences, and early neglect and abuse, be it verbal, emotional, physical, sexual, or financial. It also includes family level of functioning, family stressors, separation, divorce, peer relations, job stressors, support system, and environmental factors. For example, it would be important to identify vulnerabilities to depression, impulsivity, or specific social and environmental factors such as drinking friends, living in poverty, or working in a hostile environment. In addition to these vulnerabilities or risk factors, the predisposition can include protective factors and strengths.

Perpetuants

"Perpetuants," also called maintaining factors, are processes in which a client's pattern is reinforced and confirmed by both the client and the client's environment. Perpetuants serve to "protect" or "insulate" the client from symptoms, conflict, or the demands of others. For example, individuals who are shy and rejection-sensitive may gravitate toward living alone because it reduces the likelihood that others will criticize or make interpersonal demands on them. Because the influence of these factors seem to overlap, at times it can be difficult to specify whether a factor is a predisposition or a perpetuant. Perpetuants might include skill deficits, hostile work environment, living alone, negative responses of others, etc. Other times, predisposing factors function as maintaining factors. For instance, an individual with an avoidant style (predisposition) tends to engage in social isolation. By repeatedly distancing themselves from others to be safe, that individual is unlikely to develop the social skills necessary for making friends, developing assertive communication and intimate relationships, or engaging in conflict resolution. As a result of feeling lonely and ineffective in relating to others, the individual may unwittingly confirm her core belief that she is defective or unlovable.

Cultural Formulation

A cultural formulation supports the clinical formulation and can inform treatment focus and the type of interventions chosen. The cultural formulation is a systematic review of cultural factors and dynamics that have been described in the "Social History and Cultural Factors" section of a clinical case report. It answers the "What role does culture play?" question. More specifically, the cultural formulation statement describes clients' age, gender, social class, sexual orientation, and cultural or ethnic identity, their level of acculturation, and their cultural explanatory model (Sperry, 2010). Cultural identity is an individual's self-identification and perceived sense of belonging to a particular culture, whereas acculturation is the degree to which individuals integrate new cultural patterns into their original cultural patterns. Cultural explanatory model is an explanation of the client's condition as well as the impact of cultural factors on the client's personality and level of functioning. Furthermore, it forms the basis for anticipating if cultural elements may impact the relationship between the individual and the therapist, and whether culturally sensitive treatment is indicated (GAP Committee on Cultural Psychiatry, 2002; Wu & Mak, 2012).

The cultural formulation is based on four key cultural elements: cultural identity, acculturation level and acculturative stress, cultural explanatory model, and the impact of cultural versus personality dynamics. See Sperry and Sperry (2012), *Case Conceptualization: Mastering This Competency With Ease and Confidence*, for an extended discussion and illustration of these elements.

Treatment Formulation

The treatment formulation provides an explicit blueprint for intervention planning. It is a logical extension of the diagnostic, clinical, and cultural formulations. A treatment formulation answers the "How can it be changed?" question; it contains treatment goals, focus, strategy, and specific interventions and anticipates challenges and obstacles in achieving those goals. The following treatment formulation elements are reflected in the work of master therapists.

Treatment Goals

Treatment goals are the specific outcomes clients expect to achieve in their treatment. Also called therapeutic objectives and treatment targets, treatment goals form the basis for the work a practitioner and the client do together (Sperry & Sperry, 2012). Clinically useful treatment goals are measurable, achievable, and realistic and are effective to the extent they are mutually agreed on and the client understands them, commits to them, and believes that they are attainable. Goals can be short term or long term. Typical short-term goals are first order change goals such as symptom reduction, increased relational functioning, return to baseline functioning, and return to work. For example, the goals may be to reduce and eventually eliminate depressive symptoms or compulsive checking and counting behaviors. Long-term goals are second order change goals. A common long-term goal is pattern change; replacing a specific maladaptive with a more adaptive pattern. In short, treatment goals are the stated outcome of treatment.

Treatment Focus

"Treatment focus" refers to the central therapeutic emphasis that provides directionality to treatment and aims to replace a maladaptive pattern with a more adaptive pattern. Treatment focus not only provides direction to treatment; it also serves as a stabilizing force in maintaining a focus on change (Sperry & Sperry, 2012). A therapist's ability to track a treatment focus is associated with positive treatment outcomes. Not surprisingly, master therapists excel at establishing and maintaining a productive treatment focus.

In contrast, trainees can easily lose focus or get sidetracked in an unproductive discussion with clients. For example, a client reports that she had intended to do the mutually agreed-on homework assignment but ended up doing something else instead. The trainee then asks several factual questions about the circumstances. While collecting more data about the situation, the trainee has unwittingly colluded with the client's maladaptive pattern of making excuses instead of taking action. After running out of excuses, the client shifts to another topic and says she was really depressed (or anxious) yesterday, after which the trainee proceeds again down another track. Soon, the session comes to an end, and no change has been effected.

If therapists are guided by a specific therapeutic approach, the "direction" question has already been answered and specific guidelines given for how to process a situation therapeutically. For instance, in working with the client who failed to do agreed-on homework, the cognitive-behavioral approach is clear about directionality: focus on troublesome situations that are triggered or exacerbated by the client's maladaptive beliefs or behaviors. Here, the therapist recalls from the case conceptualization that the client's core belief is that she is inadequate and worthless, and that one of her intermediate beliefs is that if she tries and fails she will feel worthless, so she does not try (Sperry & Sperry, 2012). Thus, it is not a surprise that the client did not do the assignment and instead makes excuses. Informed by the case conceptualization, the therapist can therapeutically process the maladaptive beliefs that were activated by the homework situation. The therapist knew there was a treatment focus to follow. However, the therapist still must decide whether to follow or not follow that directive.

Treatment Strategy

Treatment strategy is the action plan for focusing specific interventions to achieve a more adaptive pattern (Sperry & Sperry, 2012). The plan involves relinquishing and replacing the maladaptive pattern with a more adaptive pattern and then maintaining that healthier pattern. The most common treatment strategies are support, interpretation, cognitive restructuring, replacement, exposure, skills training, and psychoeducation, support, biological, and corrective experiences (Sperry, 2010; Sperry & Sperry, 2012). Ordinarily, one or more of these treatment strategies is associated with a given therapeutic approach. For example, insight and corrective emotional experience are associated with the dynamic approaches, while cognitive restructuring, exposure, and skill building are associated with the cognitive behavioral approaches. However, a range of treatment strategies can be used to achieve the same or similar treatment goals.

Support. Support is probably the most common of all the psychotherapeutic strategies used by all or most therapists. It assists clients to function better by providing safety, acceptance, and caring. The therapist provides a supportive environment for clients to reflect on their life situation and feel safe and cared for while relieving symptoms or assisting clients to live with them rather than attempt personality or pattern change. Instead, it reinforces adaptive patterns of thought and behaviors to reduce stress and conflicts. This supportive relationship is critical in helping clients cope better, even if they cannot change the problems they are facing. Support helps clients cope with the challenges of daily life and is especially useful for dealing with long-term problems that are difficult to change. This strategy integrates psychodynamic, cognitive-behavioral, and interpersonal techniques and is part of a therapeutic approach known as supportive therapy.

Replacement. Replacement is probably the next most commonly used strategy, although many therapists are probably unaware of how they use and rely on it. For example, with insufficient time in the session to process a new issue with cognitive disputation, a practitioner might say, "The next time when no one is calling you to do something and you are starting to feel sorry for yourself and tell yourself that nobody cares about you, what could you do instead?" The practitioner is asking the client to come up with a replacement behavior ("I can call Jim or Jerry") and/or a replacement thought ("When I talk to them, I'll realize that others really do care about me"). Replacement is often used in combination with other strategies such as restructuring, exposure, and psychoeducation.

Guidance and Psychoeducation. Although considered anathema by many therapists, the reality is that, when indicated, responding to clients' requests or need for advice and guidance can be therapeutic. Effective therapists whom we have supervised and who have provided helpful guidance to their clients may be surprised and even embarrassed when it is pointed out. Many have internalized the clinical prohibition: "never give advice" on the questionable belief that clients always know the answer and what is good for them. Guidance typically overlaps with educating and fostering skill training, which today is called psychoeducation. Psychoeducation is a broad treatment strategy of educating and training individuals experiencing psychological disturbance to increase their knowledge, coping capacity, and skills required to solve their presenting problems. Common interventions using the skills training strategy include assertiveness training, problem-solving training, and communication skills training.

Cognitive Restructuring. Cognitive restructuring is a basic therapeutic tool for helping clients identify, challenge, and modify maladaptive and distorted beliefs so they become more adaptive. It assists clients in becoming aware of automatic thinking patterns and their influence on self and others; changing the way they process information and behavior; and learning to modify their beliefs about self, others, and the world. There are various techniques used in restructuring such beliefs that include guided discovery, Socratic questioning, examining the evidence, cognitive disputation, reattribution (i.e., modifying the attributional style), and cognitive rehearsal.

Exposure. Exposure is a treatment strategy that involves intentional and prolonged contact with a feared object combined with actively blocking undesirable avoidance behaviors. During exposure treatment, the client is confronted with a stimulus that has previously elicited an unwanted behavior or emotional response. Even though the client will experience increased anxiety in the short term, in the long term, repeated and incremental exposure to that feared stimulus in vivo (live) or in the client's imagination, anxiety and the avoidance response is extinguished because of the principle of habituation. There are a variety of exposure techniques that can be used, including systematic desensitization, guided imagery, flooding, and implosion.

Interpretation. An interpretation is a hypothesis or guess about the connection between a client's conscious thoughts, behaviors, or emotions and his or her unconscious emotions or thoughts. Interpretations can focus entirely on the present situations, called a dynamic interpretation, or it may suggest a link between the present and the past, called a genetic interpretation. In either instance, the client can gain a new frame of reference and a deeper understanding of themselves and their lives.

THE CENTRALITY OF THE CASE CONCEPTUALIZATIONS

They go beyond the client's overt words and offer new meaning or explanation. While interpretation is primarily associated with the dynamic approaches, interpretations are also used in various other approaches, including Jungian therapy, existential therapy, feminist therapy, and Adlerian psychotherapy.

Corrective Experiences. Corrective experiences are ones in which an individual comes to understand or experience affectively an event and how a significant other in the past reacted to them. Such corrective experiences may be emotional, relational, cognitive, or behavioral. In the past, corrective emotional experience referred specifically to the positive effects of experiencing the discrepancy between how clients expected a therapist to react to them regarding an important life issue or event. Today, corrective experience has a more general meaning, referring to all aspects of the therapeutic process that allow clients to experience an unexpected form of relational interaction than can help in healing a previously maladaptive pattern. This experience can continue to occur throughout therapy as therapists respond to clients in a manner that is respectful, accepting, and caring—often the opposite of their own parents or parental figures.

Biological Interventions. There are a range of biological treatments that are useful in psychotherapy. The one that usually comes to mind is medication, but there are other biological interventions that have long been used as adjuncts to psychotherapy. These include exercise, neurofeedback, controlled breathing, diet, and nutrients. Effective therapy outcomes may require the use of one or more of these adjunctive interventions.

While most trainees and many therapists regularly use one or two strategies, more proficient and master therapists commonly use several of these strategies. It should be noted that during the course of his therapeutic work with Aimee, Dr. Carlson used all eight of the strategies just mentioned.

Treatment Interventions

A treatment intervention is a therapeutic action designed to positively impact a client's issue or problem. Treatment interventions are selected based on the treatment targets, the willingness and capacity of the client to proceed with the intervention, and whether culturally sensitive treatments are indicated. While there are hundreds of treatment interventions, effective treatment outcomes involving pattern change require the selection of interventions that operationalize the treatment strategy. With regard to the journey metaphor, treatment interventions represent trip provisions such as the right grade of fuel, tires that are appropriate for the terrain, and sufficient food, water, and money.

Culturally sensitive treatment. Culturally sensitive treatment is a psychotherapeutic treatment that is sensitive to the client's culture, identity, and level of acculturation. Cultural sensitivity is the therapist's awareness of cultural variables in themselves and in their clients that may affect the professional relationship and treatment process (Sperry, 2010). Even though most therapists believe that culturally sensitive treatments are important in providing effective care to culturally diverse clients, very few therapists actually provide such treatment. The most common reason for this omission is that few have had formal training and experience with these competencies. Such training would include assessment of such factors as cultural identity and level of acculturation, indications for the use of various types of culturally sensitive treatment, and a method of selecting if, when, and how to use such treatments. There are three types of culturally sensitive treatment: cultural interventions, culturally sensitive therapies, and culturally sensitive interventions. A cultural intervention is an intervention or healing method or activity that is consistent with the client's belief system regarding healing and potentially useful in effecting a specified change. Some examples are healing circles, prayer or exorcism, and involvement of traditional healers from that client's culture. Sometimes, the use of cultural interventions necessitates collaboration with or referral to such a healer or other expert. Still, a therapist can begin the treatment process by focusing on core cultural value, such as "respito" and "personalismo," in an effort to increase clinician credibility (Paniagua, 2005).

Culturally sensitive therapy is a psychotherapeutic intervention that directly addresses the cultural characteristics of diverse clients (i.e., beliefs, customs, attitudes, and their socioeconomic and historical contexts). Because they use traditional healing methods and pathways such approaches are appealing to certain clients. For example, "cuento therapy" addresses culturally relevant variables such as "familismo" and "personalismo" through the use of folk tales ("cuentos") and is used with Puerto Rican children. Likewise, "Morita therapy," which originated in Japan, is now used throughout the world for a wide range of disorders ranging from shyness to schizophrenia. These kinds of therapy appears to be particularly effective in clients with lower levels of acculturation.

In contrast, a culturally sensitive intervention is a conventional psychotherapeutic intervention, such as cognitive-behavioral therapy (CBT), that has been adapted or modified to be responsive to the cultural characteristics of a particular client. Largely because of their structured, and educational focus, diverse clients seem to find cognitive behavior therapy interventions acceptable and are the most often modified to be culturally sensitive (Hays & Iwanasa, 2006). For example, in culturally diverse clients with lower levels of acculturation, disputation and cognitive restructuring of a maladaptive belief are seldom the CBT intervention of choice, whereas problem solving, skills training, or cognitive replacement interventions may be more appropriate.

Here are some guidelines for selecting culturally sensitive treatments. First, elicit or identify the client's cultural identity, level of acculturation, explanatory model (i.e., belief about the cause of their illness, such as bad luck, spirits, virus or germ, heredity, early traumatic experiences, chemical imbalance in brain, etc.), and treatment expectations. Second, develop a cultural formulation framing her presenting problems within the context of her cultural identity, acculturation level, explanatory model, treatment expectations, and interplay of culture and personality dynamics. Third, if a client identifies (cultural identity) primarily with the mainstream culture and has a high level of acculturation and there is no obvious indication of prejudice, racism, or related bias, consider conventional interventions as the primary treatment method. However, the clinician should be aware that a culturally sensitive treatment may also be indicated as the treatment process develops. Fourth, if a client identifies largely with the mainstream culture and has a high level of acculturation and there is an indication of prejudice, racism, or related bias, consider culturally sensitive interventions or cultural interventions for cultural aspect of the client's concern. In addition, it may be useful to use conventional interventions for related noncultural concerns (i.e., personality dynamics). Fifth, if a client identifies largely with his ethnic background and his level of acculturation is low, consider cultural interventions or culturally sensitive therapy. This may necessitate collaboration with or referral to an expert and/or an initial discussion of core cultural values. Sixth, if a client's cultural identity is mainstream and acculturation level is high but that of her family is low, such that the presenting concern is largely a matter cultural discrepancy, consider a cultural intervention with the client and the family. However, if there is a imminent crisis situation, consider conventional interventions to reduce the crisis. After it is reduced or eliminated, consider introducing cultural interventions or culturally sensitive therapy. See Sperry (2010) for an extended discussion of these guidelines.

Treatment Obstacles and Outcomes

Success in implementing a treatment plan and achieving expected outcomes may be limited dependent on a number of factors, including the capacity to anticipate and deal with treatment challenges and obstacles. Obstacles may originate from the client, the practitioner, or both client-practitioner, or factors in the treatment process itself. Anticipating obstacle challenges to the implementation of the treatment plan is indispensable in achieving treatment success. The test of an effective case conceptualization is its viability in predicting the obstacles and challenges throughout the stages of therapy, particularly those involving resistance, ambivalence, transference enactments, and issues that complicate maintaining treatment gains and preparing for termination (Sperry, 2010).

Explanatory and Predictive Power of the Case Conceptualization

Two criteria to evaluate the accuracy and sufficiency of a case conceptualization are explanatory power and predictive power. Highly effective case conceptualizations are characterized by high level of explanatory and predictive power.

Explanatory Power

The value of a case conceptualization is the degree to which it offers an accurate and compelling explanation of the client's maladaptive pattern. The degree to which it explains a pattern is referred to as its "explanatory power" (Sperry &

Sperry, 2012). Explanatory power can range from "poor" to "highly compelling." There is no theoretical approach that can best explain a client's pattern since individuals and their needs and the contexts are so unique and complex that no single approach or case conceptualization method can provide the best explanations for all cases.

Explanatory power is a function of the accuracy and "fit" of the clinical formulation between the explanation offered and case data, particularly predisposing factors and protective factors. As therapists become more competent and confident in constructing case conceptualizations, they realize that not every case conceptualization is as compelling as others. Another way of saying this is that a case conceptualization can have varying degrees of explanatory power ranging from low to very high. At a case conference, when trainees are asked: "Does this case conceptualization offer a compelling explanation for the 'Why' question?" if the response is: "Not very compelling," it would reasonable to discuss what additional predisposing factors might be included or revised to increase explanatory power. Often, the addition of other predisposing factors, like core schema or maladaptive beliefs about self, the world, and others, can boost explanatory power.

Predictive Power

By itself, high explanatory power does not increase treatment outcomes. Rather, a compelling explanation of a client's maladaptive pattern can translate into a focused plan for using tailored interventions to achieve specific treatment targets and goals informed by the case conceptualization. The real test of an effective case conceptualization is its viability in predicting the obstacles and facilitators most likely throughout the stages of therapy. This is referred to as its "predictive power" (Sperry & Sperry, 2012).

Common treatment obstacles in the therapy process typically reflect the client's personality dynamics and maladaptive pattern. An accurate and compelling explanation of predisposing factors, including personality dynamics and contextual dynamics, can be invaluable in anticipating obstacles. For example, clients with an avoidant pattern can be anticipated to have difficulty discussing personal matters and "test" and provoke their therapists into criticizing them for changing or canceling appointments or being late. Likely treatment facilitators or promoting factors include a high level of client readiness and motivation, client strengths, and protective factors, clinician credibility, an effective therapeutic alliance, mutually agreeable goals, and a tailored intervention plan (Sperry, 2010). For example, a therapy marked by an effective therapeutic alliance with a motivated client and a highly proficient therapist is more likely to achieve a second order change goal than a therapy with less optimal conditions.

Case conceptualizations that have high predictive power help therapists to anticipate and to plan for dealing with such obstacles and facilitators. In addition, case conceptualizations with high predictive power permit the therapist to make a more informed prognosis for treatment. An informed prognosis is a prediction

THE CENTRALITY OF THE CASE CONCEPTUALIZATIONS

of the likely duration and therapeutic outcomes with treatment tailored to client need and context.

Following are three reports about the same client. The writers of each report believe that they have developed an effective case conceptualization. Using the criteria of explanatory power and predictive power, decide for yourself which version best explains the client and best specifies treatment goals and outcomes.

Version 1

Jaime G. is a 27-year-old married, Hispanic man who was referred for evaluation of somatic symptoms—including alternating diarrhea and constipation, anxiety, and insomnia. He is the manager of information technology for a regional bank, and while he minimizes his concerns, he describes a number of job concerns and stressors. While he attempts to meet the increasing demands of his boss for greater productivity, his employees complain that he is too demanding and nonsupportive. He criticizes himself for not being a better manager. He reports that his wife is supportive of him, particularly since she has just been laid off from her job. Jaime is diagnosed with Anxiety Disorder NOS and Obsessive-Compulsive Personality Disorder. He denies the use of medication, alcohol, or other drugs and reports no previous psychiatric treatment nor psychotherapy. Outpatient treatment will begin with an executive physical examination and weekly psychotherapy. Treatment goals are specified as symptom reduction and return to baseline functioning.

Version 2

Jaime G. is a 27-year-old married, Hispanic man who was referred for evaluation of somatic symptoms—including alternating diarrhea and constipation, anxiety, and insomnia. These symptoms appear to be his reaction to increased job demands and stresses. Throughout his life Jaime has strove to be perfect, hardworking, and conscientious and not show "weak" emotions—like caring and concern—to feel worthwhile. All this consciousness and emotional distancing have negatively affected his relations with his workers. His reaction is understandable in light of his personality dynamics of perfectionism, criticalness, conscientiousness, and feeling avoidance, as well as his difficulty delegating tasks to his employees. Growing up, he faced similar demands for achievement and perfection from his controlling and critical father. This pattern seems to be maintained and reinforced by constant activity, conscientiousness, feeling avoidance, and related obsessive-compulsive features.

Treatment goals include decreasing his somatic anxiety, and insomnia, as well as job stressors, and increasing his ability and willingness to be emotionally available to his employees. A referral for an executive physical examination will be made to evaluate his somatic symptoms. Cognitive-behavioral therapy will be directed at his perfectionism and other operative features of his obsessive-compulsive style. Given that his stressors appear to be largely situational and job related, his prognosis appears to be good.

85

Version 3

Jaime G. is a 27-year-old married, highly acculturated Hispanic man who was referred for evaluation of somatic symptoms—including alternating diarrhea and constipation, anxiety, and insomnia. These symptoms appear to be his reaction to increased job demands and stresses and increased caffeine intake. Throughout his life, Jaime has strove to be perfect, hardworking, and conscientious and not show "weak" emotions—like caring and concern—to feel worthwhile. This over-conscientiousness and emotional distancing have negatively affected his relations with his workers. His reaction is understandable in light of his personality dynamics of perfectionism, criticalness, conscientiousness, and feeling avoidance, as well as his difficulty delegating tasks to his employees. Growing up, he faced similar demands for achievement and perfection from his controlling and critical father. This pattern is maintained and reinforced by constant activity, overconscientiousness, and feeling avoidance.

The agreed-on treatment outcome for Jaime is to become reasonably conscientious and more emotionally present to his employees. Treatment goals include decreasing his somatic anxiety, and insomnia, as well as job stressors, and increasing his emotionally availability. Treatment strategies compatible with these treatment goals and focus include therapeutic support and replacement. Finding more adaptive interpretations and behaviors that replace his perfectionistic interpretations and behaviors could modulate and limit his compulsivity. In addition, psychoeducation and processing the link between caffeine, stress, bowel concerns, and insomnia can reduce his caffeine intake. In terms of potential treatment obstacles and challenges, it is likely that Jaime will minimize certain issues, such as his relationship with his father, since he believes they are unrelated to his currents stressors. His obsessive-compulsive style can present challenges that the therapist should be prepared to address (i.e., that he will have high expectations for a successful outcome in therapy and the likelihood that he may "undermine" change efforts while appearing to please the therapist). Despite these potential obstacles, his motivation for change is high, suggesting that the agreed-on treatment outcome is likely to be achieved.

Comment

Version 3 provides a full explanation and implications for treatment, more so than Version 2. In contrast, Version 1 provides a description and distillation of facts expected of a case summary, but none of the explanation of such facts expected of a case conceptualization. Central to the Version 3 is an explanation of pertinent personality, situational, and cultural dynamics from which a tailored treatment plan is derived. In addition, it effectively anticipates potential obstacles to treatment success. In short, Version 1 has neither explanatory nor predictive power, which is typical of a case summary. Version 2 does have some explanatory power but no predictive power, while Version 3 has a high degree of both explanatory and predictive power. Accordingly, Version 3 meets the criteria for an effective and clinically usefully case conceptualization.

Developing Clinically Useful Case Conceptualizations

At first glance, it may seem that developing an effective, clinically useful case conceptualization is a difficult, time-consuming, and daunting task. It certainly can be. But, it does not have to be a long, drawn-out, and foreboding process. What follows is a relatively quick and straightforward method for identifying the basic structure and key elements of an effective case conceptualization. Once the structure is evident, everything else falls into place.

This quick and straightforward method of conceptualizing cases is centered on patterns (Sperry & Sperry, 2012). As already noted, the capacity to accurately identify patterns is essential in the case conceptualization process. Not surprisingly, master therapists excel at accurately identifying patterns quickly and effortlessly.

It may be useful to imagine the case conceptualization process as a bridge that links with assessment process with the treatment process. The case conceptualization process begins with assessing and identifying a maladaptive pattern. From that maladaptive pattern, a more adaptive pattern is derived. From that adaptive pattern, the goals and focus of treatment are derived, and tailored treatment interventions are planned and implemented. Consistent with the basic message of this book, treatment goals are specified in terms of first order and second order change. The final piece of this process involves identifying likely obstacles that may be encountered in achieving this more adaptive pattern and related treatment goals. Basically, that is the structure of a case conceptualization. In talking with or observing how master therapists work, it became apparent that this structure and process is implicit in the way they think about and conceptualize cases.

This structure also serves as an outline for writing up a case conceptualization statement. Answering eight questions can result in a case conceptualization statement that has high explanatory and predictive power. This statement can be as short as eight sentences, one sentence that answers each of the eight questions. That's right—effectively drafting a case conceptualization can be accomplished in just eight sentences. Of course, it can be considerably longer, as the writer might choose to elaborate certain features of the conceptualization.

In seminars and training programs over the years, it has been my (L.S.) experience that if therapists and therapists-in-training are encouraged to focus and answer the following eight questions, they can begin to derive clinically useful case conceptualizations and to feel confident in the process. Here are the questions. The case of Aimee illustrates the use of these questions in developing a case conceptualization.

The first question is: *What is the client's presentation and what precipitates it?* This question targets the "presentation "and "precipitant" elements of the case conceptualization. Asking questions to clarify both and the link between them is the start of the process. For example, Aimee presented for therapy with depression, fatigue, insomnia, anger at her mother, and worries about her children and ex-husband. Precipitants included increased demands to care for others and the anticipation of her ex-husband's release from prison.

The second question is: **What is the client's basic movement and its purpose?** Movement means the individual's dominant mode of relating to others. There are three basic types of relating to others: one can move toward others, one can move against others, or one can move away from others. Of course, an individual can move in two directions at the same time (ambivalence), such as toward and against. Table 4.1 can be helpful in answering these questions. For example, initially Aimee's movement was toward others and its purpose was to meet others' needs. This is consistent with the dynamics of the dependent personality that is Aimee's basic personality structure. As therapy proceeded a secondary movement also became evident. Aimee would also move against others and herself for the purpose of doing things perfectly. In addition to pleasing and meeting others' needs, it was important for Aimee to do her best and do things right and to be self-critical and feel bad when she did not achieve perfection. Table 4.1 summarizes movement and purpose and specifies the most closely related personality style.

The third question is: **What is the maladaptive pattern based on the individual's movement and purpose?** This is the "pattern-maladaptive" element of a case conceptualization and is derived from movement and purpose. For example,

Table 4.1 Identifying Patterns Through Movement and Purpose

Movement	Purpose	Personality Style
Toward	Get attention	Histrionic
Toward	Get others' help, pleaser, meet others' needs	Dependent
Against	Get special treatment	Narcissistic
Against	Protect self and/or retaliate	Paranoid
Against	Harm others	Antisocial
Away	Avoid harm; be safe	Avoidant
Away	Avoid involvement and distance others	Schizoid
Away	Act different/odd/eccentric and distance others	Schizotypal
Ambivalent [toward/against]	Resist others' demands/expectations	Passive-aggressive
Ambivalent [toward/against]	Be perfect; overachieve	Obsessive-compulsive

THE CENTRALITY OF THE CASE CONCEPTUALIZATIONS

the maladaptive pattern for Aimee was that she focused on meeting others' needs but ignored her own needs. This is her core maladaptive pattern, which is supported by a secondary pattern of perfectionism.

The fourth question is: *What is the value and origin of the maladaptive pattern?* This question taps into the "predisposition" or "predisposing factors" element of the case conceptualization. As noted earlier, the more compelling the explanation of the origins of the maladaptive predisposing factors, as well as protective factors, the greater the explanatory power of the case conceptualization. For Aimee, the value of caring for others and being pleasing is that others will like her and allow her to feel that she is needed and worthwhile. The origins of this pattern include an upbringing in which her parents were self-centered, critical, and overly demanding while emotionally absent and skill deficits in assertive communication and self-care. It also included maladaptive beliefs about herself as being nice but deficient and a view of the world as demanding, critical, and conditional. These dynamics fostered the development of her pleasing and perfectionistic pattern.

The fifth question is: *What is a clinically appropriate adaptive pattern?* This is this "treatment pattern" element of a case conceptualization. Her primary adaptive pattern is derived from her primary maladaptive pattern. Essentially, it is the mirror opposite of the maladaptive pattern. So what is the opposite of Aimee's maladaptive pattern? The opposite of meeting others' needs while ignoring her own needs is to meets others' needs and also meet her own needs. Added to this is a secondary adaptive pattern of acting in a reasonably accurate and conscientious manner in place of needing to consistently strive for perfection. The composite adaptive pattern could be stated as: meets others' needs and also meet her own needs in a reasonably conscientious way.

The sixth question is: *What needs to happen to shift from the maladaptive pattern to the adaptive pattern?* Answering this question involves considering overall structural factors in therapy such as personality and contextual dynamic beyond common therapeutic factors such as support, empathic responding, and support and empathetic responding. For Aimee, structural factors that need to shift include core beliefs and schemas and reversing key skill deficits. Specifically, she needs to become more empowered and self-confident and less perfectionistic, act more assertively, and engage in self-care without guilt.

The seventh question is: *What are clinically appropriate first order change and second order change goals?* This question reflects the "treatment goals" and "treatment focus" elements of a case conceptualization. These goals serve to operationalize the structural changes already specified in the previous question. They are the targets to which treatment is directed with tailored intervention, the "treatment intervention" element of a case conceptualization. For example, with Aimee, first order change goals are to decrease her presenting symptoms of depression, fatigue and insomnia. Second order change goals include increasing her sense of self-efficacy and empowerment, which requires a shift in core beliefs as well as increasing assertive communication. Decreasing perfectionistic striving is the related second order change goal.

The eighth question is: *What obstacles and facilitators are likely to be encountered in attempting to achieve these goals?* This is the "treatment obstacles and outcomes" element of a case conceptualization. As noted earlier, the real test of the value of a case conceptualization is its viability in predicting therapeutic obstacles and outcomes. For example, because of Aimee's highly critical and demanding parents, working successfully with her will mean being mindful of this history and avoiding transference-activating comments that she could construe as critical and demanding. It means being prepared to deal with the possibility of clinging to the therapist and to therapy (i.e., difficulty with termination). These are some of the potential therapeutic challenges and obstacles in this case. Table 4.2 suggests likely obstacles and challenges for various personality types. At the same time, it means that because of a positive therapeutic alliance and her history of successfully leaving an abusive partner, her therapist can reasonably expect that she could confront her abusive mother, something she has avoided, so far. These are some of the potential therapeutic facilitators in this case.

Table 4.2 Anticipating Treatment Challenges Based on Personality Dynamics

Avoidant Personality	
Engagement	Premature termination; "testing" behavior, e.g., canceling appointments; fear of being criticized; difficulty with self-disclosure
Transference	"Testing"; overdependence
Countertransference	Frustration and helplessness
	Unrealistic treatment expectations
Pattern triggers	Close relationships and public appearance
Maintenance	Homework avoidance
Termination	Anxiety and ambivalence about termination
Borderline Personality	
Engagement	Client's difficulty viewing clinician as helpful/collaborative
Transference	Dependency, merger fantasy
Countertransference	Anger, rescue fantasies
Pattern triggers	Personal goals, close relations
Maintenance	Focus on feeling good vs. changing
Termination	Abandonment fears, relapse proneness

(*Continued*)

Table 4.2 (Continued)

Dependent Personality	
Engagement	Silent demand for clinician to make decisions and solve their problems; comply rather than collaborate
Transference	Clinging resistance; multiple requests; idealize clinician
Countertransference	Rescue fantasies; directive role; failure to confront limited progress
Pattern triggers	Demands for self-reliance and/or being alone
Maintenance	Resist increasing independence, assertiveness
Termination	Fear of termination/abandonment with paradoxical worsening of progress

Narcissistic Personality	
Engagement	Demanding mirroring; easily narcissistically wounded
Transference	Idealizing to devaluating; projective identification
Countertransference	Not recognizing one's own narcissistic needs; boredom; feeling controlled, angry, hurt, impotent
Pattern trigger	Evaluation of self
Maintenance	Difficulty relinquishing specialness, entitlement
Termination	Premature termination

Histrionic Personality	
Engagement	Quickly develops therapeutic alliance; believes clinician can understand them intuitively
Transference	Fantasy of being rescued; erotic or eroticized transference
Countertransference	Messiah/rescue role; aloofness, anxiety; exploitation
Pattern triggers	Opposite sex relationships
Maintenance	Resist being ordinary
Termination	Fantasies of continuing relationships; fear of termination

Obsessive–Compulsive Personality	
Engagement	Appear eager to comply in and between sessions
Transference	Obsessive rambling and lists; discounting clinician
Countertransference	Disengagement; isolated affect; anger; collude with client's defenses
Pattern triggers	Authority issues; unstructured situations; close relationships
Maintenance	Resists getting in touch with "soft" feelings
Termination	Ambivalence about termination

Case of Aimee: Transcription and Commentary

In this transcribed segments that follow from the first session, you can follow how Dr. Carlson expertly focuses his questioning and clarifications in identifying Aimee's maladaptive pattern, a key element in his provisional case conceptualization.

AIMEE: Mhmm . . . I don't want to hurt her feelings, I feel like if I tell her I really am angry, I really do resent you, you know, to a degree . . . I can't do that . . . So, I kind've walk around with these feelings inside me that have never really come out.

DR. CARLSON: Any idea why that might be? I guess, would that be being honest with your feelings?

AIMEE: Yeah, I guess it would be but I have a hard time expressing how I feel to people, well unless it's something good, because I don't want to hurt anyone's feelings so I'm very nice even at the expense of myself . . . I'm a very passive person.

DR. CARLSON: Nice, but it sounds like you're not honest?

AIMEE: No [*says while laughing*]

DR. CARLSON: And how does that work in relationships?

AIMEE: It doesn't [*laughing*] . . . No, I don't really have many relationships that last. I really don't have too many relationships, I'm kind've a loner.

DR. CARLSON: So, that would be a lot like your dad?

AIMEE: Mhmm, yeah.

DR. CARLSON: I see and how about your mom?

AIMEE: She's very social. I'm very social but um as far as adhering to a relationship . . . I'm a chauffeur, I talk to a lot of people, conversing is a part of my job, but to make a relationship, to build a relationship is very hard for me.

DR. CARLSON: And what does hard mean?

AIMEE: Difficult letting people in, difficult letting them see a different side of me other than what I want them to see . . . you know the friendly, happy me.

DR. CARLSON: And that's the thing that you learned from your mom?

AIMEE: Yeah, probably . . . she's a very outgoing, very charismatic person.

DR. CARLSON: But you learned this idea that it's important to be what somebody wants you to be other than to be yourself?

AIMEE: Yes, probably. I'm not ashamed of who I am, but I just don't want anybody to know that I have these bad sides too . . . I guess everybody is sort of like that in a way.

DR. CARLSON: But the bad side, for you, is that you don't want to hurt anyone's feelings?

AIMEE: Yeah, I have resentment and anger toward a family member, and I feel sort of guilty for that because I feel like I should be an obedient child . . . and I was a very obedient child growing up. I was good all the time I still am like that, I never disappointed my parents and to disappoint my parents makes me feel really bad . . . it makes me feel very bad about myself so I sort of over-achieve in order to gain [their approval] . . . I mean I know they love me but there's no room for failure, but I'm always doing and doing to try to please everybody else.

DR. CARLSON: No wonder you don't relax . . .

AIMEE: No, I don't.

DR. CARLSON: There's no time. Do you think this is the way you'll be forever?

AIMEE: I hope not.

DR. CARLSON: How would you like to be?

AIMEE: I would like to be able to sit down and not think about the day, what needs to be done. I mean everybody . . . you can't really automatically shut your mind off of the different things you're thinking about and worrying about . . . anticipating, but just sort of serenity inside, that would be nice, just to sit down and enjoy the day.

DR. CARLSON: But I'm wondering how much a day you have?

AIMEE: Not much.

DR. CARLSON: I mean you work, you're going to school, and you're taking care of your father . . .

AIMEE: My kids too . . .

DR. CARLSON: Two children you're taking care of . . .

AIMEE: And my grandmother . . .

DR. CARLSON: And your grandmother?

AIMEE: Yeah, my grandmother, she's 80 now. She'll be 80 in a couple weeks and so I take care of her also. I go over and clean her house and you know just visit her, she's very lonely.

[SKIP]

AIMEE: In a sense, I take care of my parents. So, I liked the company of her too, it's not burdensome, I don't go over there and think I have to clean her house again, it's sort of time with her.

DR. CARLSON: But being a single mom . . . you are a single mom?

AIMEE: Yeah.

DR. CARLSON: And what does that word you used "serenity" ... how does that fit in?

AIMEE: I don't know I'd like to fit it in somehow, some way, you know, because right now it really wears me down and I also have problems sleeping and I'm very tired when I go to bed at night. I lay in bed and start thinking about what I have to do and so the process starts all over again and it just doesn't seem like I even have time to just take five and, you know, just watch TV, and lay around.

[SKIP]

AIMEE: ... and I still play once in a while, but to be in a band it's really demanding if you want to be good at it you have to practice a lot and I'm sure my neighbors wouldn't enjoy that either.

DR. CARLSON: So again, you're always thinking of others. Thinking of the family, thinking of the neighbors, thinking of ...

AIMEE: Mhmm, yeah, always.

DR. CARLSON: But there's somebody we're not thinking about?

AIMEE: No, no, I don't know why. I need to start thinking about myself because I feel like I don't know who I am anymore I'm running so much that I never took time to know who I was as a person. I became a mother at sixteen, I was married out of high school I ... it was just a rat race so I never really stopped to think what I really want or like, I just do ... I don't stop to think of who I am as a person.

DR. CARLSON: I don't know who I am, so I do everything because I do everything, I'm too tired to figure out who I am.

AIMEE: Yes, that sounds like a good song.

Commentary

In his initial session with Aimee, Dr. Carlson uses strategic questioning to develop a provisional case conceptualization while collecting developmental and social history. His provisional conceptualization is that she must please others and take care of their needs, while ignoring her own needs. This part of the assessment focuses primarily on key relationships in Aimee's life, primarily her mother, father, and maternal grandmother who essentially raised her. We learn briefly that she has two children and an ex-husband. She is queried about her reason for seeking therapy (to deal with her anger and resentment toward her mother). We will learn in a subsequent session that she has also been increasingly concerned about the effect her ex-husband's release from prison in approximately three months will have on her life and that of her children.

THE CENTRALITY OF THE CASE CONCEPTUALIZATIONS

Aimee has some insight into her daily life situation. She knows what she would like to be able to do: sit down and feel serene and enjoy the day. Instead, she ruminates about the mounting expectations and demands on her that day and when the demands become overwhelming she experiences symptoms like anxiety and insomnia and engages in unhealthy efforts such as drinking beer to induce sleep. She is able to rather accurately describe her basic life dilemma: "I have a hard time expressing how I feel to people, well unless it's something good, because I don't want to hurt anyone's feelings so I'm very nice even at the expense of myself . . . I'm a very passive person." She seems to have captured the essence of her maladaptive pattern and its effect on her, i.e., " . . . at the expense of myself." Despite this awareness she has been unable to find a way to care for others *and* care for herself. This, as the reader will note, becomes the focus of the therapeutic process.

From this segment of their very first session together, a central element of Aimee's case conceptualization—a provisional case conceptualization to be sure—emerges for Dr. Carlson. Aimee's primary pattern is pleasing. Her basic movement is toward others, and puts their needs before her own. She reports that she consistently thinks about others and their needs and then meets those needs. But she rarely thinks about her own needs. Consequently, she has little time for self care because she is so over-focused on caring for others. It should be noted that Aimee seems to agree with Dr. Carlson's provisional case conceptualization, particularly her maladaptive pattern and the need for a more adaptive one. She says "I need to start thinking about myself because I feel like I don't know who I am anymore." In his taped commentary after their first session, Dr. Carlson noted that Aimee was able to see her maladaptive pattern and role "as one who can take care of others, but does not do a good job of taking care of herself."

There is ongoing discussion of this primary pattern in subsequent sessions. It is noteworthy that in a follow-up conversation seven years after the sixth and last therapy session, the pattern was uppermost in her memory about her therapy experience. This is discussed in considerable detail in Chapter 7. Central to that follow-up conversation is how Aimee has come to balance self-care with caring for others. Aimee had replaced her maladaptive pattern with a much more healthy and adaptive pattern. In other words, second order change occurred during the course of therapy and was sustained in subsequent years.

Dr. Carlson's provisional case conceptualization was on the mark. But it was not the full and complete case conceptualization, and that fact became increasingly clear in Session 2. What emerged was a secondary pattern of the case conceptualization. It involved moving against others and herself. Now, this movement against was neither aggressive nor openly manipulative. Instead, Aimee acted in a manner that was perfectionistic and self-critical, and maintained overly high expectations for herself. Both patterns are contradictory in that her movement is both toward and against. To fully understand Aimee and the course of therapy with Dr. Carlson, one must recognize that both patterns were operative simultaneously. To the extent to which a therapist did not recognize these two movements and patterns, and tension between them, would predictably complicate the therapy process and possibly result in premature termination.

Let's be more specific. As a result of her longstanding pleasing pattern Aimee refrains from communicating her needs to others and has difficulty saying no to their demands, particularly those of her mother and father. She typically relates to others in an openly agreeable manner (pleasing pattern). Even though she has strong opinions of her own (perfectionistic pattern), she rarely takes issue with others or stands up in her own defense. Her nonresponsiveness in the face of personal and political opinion which she found intolerable demonstrated her lack of assertiveness and fear of not being liked and accepted by others (pleasing pattern). But, there was at least one exception. Although she describes it as extraordinarily difficult and distressing, Aimee was able to stand firm with her ex-husband and leave him after years of physical, emotional, and verbal abuse. This exception is notable and greatly increased the likelihood that Aimee could be successful in therapy. She knew it was the right thing to do (perfectionistic pattern) and was able after much deliberation to act in her best interest and that of her children and against her tendency to acquiesce to his abuse and demands (pleasing pattern). In subsequent sessions, Aimee's need to phrase her words perfectly, say them at just the right time, and not make a mistake, are other indications of her secondary pattern of perfectionism.

Because Aimee did demonstrate assertiveness in leaving her abusive husband, Dr. Carlson could reasonably encourage Aimee to assertively communicate with her mother, another important figure in her life. The fact that it took Aimee two weeks of procrastinating until she had the right words and the right time (perfectionistic pattern) was therapeutically predictable. On the one hand, Aimee felt compelled to please and acquiesce to this therapeutic task (pleasing pattern), and on the other hand, she felt compelled to make no mistakes and not sound harsh or hurt her mother's feelings. The fact that Aimee was crushed after she gently confronted her mother reflects both pleasing and perfectionistic patterns being operative and her subsequent, and predictable, depressive symptoms.

A more adaptive pattern for Aimee would be to care for others *and* also care for herself. It is not surprising then that Dr. Carlson makes this more adaptive pattern the central focus of the treatment throughout the rest of the therapeutic process. Because this new pattern is so essential for Aimee to achieve second order change in her life, he begins helping her in this first session to speak up and use more assertive communication with her mother. Why did Dr. Carlson focus on Aimee's relationship with her mother? The answer is that Aimee's stated purpose for seeking therapy was to resolve her negative feelings toward her mother.

It is also worth noting that the psychological inventory that Aimee completed and Dr. Carlson saw before their first session was only partially accurate. Dr. Carlson notes in his taped commentary before the first session that the *Kern Life Style* showed high scores on two scales, i.e., needing to please others, and victimizing herself by a lack of assertive communication and by surrounding herself with self-centered individuals. These relate closely to her primary maladaptive pattern, but do not speak to her secondary pattern. Fortunately, Dr. Carlson's clinical acumen made up for the shortcoming of this inventory. Finally, in diagnostic terms, Aimee meets DSM criteria for Depressive Disorder-NOS and Dependent Personality Disorders and Obsessive-Compulsive Personality avoidant traits.

Dr. Carlson's Commentary

I continue to concentrate on the important components of creating and maintaining a positive relationship with Aimee. She was similar to many of the clients I have worked with who have had a challenging relationship history complete with many negative and unfulfilling encounters. Many therapists-in-training or average therapists stop with being a nice person with their clients and are afraid to participate with the client in a normal fashion of give and take. I wanted Aimee to know that I valued her and viewed her as a competent person and would treat her in this fashion. It is important for the client to know that you are being honest and truthful and will respond with validation *and* criticism. When working with the client's diagnosis of dependent personality, it is important to continue to validate them and show through your actions that you see them as able. Although Aimee does meet the criteria for Depressive Disorder NOS, she is additionally suffering from loneliness. Her personality structure works to keep her at a distance from others, leaving her experiencing deep loneliness despite her many attributes and social skills.

The case conceptualization using the model of Sperry and Sperry (2012) seems to be right on target and parallels my conceptualization and therapy with Aimee. It is nice to see the conceptualization so nicely and logically represented in print, but I must confess that I did not consciously operate with such a deliberate model. Much of what I did with Aimee and other clients occurs intuitively. I worked very hard at understanding Aimee's world while at the same time gently questioning or challenging her statements when they seemed limiting and destructive to herself. I think it is important for therapists to be real people and genuinely engaged. Too many average therapists seem to be playing the "therapist's role," making sure that every response, reflection, or utterance is like a videotape they observed. In essence, they are busy being somebody else, which distracts or takes away from what can potentially be achieved in therapy. I guess in many ways they are like Aimee and trapped trying to please others and unable to really be helpful at a very deep level.

I have probably modeled more master therapists than anyone in the world today. This is because I have made so many videos with the various master therapists and watched each of them work with several challenging clients. I noticed that I find myself unconsciously doing things that I watched the masters do without even realizing it. My treatment formulations have gained complexity, and my arsenal of treatment strategies has been expanded through this exposure.

I became aware that in Aimee's cultural background, she had no guide for who she wanted to become or where she wanted to go. She had already gone beyond all of her family members by finishing a college degree, and now she was in graduate school thinking of doctoral study. For her to be successful, it would be necessary for her to have a mentor to help her through the process. In a sense, Aimee had moved away from her cultural roots and found herself with no one to talk to, leaving her feeling lonely, isolated, and depressed. Effective therapy needed to understand the complexity of her situation and realize that biological interventions such as antidepressant medication would not reach the depth of her problem.

In working with Aimee, it was necessary to be aware of her secondary pattern of perfectionism. She would only move forward in a very careful fashion, making sure that she could perform in a "perfect" fashion. It is likely that her need to be perfect slowed down her challenging her mother until she could create the "perfect" message. Aimee's deep need to be loved and accepted provided the motivation for her needing to care for and please others. It was important to realize that Aimee viewed herself as nice but deficient and therefore needing to compensate, be careful, and cover up to survive in a critical and limiting world.

In my work with Aimee, I remained aware of her need to please others and take care of their needs at the expense of her own needs. I carefully monitored each session to insure that I did not become yet another person for Aimee to please at the expense of her own happiness and satisfaction. Understanding this feature of her personality was largely responsible for the success of her treatment. I was pleased when I learned that she had made progress in pleasing others as well as herself (this will be discussed in Chapter 7 long term).

Concluding Comment

For a therapist with a case conceptualization with low explanatory and predictive power, Aimee's behavior in the first three sessions might have seemed baffling. In the first session, she appears willing and agreeable to confront her mother before the second session, but she does not. In the second session, she restates her willingness and does so, but she comes to the third session crushed and depressed. This scenario could have been anticipated had the therapist developed a case conceptualization with a higher level of explanatory and predictive power. That is why Dr. Carlson was able to continue to confidently assist Aimee's transformation despite her momentary stumbling. Guided by such a case conceptualization, Dr. Carlson intuitively knew the kind of transformative journey Aimee needed to take and was there to confidently guide her along the way. Most of those who watch this DVD series with me (L.S.) admit that it is remarkable that second order change could occur this early in the therapeutic process. While trainees and beginning therapists may be in awe of such early transformative therapeutic outcomes, this is typically how master therapists work.

References

American Psychiatric Association (2013). *Diagnostic and Statistical Manual of Mental Disorders*, fifth edition. Arlington: VA: American Psychiatric Association.

Eells, T. (2007). History and current status of psychotherapy case formulation. In T. Eells (Ed.), *Handbook of psychotherapy case formulation* (2nd ed., pp. 3–32). New York, NY: Guilford.

Eells, T. (2010). The unfolding case formulation: The interplay of description and inference. *Pragmatic Case Studies in Psychotherapy*, 6 (4), 225–254.

Eells, T., Lombart, K., Kendjelic, E, Turner, L., & Lucas, C. (2005). The quality of psychotherapy case formulations: A comparison of expert, experienced, and novice cognitive-behavioral and psychodynamic therapists. *Journal of Consulting and Clinical Psychology*, 73, 579–589.

GAP Committee on Cultural Psychiatry. (2002). *Cultural assessment in clinical psychiatry*. Washington, DC: American Psychiatric Press.

Hays, P. & Iwanasa, G. (Eds.) (2006). *Culturally responsive cognitive behavioral therapy: Assessment, practice, and supervision*. Washington, DC: American Psychological Association.

Paniagua, F. (2005). *Assessing and treating culturally diverse clients: A practical guide* (3rd ed.). Thousand Oaks, CA: Sage.

Sperry, L. (2005). Case conceptualization: A strategy for incorporating individual, couple, and family dynamics in the treatment process. *American Journal of Family Therapy*, 33, 353–364.

Sperry, L. (2006). *Cognitive behavior therapy of DSM-IV-TR personality disorders*, second edition. New York, NY: Routledge.

Sperry, L. (2010). *Core competencies in counseling and psychotherapy: Becoming a highly competent and effective therapist*. New York, NY: Routledge.

Sperry, L., Blackwell, B., Gudeman, J., & Faulkner, L. (1992). *Psychiatric case formulations*. Washington, DC: American Psychiatric Press.

Sperry, L., & Sperry, J. (2012). *Case conceptualization: Mastering this competency with ease and confidence*. New York, NY: Routledge.

Wu, E., & Mak, W. (2012). Acculturation process and distress: Mediating roles of sociocultural adaptation and acculturative stress. *Counseling Psychologist*, 40, 66–92.

5
EFFECTING CHANGE: INCORPORATING SECOND ORDER CHANGE

Any therapist working with a challenging client like Aimee is faced with a critical question: How can this client be helped to change? In particular, how can she be helped to relinquish the maladaptive patterns and ineffective coping strategies that she has relied on for much of her life? For Dr. Carlson, the question was more specific: How can I help Aimee change the relational pattern that has caused so much distress and impaired functioning with her mother, as well as others? One answer and option for some therapists is: She can engage in a caring relationship with a therapist who will support her as she faces life challenges. We suspect that this approach would effect little or no change based on the experience of others with long-standing abuse histories who fail to change in generic, reflective forms of therapy. A second answer and option for other therapists is: She can develop insight into her situation and then change. We know this answer is limited since clients like Aimee already had achieved a relatively high level of insight into her situation, but it effected no change. A third answer and option might be: Provide her with a problem-solving therapy in which she is provided specific advice on identifying past successes and repeating them. The problem is that she has had little success in most areas of her life. A fourth answer and option might be to refer her for a medication evaluation for her symptoms of insomnia, depression, and anxiety, or use skill training to teach her to cope with these symptoms. By itself, symptom-based therapy that is focused on first order change is unlikely to effect more than short-term, symptomatic change. Unfortunately, most trainees and many therapists would likely offer a client like Aimee one or more of these four treatment approaches.

Master therapists, by contrast, are less likely to consider these options after hearing Aimee's story. Instead, they would identify maladaptive patterns and consider options that could effect deep change. They might formally articulate specific second order change interventions and core treatment strategies, like exposure and corrective experiences. Or, they might not. But, they would focus their therapeutic efforts at effecting deep and enduring change. This is exactly how Dr. Carlson proceeded in this case as the transcription of Session 3 illustrates.

This chapter describes second order change and the process of effecting such second order, also called transformational, change. It begins with a discussion of pattern change and the orders of change. Then, it details second order change and five second order change strategies and interventions. Next, it compares core treatment strategies with these second order change strategies. This is followed by the full transcription of Session 3, which emphasizes second order change. Finally, there are two commentaries on the session and second order change. It should also be noted that the discussion of the orders of change is continued in subsequent chapters. Chapter 6 addresses first order change, while Chapter 7 addressees third order change.

Pattern Change and Orders of Change

It has been said that psychotherapy does not effect cures in clients but rather effects change in clients. Since this book is primarily about effecting change, it may be quite useful to formally describe and delineate the change process and the types or orders of change. Let's begin with the change process and then describe the orders of change.

Pattern Change

In our experience and that of the master therapists we know, the primary focus of change is on patterns. Pattern change refers to modifying a maladaptive pattern by reducing its intensity and frequency and at the same time putting in place a more adaptive pattern by increasing the healthier pattern's intensity and frequency (Good & Beitman, 2006). In other words, the goal is to change by shifting from a maladaptive pattern to a more adaptive pattern. Typically, in the course of therapy the client and therapist collaborate to change a pattern or patterns. Pattern change occurs as a result of what the client does with the assistance of the therapist (Sperry, 2010). As will later be explained, this is the common scenario in effective therapy, and is called second order change.

This process of pattern change consists of three steps. The first step involves modifying the client's maladaptive pattern by first reducing its severity and frequency. The second step involves developing a more adaptive pattern and increasing the intensity and frequency of this new pattern. The third step is maintaining the adaptive pattern (Beitman & Yue, 1999).

For example, an individual has a maladaptive pattern that includes the belief that she is responsible for the negative events surrounding her and experiences considerable distress and guilt. As this pattern shifts to become more adaptive, she may continue to believe that she has some responsibility for negative events but experiences considerably less distress and guilt.

Indicators of the first step are a decrease in fearful thoughts, less avoidance of situations requiring assertive communication, and less frequent discomfort in social interactions. Indicators of the second step are more capacity to relax in the face of fearful and difficult situations, some degree of confidence in assertive communication, and more ease in social interactions. Indicators of the third step are being relaxed in the face of difficult situations, confident in assertive communication, and ease in social interactions (Good & Beitman, 2006).

It should be noted that while new awareness and insight can and often do occur in this process of shifting from a maladaptive to a more adaptive pattern, it does not mean that the shift or change occurs automatically or suddenly (Beitman & Yue, 1999). Actually, pattern change tends to occur in a start-and-stop fashion. Individuals will make progress only to experience some regression back to the old pattern. Progress is likely to involve two steps forward with one step backward. This is certainly borne out in the case of Aimee, who shifted from a maladaptive pattern to more adaptive one and then back to her maladaptive one on occasion. However, in the long term, her shift to the adaptive pattern persisted.

Orders of Change

It can be clinically useful for trainees and therapists to conceptualize the change process in terms of orders of change. While originating in the family therapy literature, similar orders of change are described in the psychotherapy literature (Good & Beitman, 2006; Fraser & Solovey, 2007). The basic assertion of this perspective is that when therapy is effective, a transformation of current efforts is needed to effect change in contrast to therapy that produces stability or a return to baseline functioning.

Three orders of change can be specified, and all three are the domain of the master therapist. Of these three, the first two seem to be the focus of most therapists. "First order change is defined as a class of resolutions that do not change a problem or make a problem worse. In contrast, second order change is a change of those first order resolutions, which results in a resolution of the problem" (Fraser & Solovey, 2007, p. 15). In short, first order change is related to stability, while second order change is related to transformation. Third order change is similar to second order change but without the involvement of a therapist.

For example, an unemployed client with the diagnosis of social anxiety disorder might take medication that effectively reduces his anxiety symptoms but does not replace his maladaptive pattern of fearfulness and avoidance. Thus, he might fill out a job application online, but out of fear decides he cannot tolerate the prospect of a job interview when it is offered. If medication reduces his symptoms, a degree of stability has been achieved. This represents first order change. However, if the client is helped by a therapist to learn to face his fears and avoidance behavior directly so that he can be interviewed, offered, and start the job, a more adaptive pattern is achieved. Such positive actions reflect a more adaptive pattern and constitute second order change. If this same client is then able to disengage from excessive fearful and anxious feelings on his own, without the assistance of a therapist, he has achieved third order change. This represents the ultimate goal of therapy wherein clients function "as their own therapists." Table 5.1 summarizes the orders of change. Subsequent discussion in this chapter focuses on second order change.

Table 5.1 Orders of Change

Order	Description
Zero	Client is not assisted in making change; this may negatively impact treatment
First	Clients assisted in making small changes, reduce symptoms, or achieve stability
Second	Clients assisted in changing a maladaptive pattern to a more adaptive pattern
Third	Clients change patterns on their own; "become their own therapists"

In our clinical and supervisory experience, we can add another order of change. Zero order of change, if we can call it that, represents situations when no change is effected for any number of reasons. This situation is particularly common when trainees, often to reduce their own anxiety about how to proceed, employ the tactic of continually asking factually oriented questions rather than process the client's issues or adequately engage the client. Unfortunately, the unspoken message of this tactic is that "I don't know what I'm doing, and I don't really expect you will get better." Or, therapists are unable to establish and maintain a treatment focus, a prerequisite for engaging the client in the change process. The result is that clients may continue to experience symptoms, become demoralized about their situation ever improving, or not improve because they may not want to face the responsibilities that come with getting better (i.e., finding a job, returning to work, or making a relationship work) (Sperry & Sperry, 2012).

Second Order Change

Second order change involves therapist-assisted pattern change. In this order of change, a therapist assists clients to alter their patterned thinking and behavior within the situation in which their maladaptive pattern is occurring. The heart of second order change is transformation—specifically, a transformation of pattern. In this order of change, a new and more adaptive pattern transforms or replaces the maladaptive pattern.

For example, an individual with panic attacks may begin working with a therapist to face his fears directly. Facing a dreaded fear is not simply symptom reduction (first order change), but, if the treatment is successful, symptoms will not only be reduced but also eliminated. It is second order change because the maladaptive pattern of avoidance of painful thoughts and feelings is transformed and replaced with a more adaptive pattern. The pattern of avoiding fears is replaced with a new pattern in which the individual can now realistically face fears that were avoided in the past.

Second Order Change View of Clinical Conditions

Understanding the most common clinical conditions in light of first and second order change is helpful in planning and implementing change strategies. The first and second order change views of three common clinical conditions are briefly described.

Anxiety Disorders

Anxiety is typically viewed as the result of attempting to master anxiety by avoidance of it. This is the prototypic first order solution, which serves not only to increase symptoms of anxiety but also to engender anticipatory anxiety. The second order view of anxiety offers a different rationale for it and prescribes reversals in the pattern so that individuals move toward (rather than avoid) their anxiety so that they can master it (Fraser & Solovey, 2007).

Depression

Depression is commonly viewed as a cynical cycle of efforts to cope with overwhelming stress by self-disconfirmation, cognitive oversimplification, and withdrawal. The first order solution typically results in self-doubt, blame, and further withdrawal. By contrast, second order interventions offer various rationales to affirm the experience of depression as appropriate to the context. Then they reverse the pattern through exercises in which individuals check out their assumptions and address their challenges (Fraser & Solovey, 2007).

Substance Dependence

Alcohol and other substance dependencies are commonly viewed as the result of an attempt at mastery through avoidance. This means the individual either fails to attend to addictive behavior or fails to take necessary action for change. Two first order solutions or cycles are involved. In the first cycle, the more the individual denies dependence, the more they become dependent. The other cycle is triggered when significant others attempt to coerce addicts out of their addiction.

One effective second order intervention is to have the addict win over their addiction by admitting defeat in a 12-step program. Significant others are counseled to stop their initial solution of persuading the addict to become abstinent and stand back and allow the addict to seek his or her own resolution. The other effective second order intervention involves therapists using reversals. So instead of attempting to make the addict acknowledge and change the addiction, therapists validate the addicts' "position on change and collaborate with the person on what he or she might decide to change, if anything" (Fraser & Solovey, 2007, p. 277).

Second Order Change Strategies and Interventions

A number of clinically useful second order change strategies have been described (Fraser & Solovey, 2007). These strategies are based on the premise that first order solutions do not change or resolve the problem, and often make the problem worse. In contrast, second order solutions can and usually do resolve the problem. These second order change strategies include reversal; blocking and acceptance; framing, reframing, and deframing; prescribing; and predicting.

Reversal

Reversal is the most basic of second order changes. In fact, it was the primary strategy employed in the early days of behavior therapy. Starting in the 1960s, behavior therapy was largely focused on the treatment of anxiety disorders, particularly phobias and panic disorder. Desensitization and exposure therapy were interventions directed at gradually exposing individuals to feared objects or situations. CBT continues to use reversal in the form of exposure therapy.

Today, it refers to a wide range of strategies across a number of approaches for countering the ineffectual solutions (avoidance) used by the individual to solve problems. It blocks the first order change processes the individual had been using. So, if the individual with panic symptoms had used avoidance, the opposite would be for the individual to face the fear by imagining successfully more anxiety-provoking situations while remaining relaxed. The basis for this strategy is that doing "something willfully" is the opposite of having it occur involuntarily. This reverses the cycle. Instead of experiencing panic attacks involuntarily, "the problem solver is now trying to have a panic attack on purpose.... This shift re-establishes the problem solver's confidence in her ability to control herself" (Fraser & Solovey, 2007, p. 57).

Behavioral activation is one of the most powerful interventions in reversing depressive symptoms (Chartier & Provencher, 2013). The purpose of behavioral activation is to increase the depressed individual's activity level and to reverse and prevent the individual's avoidance behaviors such as oversleeping, laying around during the day, and social isolation instead of getting out of bed, taking a walk, and talking to others. As a result of engaging in positive, energizing, and rewarding activities the client's mood improves. Because it reverses avoidance behavior, behavioral activation is a second order change strategy.

Acceptance and Blocking

Acceptance and blocking strategies are designed to stop solutions that fail to solve a problem. This strategy is embedded in various interventions including psychoeducation. For example, individuals are educated about the psychophysiology of a panic attack. They learn that the panic response is natural and normal. This allows individuals who had mistaken their reaction as unnatural or pathological to accept it. For some individuals, this is enough to help them relax without reliance on their previous avoidance solution. As a result of this acceptance, their panic symptoms may cease.

Framing, Reframing, and Deframing

These strategies have been a mainstay of family therapy for years and have been a go-to intervention of master therapists doing individual therapy. They can directly reverse meanings that drive the individual's ineffective first order solutions. They can also serve as building blocks for prescribing alternative actions in the problem-solving process. "Toward this end, framing, reframing, and deframing are generally used to place a problem or problem solver in a more favorable light, to assist a problem solver with seeing the discrepancy between his solution attempts and goals, and to make new actions seems attractive" (Fraser & Solovey, 2007, p. 105).

Prescribing

In this strategy, the therapist directs the individual to deliberately enact a symptom on purpose in order to gain mastery over it. This strategy is effective because it requires the individual to reverse direction and move toward the symptom instead of moving away from it. Because it serves as an implicit permission from the therapist to engage in the symptomatic behavior, the client feels validated despite having the symptoms. The result is that the client is encouraged to embrace the problem (Fraser & Solovey, 2007, p. 105).

Predicting

In this strategy, the therapist predicts that change will be difficult to maintain and that setbacks may occur. But setbacks are reframed "as opportunities to consolidate gains by reencountering old dangers. . . . Pressure is lessened for maintaining change, which may prevent future reoccurrences of the problem" (Fraser & Solovey, 2007, p. 106). This strategy is particularly useful in preparing for termination wherein the client is informed she may return to treatment for an additional learning opportunity.

Core Treatment Strategy and Second Order Change

Chapter 4 described a core treatment strategy as the action plan for focusing specific interventions to achieve a more adaptive pattern. The purpose of the action plan is to replace the maladaptive pattern with a more adaptive pattern and then maintain that pattern. Eight common treatment strategies were described: support, interpretation, cognitive restructuring, replacement, exposure, skills training and psychoeducation, biological, and corrective experiences.

EFFECTING CHANGE: INCORPORATING SECOND ORDER CHANGE

Of these eight, support and the biological (particularly medication) are primarily first order change strategies. Others like interpretation, cognitive restructuring, and replacement are second order strategies. Generally speaking, these are relatively weak interventions in effecting transformation. By comparison, corrective experience, exposure, and skill training and psychoeducation are more potent. Described in this chapter are five second order change strategies: reversal; blocking and acceptance; framing, reframing, and deframing; prescribing; and predicting. Some of these are similar to the eight basic treatment strategies. For instance, reversal and exposure share similarities, as do blocking/acceptance and skill training/psychoeducation.

Transcription of Session 3

This section includes a transcription of the entire third session. The reader can note several therapeutic tactics and strategies are used by Dr. Carlson.

DR. CARLSON: Aimee, it's good to see you.

AIMEE: It's good to see you too.

DR. CARLSON: And what I'd like to have us work on today is a couple things I want to address the questions that you wrote down on the sheet that you wanted to talk about today and what's been different and then to go over the things that you had talked about doing last week, but on the top of this sheet you wrote I've been very down lately. I have feelings of overwhelming responsibility . . .

AIMEE: Yeah.

DR. CARLSON: Can you talk about that?

AIMEE: I've I think . . . I've kind of hit a wall sort of because I know that . . . alright the thing with my mother that happened, but it's like I've been kind of dragging my feet.

DR. CARLSON: So you talked to your mom?

AIMEE: I talked to her yes.

DR. CARLSON: How did that go?

AIMEE: That was very weird because uh . . . she said to me . . . she said to me that . . . she goes why did you tell me that now and she started crying. So, she asked a question and I wasn't ready for her to ask me a question. I was like I don't know why, so it felt really strange.

DR. CARLSON: So you asked her a question and she didn't answer the question and put it back on you?

AIMEE: Well, yeah sort of. I told her I'm glad that you're my mother now . . . I'm glad that you're stepping in and she goes well why did you tell me that, then she started crying it was kind of a neutral reaction . . . it was strange to me, I don't know what she meant, it was mixed signals. I don't know if she accepted it, it was kind of a weird reaction.

DR. CARLSON: You didn't talk anymore about that?

AIMEE: Well, yeah we did. She said she wanted to come over the next day and hang out . . . she's wanting to hang out with me a little more so that's nice, but I, you know, we didn't really . . . it was kind of a strange . . . I don't know I didn't want to delve too far . . . it was kind of weird and then she was crying, so I didn't want to keep on going.

DR. CARLSON: So, when she cried, you kind of shut down?

AIMEE: Sort of yeah, I was kind of sort of crying too and I just said that it was not right and I kind of left it at that . . . it was so hard for me to do it though because um I actually was nauseated, before it happened, like I was thinking about it, I couldn't eat and . . .

DR. CARLSON: So, this was really difficult?

AIMEE: Yeah, really difficult to the point where I almost stopped functioning from it . . .

DR. CARLSON: Well, congratulations for doing something so difficult.

AIMEE: Yeah, well now it seems like that . . . I've gone through that and I know that I'm going to have to go through a lot more in order to start to grow and it scares me to think about . . . I don't know about doing instead of not doing.

DR. CARLSON: So as you thought about that, and I know I heard you say it scares you, but what do you think the next step is going to be with your mom?

AIMEE: I don't know . . . right now I'm really physically exhausted from thinking about all of this and . . .

DR. CARLSON: So, that may have a lot to do with feeling overwhelmed and down?

AIMEE: Yeah, yeah . . . I've been really depressed lately . . . just I'm afraid. I'm afraid about where I'm going with my life, what I'm going to do. I mean, I know I have it mapped out already, but the means of getting there. I've had a lot of self-doubt, lately, and it's like my mind wants me to go back into that little comfort zone instead of going out and doing what I have to do in order to progress. So, I've been battling myself inside over this past week.

DR. CARLSON: I see, so one of the reasons you're not feeling so good is because you've not given in to that?

AIMEE: Yeah, well yeah of course. It's like fighting . . . it's going against what my body wants me to do and it's like a battle inside my head, it's very strange.

DR. CARLSON: So how does that battle go? Is there kind of talk at both sides of the battle? What would it be like?

AIMEE: Umm, well the one side, the comfort side would be like don't talk to your mom you could do it another day . . . procrastination . . . you don't have to do this that whatever, it's like bad. But, then the other side says you have to do in order to get over this, you have to do this to progress, to heal inside.

DR. CARLSON: So, it's sort of like there's a good me and a not so good me?

AIMEE: Yeah, yes exactly.

DR. CARLSON: And you talk to both of them?

AIMEE: Yeah, yeah, I do, but it's really hard to start living a different life when you just found a niche to be comfortable . . . like I keep thinking about being more assertive and it scares me, I don't know why, what is . . . I've gone through so much and I've overcome a lot; I don't know why I'm afraid, I'm very afraid of it.

DR. CARLSON: Is that back to the anxiety that we talked about last week, is that a performance anxiety? Is that a good thing that will help you to get ready and kind of motivates you?

AIMEE: Yeah, it does, but now I've . . . it's just really physically it's really happening like I can't eat very much and I'm not sleeping and uh . . .

DR. CARLSON: So, not eating much?

AIMEE: No, I have like kind of a knot in my stomach and even though it felt really good to tell my mom that, it was like . . . I don't know it was just like this is only the beginning. So instead of like rejoicing the fact that I achieved what I wanted to achieve, I immediately started thinking well this is this, now you have this instead of basking in . . .

DR. CARLSON: Ahhh . . . so, you're seeing this rather than as the finished paper, you're seeing this as like maybe you wrote the first page, now you've got to write the second page?

AIMEE: Yeah, definitely, yes. So, um . . .

DR. CARLSON: And when you're writing a paper, how do you do that?

AIMEE: I just flow that's it . . . I'm very good at that.

DR. CARLSON: I see, so you don't stop along the way?

AIMEE: Not really

DR. CARLSON: So this is an incredible first page?

AIMEE: No, not really, I just let it go and then I edit.

DR. CARLSON: But with the relationships you want to kind of check along the way?

AIMEE: Yeah.

DR. CARLSON: It sounds like when you write it's like planting a tree and you put the tree in the ground and you put a lot of water and fertilizer, then you get out of the way and just let it go. But with your mom, it's like you keep pulling out the tree and say how's it doing and sticking it in the ground.

AIMEE: Yeah.

DR. CARLSON: Do you think you could be more like writing with your mom?

AIMEE: Oh yeah, definitely. I can write, you know, that is one of the ways I could . . .

DR. CARLSON: But act like your writing with your mom, but to call her up and say mom we didn't finish our conversation?

AIMEE: Yeah.

DR. CARLSON: I didn't get an answer back from you.

AIMEE: Yeah, I mean, it was very strange I didn't know how she felt about it . . . what she said to me was not the reaction I expected.

DR. CARLSON: And you didn't . . . well you didn't get an answer.

AIMEE: Yeah.

DR. CARLSON: And I think you need to return to that. Sometimes crying is used to stop somebody from asking a question. I mean, it sort of worked for you.

AIMEE: Yeah, definitely. So, she's coming over tomorrow, maybe that's an opportunity there.

DR. CARLSON: And you would start it how?

AIMEE: Uh . . . you know, I don't know. I haven't thought about that.

DR. CARLSON: Mhmm . . . right.

AIMEE: I guess I'll have to think about how I'm going to start it out.

DR. CARLSON: Right. What would happen if you didn't think about it and just did it?

AIMEE: I think it will be better if I didn't think about it and just do it because then maybe I won't convince myself not to do it.

DR. CARLSON: Oh soo, it would be better on one level and not on another level, it wouldn't get done.

AIMEE: But, at least I've done that much so I kind of feel better about it now. I'm looking forward to her visiting me and yeah it's not so hard for me to think about it right now after I've already done what . . . done that much.

DR. CARLSON: Oh, OK so you're actually not dreading her visit?

AIMEE: No, where I was dreading telling her how I felt all this week.

DR. CARLSON: Well, it will be interesting to see what tomorrow brings.

AIMEE: Yes.

EFFECTING CHANGE: INCORPORATING SECOND ORDER CHANGE

DR. CARLSON: Yeah, and so this has been a difficult time, you also wrote down your depression and your fear that you wanted to talk about and last week you were working on some other things as well. You were working at talking to other people, taking some action, giving yourself permission to feel certain ways.

AIMEE: Yes and I've kind of had a setback there because when I get depressed, I isolate myself from everybody. That's what I've been doing and I've been at home. I haven't been working much; it's slow so I don't have much work. I'm on the couch a lot, not doing much of anything and . . .

DR. CARLSON: I see, so when you do depressing things like not get out and hang on the couch, then you feel depressed?

AIMEE: Yeah.

DR. CARLSON: Oh, OK. So, it sounds like you're pretty normal.

AIMEE: Yes, but I have this fear like last night I was lying in bed and I could not fall sleep and I was thinking about how crazy it's going to be to have to go to school and I've already done it, but for some reason, I started thinking oh it's not going to be . . . I'm not going to be able to achieve this, it's going to be hard, am I up for this? I don't know, I just had anxiety.

DR. CARLSON: So, what can you do with those voices? I mean, it sounds like there needs to be a way to hear more from this person who wants you to grow and less from this person who keeps doubting you.

AIMEE: Umm . . . I'm gonna have to overcome them.

DR. CARLSON: What strategies have you used before?

AIMEE: I don't know, I really haven't . . . I kind of just let one override the other.

DR. CARLSON: So, would you be interested in looking at one possible way?

AIMEE: Yes.

DR. CARLSON: Now, I'm wondering what would happen if you could become more aware of these thoughts once they start? Because it sounds like once they get started, then they tend to have a life of their own like last night . . .

AIMEE: Definitely.

DR. CARLSON: As I was hearing you, one after another after another.

AIMEE: Yes.

DR. CARLSON: And there's one strategy that people have found pretty helpful; it's called meditation and I don't know if you've ever learned how to do meditation?

AIMEE: No, but I'm interested in it . . .

DR. CARLSON: OK, so you wouldn't be opposed to doing some meditation?

AIMEE: No.

DR. CARLSON: What happens with meditation is that you learn to . . . really learn to breathe, breathing slowly and breathing deeper. Like, right now I see that you're breathing very shallow, did you know that?

AIMEE: Yes.

DR. CARLSON: Can you picture the inside of your lungs are like a jar and when you pour water into a jar you fill the bottom all the way up to the top. So, can you imagine breathing deeply like that where you start and you fill up the bottom and go [*breathes slowly giving an example*] then blow it out the same way and take a slow deep breath. Maybe you learned that when you sang and do this diaphragmatic breathing that singers usually do?

AIMEE: Mhmm.

DR. CARLSON: Where you really use your diaphragm. So, can you practice breathing in slowly and breathing in deeply?

AIMEE: Yes.

DR. CARLSON: And as you do that, you know, maybe you might want to close your eyes and practice right now and see how it goes OK?

AIMEE: OK. [*Closes her eyes and begins deep breathing*]

DR. CARLSON: All the while, while you're breathing in slowly and breathing deeply, that's right. Now, as you breathe in slowly and deeply you'll probably have thoughts that are going to come into your mind, and when these thoughts come into your mind and what I'd like you to do is just to continue to focus on your breathing.

AIMEE: [*focuses on breathing*]

DR. CARLSON: That's right, nice in and out. You might imagine waves on a shore as they flow in and as they flow out and as any thoughts come to your mind just send them away and go back and focus on the breathing. Breathing in slowly and breathing in deeply and as you're breathing in become aware of all of yourself. Become aware of your body sitting in a chair, become aware of any noises or sounds that you hear, and all the while focusing on your breathing. Breathing in slowly and breathing in deeply. Only you and your breath exist. And if you could take three more breaths and on the third breath just open your eyes . . .

AIMEE: [*takes three slow and deep breaths, then opens her eyes*]

DR. CARLSON: What was that like for you? Were you able to stay focused on your breathing?

AIMEE: Mhmm.

DR. CARLSON: Did your mind wander or did you have to bring it back?

AIMEE: No.

DR. CARLSON: Wow, that was very good.

AIMEE: It feels really good too.

DR. CARLSON: And see we often don't take the time to become aware of how we're doing and we're finding that as you become aware, when you find yourself getting stressed, as you practice you can just breathe the thoughts away; the thoughts that are the negative thoughts and just be present. So, in your mind when your mom starts to cry, rather than thinking I'm a terrible person now look what I've done, you just go [*breathes deeply*] and choose to say: I'm sure she'll get over it she's a big person and she's cried before. . . .

AIMEE: Oh, yeah.

DR. CARLSON: I just want my question answered. It's a fair question.

AIMEE: Yeah.

DR. CARLSON: All the while, while you're breathing slowly and breathing deeply, now what I'd suggest you might do is to see this as something you can use at any time. At night, for example, when you can't sleep just focus on your breathing; people count backwards from a hundred. On the exhale, you go one hundred, and the next exhale would ninety-nine, and you find that your mind wondered off and you're thinking about school and not being successful, and how you're going to fail, and you just send those thoughts away and come back to one hundred and before you know it you come back down to one. But, the important part is that you become more and more aware of these thoughts and you have something you can do to send them away if they come back, send them away and send them away again. There's something sort of like a wave . . . you know.

AIMEE: Mhmm.

DR. CARLSON: Have you ever seen surfers on a wave when the wave gets higher and higher and higher and then what happens? It breaks.

AIMEE: Yeah.

DR. CARLSON: And those thoughts break too, those thoughts will go right away. It's a way of developing a sense of control and I think when those thoughts come that's when the fear comes, that's where the anxiety comes, that's where the depression comes. And, I was starting to feel depressed as I was hearing your voice talk about you.

AIMEE: Yeah.

DR. CARLSON: Your pretty convincing, you know that?

AIMEE: Well, I've been really depressed and I'm usually . . . I was in great spirits last week, but I kind of had some setbacks with just thinking about what's next.

DR. CARLSON: Uhuh . . . and sometimes that happens, but it's important that when you have the thoughts that it's important to do the non-depressing things, things that's we talked about.

AIMEE: Yes, uhh . . . when I get depressed it seems like I just don't want to do anything else and the whole world stops. I don't want to put make-up on, I don't want to get off the couch, and I don't want to do the dishes, and . . .

DR. CARLSON: Do you think that's a choice?

AIMEE: Yeah, it's a choice. I choose to do that.

DR. CARLSON: Mhmm . . . and what do you guess is the purpose of choosing depression? I kind of wondered about that before . . . you know, you . . .

AIMEE: Perhaps it's because it's better than feeling or confronting what I want to do. It's a way of retracting, it's procrastinating, you know, and it's an excuse really.

DR. CARLSON: So the purpose, then of depression for you is avoidance?

AIMEE: Yeah.

DR. CARLSON: That was quite a smile you had there.

AIMEE: Yeah, it is that's one way I don't do what I want to do because this is really difficult for me to even think about. And then I had another . . . something happened and I was thinking about what we were going to talk about and I've been down on myself because I chose to do what I would normally do instead of being assertive in this situation. So, it was at my emotional cost again and it happens a lot. I know I don't have to be mean to people, but I'm just not assertive enough to even tell somebody how I feel in a friendly way. I'm just afraid of. So, I'm afraid of it . . . assertiveness, that's what I've been thinking about because I endured it instead of telling this how I felt about it.

DR. CARLSON: And so you're afraid of assertiveness so far?

AIMEE: Yeah, so far.

DR. CARLSON: Did you find yourself saying "yet" or "so far" at all this week?

AIMEE: Yes, a few times, but like I said I focused on the negative aspect of not doing what I wanted to do.

DR. CARLSON: So, one of the things that you're saying is that you use the depression and the fear to avoid things?

AIMEE: Yeah.

DR. CARLSON: Is that true?

AIMEE: It is true.

DR. CARLSON: I added fear with the depression . . .

AIMEE: It's true.

DR. CARLSON: Then what you do is kind of a negative way for you to not do anything. Can you give yourself permission to not do anything?

AIMEE: Yes.

DR. CARLSON: So, rather than . . .

AIMEE: Yes, but I . . . thinking back on what I'm afraid of most it is to being assertive with other people. It's what I fear most and I've thought of everything and I've thought a lot about it and it scares me to think about being assertive. I don't know why I . . . I just . . . it's like somebody jumping out of an airplane . . . I just don't . . . someone's got to push me.

DR. CARLSON: And I hear you saying that and, I guess I'm not sure why you do it though . . . because it seems like when you do that though again it creates a lot of pain for you.

AIMEE: Oh, it does because . . .

DR. CARLSON: And I'm not sure what about the pain you like . . . and if you are not going to do something why don't you go play music? You know, go play the drums rather than lay on the couch or . . . as long as you're not going to do anything go call up a friend or go out and give yourself permission to avoid doing something.

AIMEE: That would be a better choice.

DR. CARLSON: OK well, it would be a less depressing choice . . .

AIMEE: Yes.

DR. CARLSON: I mean, the one thing is you've got the problem that you're not going to face and another thing is you're going to be depressed. At least we can take care of the problem.

AIMEE: But I won't . . . I'm usually not depressed if I have company or . . .

DR. CARLSON: Right.

AIMEE: I'm kind of a loner, I don't have many friends or anything . . . but uh so I need to make some friends, I guess because I don't really have anybody.

DR. CARLSON: Yeah, we talked about that last week . . . you were going to . . .

AIMEE: I tried to open up to a few people and I don't know I'm still afraid a little bit. I'm still sort of dragging my feet on that issue.

DR. CARLSON: But the purpose of the fear is to not do it.

AIMEE: Mhmm.

DR. CARLSON: Alright, and I'm suggesting that you give yourself permission not to do that. I mean, if you're trying to be friends with lots of people, pick one who's maybe more friendly . . . is there such a person?

AIMEE: Oh, I'm sure there is out there somewhere, but I feel like afraid to connect. I think that I'm not going to be able to connect with anyone.

DR. CARLSON: Mhmm . . . well, especially if you don't try.

AIMEE: Yeah well, or if you go in it with a negative attitude also because maybe they're reading off me . . . maybe they sense that and they aren't as friendly towards me as I want them to be. I expect people to throw themselves at me, you know, not throw themselves, but to be the assertive one and I'm just kind of mousey.

DR. CARLSON: And again all of that becomes a self-fulfilling prophecy when we think that way.

AIMEE: Mhmm... definitely.

DR. CARLSON: Now do you think by working on your breathing that that might allow you to make a little bit of a different choice?

AIMEE: Yes, I need... I need some type of a medium, I've already... I've thought about this too. I need to learn some type of meditation, maybe go to a yoga class something because I don't take... I'll either be depressed or on the couch or I'm doing so much that I don't, you know...

DR. CARLSON: Right, so you have two speeds.

AIMEE: Yes.

DR. CARLSON: Stop, then...

AIMEE: Never have time to just relax and take five.

DR. CARLSON: Unless you're depressed.

AIMEE: Mhmm... I don't really have depression too much... I don't experience it that often, but like right now it's happening because I want to confront these things so...

DR. CARLSON: And again it's the things that you don't want to confront?

AIMEE: Umm... Being more assertive...

DR. CARLSON: But that's kind of vague to me can we break it down to something specific?

AIMEE: Umm... telling family members how I feel about certain things and showing people my true colors... getting out of the mask.

DR. CARLSON: Can you... do you want to do this all at once or can you do it one step at a time?

AIMEE: No, I could do it one step at a time. That's how I am. Thinking ahead and always thinking about what I'm going to do next.

DR. CARLSON: It sounds like what you said with your mom is that you, you know, talked to her and got up the courage to do that and now you don't dread her coming over tomorrow.

AIMEE: No.

DR. CARLSON: And I'm wondering if it would be a good formula for you to tell yourself like we talked about last week that bringing about change is difficult first, but then it tapers off.

AIMEE: Yes, it seems very difficult right now.

DR. CARLSON: At first.

AIMEE: So far.

DR. CARLSON: At first and so far... so is there... did you want to work on talking with family a little more or last week it sounded like you wanted to make a friend at the university?

EFFECTING CHANGE: INCORPORATING SECOND ORDER CHANGE

AIMEE: Yeah, I talked to a few people here.

DR. CARLSON: Is there somebody that seems like more interested or less interested in talking to you?

AIMEE: I don't know, I think . . . I can't really . . . I try to strike up a conversation, but it seems like a lot of the time when I do that . . . and I do that out loud in public also, I'm very friendly patron and umm . . . people will kind of look at you like why are you talking to me more than . . . here's your change goodbye.

DR. CARLSON: Friendliness is kind of like that isn't it?

AIMEE: Yeah, it's weird . . . like, it doesn't feel right, but I'm very friendly and it's I don't know . . . maybe people are very leery of that . . . I don't know.

DR. CARLSON: Well, I think at first they are, I think most of us are.

AIMEE: So, I've been talking to a woman and I have her phone number.

DR. CARLSON: Really!

AIMEE: I called her and she never got back to me, but that happens, everybody is busy . . . I'm not thinking oh well, she doesn't like me but it was hard for me to do that.

DR. CARLSON: But another thing that you did.

AIMEE: Yes.

DR. CARLSON: Are you anticipating that if you change it's not going to be difficult?

AIMEE: I don't know, what do you mean by that?

DR. CARLSON: I think my mother used to say "no pain no gain" . . . did you ever hear that?

AIMEE: Oh yes definitely. Well, I've lived for so long by avoiding the issues in one form or another.

DR. CARLSON: I don't know that that's true . . . it seems like what you done is live for a long time making yourself kind of miserable . . .

AIMEE: Yeah.

DR. CARLSON: But I don't know that you've avoided things . . . I mean, you graduated college, you've turned your papers in, you had some kids, you've been taking care of your dad or grandma, and you've had a job . . . I mean that's not somebody who's avoiding all kinds of things. You confronted your mom . . .

AIMEE: Yeah.

DR. CARLSON: And you ended a marriage; I mean you know you . . .

AIMEE: I think I really need to start to learn to take care of myself, you know and it's hard for me to do that.

DR. CARLSON: Well, it sounds like you're taking care of yourself too.

AIMEE: Yes, but for some reason I view that as kind of being idle or I don't know.

DR. CARLSON: But I say I see you doing all of these things that you don't acknowledge very much.
AIMEE: No.
DR. CARLSON: And you have a strange way of keeping score.
AIMEE: Yes, I do.
DR. CARLSON: As we talked about last week, you do a paper, you know, you get an A+ and you think it isn't any good.
AIMEE: Yeah.
DR. CARLSON: So, what's the purpose of keeping yourself miserable?
AIMEE: I don't know, I really don't it's just sort of how I've always lived. As a child, I was kind of a melancholy kid.
DR. CARLSON: Is that a familiar feeling?
AIMEE: Yeah, it is and I feel like happy-go-lucky jolly me is . . . like going to miss something . . . it's going to screw up or you know not get up or something.
DR. CARLSON: Yeah, uhuh.
AIMEE: Or not turn in the paper because I was busy being happy.
DR. CARLSON: Right. Well, it sounds like you've got all those you's . . . you've got the happy you, you've got the melancholy you, you know? You've got that whole gamut of things.
AIMEE: I do, but I know that's how I feel if I'm doing something for me, then I might not be doing something for somebody else and therefore they're disappointed.
DR. CARLSON: OK, well that's a thought.
AIMEE: Yeah.
DR. CARLSON: That's not a feeling.
AIMEE: Yeah, OK.
DR. CARLSON: If I'm doing something for me other people might be disappointed . . . that's the thought.
AIMEE: Yeah.
DR. CARLSON: Uhh . . . and? What will they do about it?
AIMEE: I don't know. Maybe tell me that I'm selfish or something.
DR. CARLSON: And, so if they said why didn't you do that for me you'd say? . . . . sure.
AIMEE: Well, it depends on what it is, but uhh..
DR. CARLSON: I mean, I think isn't it OK to say you're doing something for yourself? I think people get in trouble if they're just doing things for themselves.
AIMEE: Yeah.
DR. CARLSON: But I mean it doesn't sound like that's you. I mean you're cleaning your grandmother's house, taking care of your dad, your kids . . . I mean you're . . .

EFFECTING CHANGE: INCORPORATING SECOND ORDER CHANGE

AIMEE: Sometimes, I think I would like somebody to take care of me for a while. I think that would be nice. Not like doting over me, but like . . .

DR. CARLSON: Mhmm . . . but you've also said that it's not something that you're very comfortable with.

AIMEE: No, then again, I would probably not accept it. I'd feel weird about it . . . you know, so I don't know . . .

DR. CARLSON: Wow.

AIMEE: I would probably not accept it. I'm not very good at taking compliments or praise.

DR. CARLSON: It sounds like that's a much bigger step to do that right now?

AIMEE: Yeah.

DR. CARLSON: I mean that's a much bigger step right now, but that's not something that you're very comfortable with right now?

AIMEE: No, so far.

DR. CARLSON: So far, and that's exactly right so far. You're feeling pretty good though that you talked to your mom?

AIMEE: I was thinking about doing something and I don't know if this sounds corny or not but like just posting little signs around my house and telling me what I've done. Just to kind of remind me of the good things that I've accomplished. Instead of well I didn't do this or I better make sure they're all right.

DR. CARLSON: Mhmm . . . so that's one of those choices about what you think about.

AIMEE: Yeah and at least then it's like . . . I mean I could do all those things in my head, but at least when I turn around it's there behind me . . .

DR. CARLSON: Mhmmm..

AIMEE: And maybe then sooner or later I wouldn't need the signs anymore I would just do it in my head.

DR. CARLSON: Well, it sure sounds like it's worth a try!

AIMEE: Yeah.

DR. CARLSON: I mean, what you're saying is maybe this will help not only break a pattern, but make you aware of the things that I think about. Yeah, I sure think it's worth a try. And like what would you write on a piece of paper as an example?

AIMEE: Um . . . you're a wonderful mother, uhh, you know, I'm amazed at some of the cars I drive, I mean sometimes . . . I mean anyone can drive a vehicle, but it's a hard job. I don't give myself credit for that.

DR. CARLSON: OK, so good driver.

AIMEE: Yeah, just . . .

DR. CARLSON: Good mother.

AIMEE: Yeah.

DR. CARLSON: Yeah, I think those reminders are really important because that goes back to the choice.

AIMEE: Mhmm.

DR. CARLSON: If we choose to think of what's wrong then we feel bad . . .

AIMEE: Exactly.

DR. CARLSON: If we choose to think of what's right, then we'll feel differently.

AIMEE: And that happens to me every day because I may overlook one thing and then I dwell on that . . . you know, the kids or whatever . . . instead I should be thinking about all the great things I've done.

DR. CARLSON: Well, I don't know if you should, but if you did you might feel better.

AIMEE: Yeah.

DR. CARLSON: For more of the time, again, I don't think this is going to happen overnight.

AIMEE: No, it's really difficult right now though just the way I'm thinking about all these things. I mean, I know I'm going to have to move on and progress in order to heal inside and it's stewing over it, it's difficult.

DR. CARLSON: Well, it's a choice too. I mean it's a choice to stew.

AIMEE: Yeah.

DR. CARLSON: I mean, I'm not sure why you're choosing that though when you have other choices. It doesn't particularly help you.

AIMEE: No, no not at all.

DR. CARLSON: I mean you could avoid doing something and not stew, if you wanted to.

AIMEE: I mean that's better or lesser of two evils isn't it?

DR. CARLSON: It's a different one. You know, it's a different one. I mean you create two problems . . . you don't do it and you feel bad . . . this way you just wouldn't do it. Maybe you could do something where you'd feel good.

AIMEE: Well, you're convincing.

DR. CARLSON: Well, I don't know if I'm convincing, but it might be a way to come up with some alternatives to stop you from the patterns that bring you down; because last week you felt pretty darn good.

AIMEE: Yeah, I know . . . but then I started thinking about what I have to do and . . .

DR. CARLSON: Well, you know those formulas you had here were that you were going to try to find out what makes you feel good and you said talking to others and taking action.

AIMEE: Mhmm . . .

EFFECTING CHANGE: INCORPORATING SECOND ORDER CHANGE

DR. CARLSON: Those were the two things so if you were going to take action tomorrow with your mom it sounds like, who could you talk to? Is there somebody you could talk to say today or tomorrow?

AIMEE: Yes.

DR. CARLSON: Like who? Give me a name.

AIMEE: I have a friend named Henry. Umm . . . that's uhh . . . were just Internet pals, but it's better than nothing.

DR. CARLSON: Well, that's not better than nothing; you kind of made that seem like not a good thing. Is there somebody you could call that you'd feel good about?

AIMEE: I could call him too. You know, it's just like the Internet I don't really believe it to be like . . . it's not a . . . it's not a real relationship, it's just people talking and writing. Human contact is something that I really need.

DR. CARLSON: So is there a human contact that you could have in the next 24 hours? I know you're going to talk to your mom tomorrow, but is there somebody else?

AIMEE: I have a friend named Carrie and she lives in Chicago, but I'll make the track up there, I don't mind.

DR. CARLSON: Mhmmm. And what will you do when you find Carrie?

AIMEE: Talk about my mom and the stuff I want to do.

DR. CARLSON: What would happen if you talked about anything but that?

AIMEE: I don't know, I'd probably feel a lot better I guess.

DR. CARLSON: So, what could you talk about?

AIMEE: Music, books . . .

DR. CARLSON: You see, I think when we're going away and we're going to have some fun and we could actually feel better because we're getting away we're going to pick a depressing topic like your mother to talk about and then we're going to wonder why we don't feel so good when we go to see Carrie.

AIMEE: Yeah, I understand.

DR. CARLSON: So, you'll go see Carrie and you won't talk about any stink . . . you won't talk about anything that's negative. You could talk about music, you could talk about your newfound skill of meditation . . .

AIMEE: Yes . . . but I'd like to learn more about that or other forms of relaxation.

DR. CARLSON: Well, what I'd like you to do is I'd like you to start taking it one step at a time. When do you arise in the morning usually?

AIMEE: 6:30 a.m.

DR. CARLSON: And do you need to get out of bed at 6:30?

AIMEE: Mhmm . . .

DR. CARLSON: Could you get up at 6:15?

AIMEE: Yeah.

DR. CARLSON: What would happen if you got up at 6:15 and took that time each time first thing in the day to work on meditating?

AIMEE: That would be a good idea because that would be a good start to a day instead of . . .

DR. CARLSON: Well, it would be a start to a day.

AIMEE: Yeah, a positive start to a day instead of out the door and running around.

DR. CARLSON: Well, it would be a different way. You know it's kind of a way to get centered first thing in the day. So, that's something you could do and if you're tired do it anyway. If it feels really good only do it for 15 minutes.

AIMEE: OK.

DR. CARLSON: You just take what you could get; some days will be better than others and that gives you something to focus on. When the thoughts come in to your mind, you're going to send them away. The only way to do it wrong is to not do it.

AIMEE: OK.

DR. CARLSON: OK. So, you're going to meet with Carrie, you're going to put up . . . boy you already committed to doing a lot of things. We're not going to meet for three weeks so you've got a little bit more time to get this done.

AIMEE: Oh, OK.

DR. CARLSON: So, you're going to meet with Carrie and only talk positive, you're going to talk to mom tomorrow about not having your question answered, you were going to put up these post up notes . . . post-it notes . . .

AIMEE: Yes.

DR. CARLSON: And then at 6:15 you're going to do some meditation each day. Are you pretty good at doing things like that if you decide to do it?

AIMEE: Yes, oh yeah.

DR. CARLSON: I mean if you pick a time you'll do it?

AIMEE: Yes because if I don't then I'll feel guilty inside. I'm hard on myself, so if I don't do what I'm set out to do than it's worse than ever.

DR. CARLSON: Mhmm, so this is maybe a way to get yourself to do something good. I'm wondering if there are people that you could talk positively with as well? I mean you don't need to, but just think about that.

AIMEE: Yeah, well my mother she's a very negative person also, so I really don't, I can't guarantee that tomorrow's conversation will be all that great as far as well it's not going to be positive . . .

DR. CARLSON: Right now.

EFFECTING CHANGE: INCORPORATING SECOND ORDER CHANGE

AIMEE: She's just . . . she is one of those pessimistic types.

DR. CARLSON: Well, I'm not sure that that's what this is about just saying hey mom you didn't answer my question.

AIMEE: OK.

DR. CARLSON: You know we want to really revisit that. So we could . . . you know your mom could be your mom, but I want you to be you.

AIMEE: Mhmm.

DR. CARLSON: I mean evidently she's learned that if she cries she doesn't have to answer tough questions.

AIMEE: Yeah.

DR. CARLSON: And does anybody else have a plan like that that they could avoid tough things when they're troubled with their emotions?

AIMEE: Yeah.

DR. CARLSON: Who might that be?

AIMEE: Me.

DR. CARLSON: I think that's a pattern that's there too, and it's not a very good pattern.

AIMEE: No.

DR. CARLSON: Because it leaves you feeling bad and your mom feeling bad and when you're with other people and you do that there's two people left feeling bad.

AIMEE: Yeah.

DR. CARLSON: OK, well that's a lot to talk about. How are you feeling right now?

AIMEE: I'm a little more relaxed then I was when I got here . . . I feel still a little overwhelmed, but not as bad. I feel relaxed.

DR. CARLSON: You remember you could send those away and I remember one of the things we were talking about was finding a mentor. Any luck on that? Did you narrow it down?

AIMEE: Yes.

DR. CARLSON: OK, so that's a plus and you made some contacts about the possibility of doing that too. Good! I can't wait to see what happens with your mom in installment two. Oh, by the way, just so you don't get the wrong idea, it often takes doing something two or three or four times to change a pattern like that. Very seldom does someone talk to someone once. Only in the movies does that happen where everything becomes wonderful. But it in real life it takes a few times. I wonder how your friends are gonna like a happy you?

AIMEE: I don't know.

DR. CARLSON: OK well I look forward to seeing you in three weeks; thanks!

Commentary

In Chapter 4, we indicated that Dr. Carlson used all eight core treatment strategies throughout this entire six-session therapy. The result is a radically reconfigured relationship between Aimee and her mother. In addition to these core treatment strategies, Dr. Carlson seems to have used four of the five second order change interventions described in this chapter. The main second order change intervention evident in this therapy was reversal, which is the equivalent of exposure. By reversing or acting against her maladaptive pattern of pleasing and meeting only others' needs, she was able to increase her assertiveness in relating to others and to achieve a balance between meeting others' needs and caring for her own needs. It is noteworthy that, in talking about her inability to confront her mother on several matters, Aimee identifies that avoidance has been her primary strategy of dealing with her mother: "Well, I've lived for so long by avoiding the issues in one form or another." This ineffectual solution is what Aimee needs to reverse if real, transformational change is to occur.

Dr. Carlson also used blocking/acceptance in his careful use of psychoeducation in assisting Aimee to understand performance anxiety, and her insomnia and depressive symptoms, and what he referred to as "guidance" about parenting and other current life problems. Similarly, he utilized reframing and predicting.

Corrective experience was another key strategy in the case of Aimee. In the first session, Dr. Carlson acknowledges that Aimee already possesses insight into her troubled relationship with her mother. But, as with many clients, this insight has not resulted in a change in Aimee or in the relationship. He also seems to have recognized the need for a corrective relational experience between Aimee and her mother. Dr. Carlson specifically asked her about the effect of her insight, and she replied that it had no effect. Based on this response he proceeded to prepare her for the specifics of the corrective experience. Essentially, she would confront her mother's lack of maternal support over the years. Aimee would then struggle, largely because of conflicting personality dynamics, in carrying out this mutually agreed upon therapeutic task. But the corrective relational experience succeeded. It turned out to be the major turning point in her therapy and her personal development.

Dr. Carlson's Commentary

I began the third session by actively structuring the session and taking control by using Aimee's responses to the three questions. I asked Aimee to talk about what she meant by being down and having feelings of overwhelming responsibility. Too often, therapists believe they know what the client means without asking and making sure that accurate understanding has occurred. Too often, client and therapist are not talking about the same thing nor really collaborating.

As Aimee talked about how things had not gone very well this week, I listened and let her know that this was not a big deal. I let her know that ups and downs are an important and normal part of real change. Things frequently get worse before improving. Too many therapists panic or feel defeated when less than desirable results occur.

Aimee described how difficult it was talking with her mother. Her nausea was an important physical statement as to how difficult it was for Aimee to "stomach" this new lifestyle. A master therapist sees her strength and does not get sidetracked by her symptoms but instead processes the "organ jargon" of the client. In this case I didn't lose track of her strength and determination. I interpreted her not giving in as a sign of her strength rather than a weakness. Aimee talks about the struggle of the change process and I re-frame her anxiety as a positive sign.

Aimee found the use of metaphors of writing a paper and planting a tree helpful in personalizing the change process. Rehearsing Aimee's response and teaching her meditation was so helpful because it was tailored to her challenges. The session also empowered Aimee by helping her realize the power of choice.

Aimee did a lot of work in this session. Her thinking and increased verbal participation showed her level of engagement. My role was to facilitate the discussion by asking questions and challenging her thinking in a positive manner. The use of psychoeducation was a powerful tool as Aimee was bright and such an eager learner. It was necessary to give her permission to do things for herself and to accept that this was a good thing.

Aimee described the strategies that she created and the master therapist knows it is important to encourage the use of her solutions whenever possible. She could easily see how she made choices to be depressed and that she also has other less depressing choices available like playing the drum or calling/emailing a friend. She easily could see how she does not avoid everything in her life, after all she completed college, is raising two children, is taking care of her father and grandmother, keeping her job, confronted her mother, and even ended her marriage. She also designed plans to put motivational notes around her house and to make meditation a part of her daily life. Much of the session involves going over her homework and providing guidance for the next three weeks.

She was beginning to understand that change or transformation is a process where you take one step at a time. Using words like "so far" and "yet" helped Aimee to understand how her actions were not permanent and that tomorrow is another day where she will be able to make new choices. I was encouraged when Aimee suggested creating signs to leave around the house to help remind her of the process that she was creating and how she was re-authoring her life. A lot of my responses were to normalize the change process and to help her to look at herself as "work in progress." Once she can begin to notice and appreciate the movement she is making toward her stated goals, her internal motivation gets an exponential boost forward.

Concluding Comment

A basic premise of this book is that effective and lasting therapeutic change requires second order change, and later third order change. Such change always involves a transformation that impacts all aspects of an individual's inner and outer life, including their thoughts, feelings, behaviors, and expectations. As briefly noted in the first chapter, the word transformation is derived from the prefix "trans," which means changing thoroughly, and the root word "form," which means structure, character, or pattern. In other words, transformation means being able to think and act in a manner that is thoroughly different from the way one was formed or grew up. More specifically, transformation always involves a basic change in pattern. For the anxiety-prone individual whose basic pattern is to run from and avoid fearful situations, transformation means facing those fears head on.

Second order change involves changing from a maladaptive pattern to a more adaptive one. Such pattern change is transformative in that the clients not only change their behavior but also change their self-others schemas. Second order change is the primary focus of the therapeutic work of the master therapists we know, and it clearly was the primary focus of Dr. Carlson's therapy with Aimee. For Aimee, whose pattern had been to please and care only for others and do it perfectly, transformation means to care for herself and others in a reasonably conscientious way. It means facing and dealing with differing or conflicting expectations. In the first two therapy sessions, Aimee is encouraged to come to terms with such differing expectations. There were at least three conflicting sets of expectations she was helped to face. First is a set of expectations of her mother to be a pleasing, dutiful, and nonassertive daughter who will not confront her mother's narcissistic and abusive manner. Second is a set of therapeutic expectations for her to become more assertive and self-caring. Third is a set of self-generated expectations that are to be pleasing to and caring for others—at the expense of her own needs—and to do everything perfectly without complaining or counting the costs. To resolve these conflicting expectations—and achieve some level of transformation—she must be pleasing to both her mother and to her therapist who have conflicting expectations, two sets of expectations that conflict with the expectations she has of herself.

References

Beitman, B., & Yue, D. (1999). *Learning psychotherapy*. New York, NY: Norton.

Chartier, I., & Provencher, M. (2013). Behavioural activation for depression: Efficacy, effectiveness and dissemination. *Journal of Affective Disorders, 145*, 292–299.

Fraser, J., & Solovey, A. (2007). *Second-order change in psychotherapy: The golden thread that unifies effective treatments*. Washington, DC: American Psychological Association.

Good, G., & Beitman, B. (2006). *Counseling and psychotherapy essentials: Integrating theories, skills, and practices*. New York, NY: Norton.

Sperry, L. (2010). *Core competencies in counseling and psychotherapy: Becoming a highly competent and effective therapist*. New York, NY: Routledge.

Sperry, L., & Sperry, J. (2012). *Case conceptualization: Mastering this competency with ease and confidence*. New York, NY: Routledge.

6
EFFECTING CHANGE: INCORPORATING FIRST ORDER CHANGE

If you've read the preceding chapters, the message is unmistakable: pattern change (second order change) is the heart of effective psychotherapy. But what about first order change? What is its role in therapy process? After all, most clients do not present for therapy requesting pattern change. Rather, they come with specific symptoms, like depression, guilt feelings, or panic attacks. Or, they come with specific life problems such as relationship issues, parenting concerns, job loss or work-related concerns, procrastination, and the like. In other words, their presenting concerns are first order considerations, and these presenting concerns typically reflect an underlying maladaptive pattern. Therapy could focus just on these first order considerations or it could focus on both first *and* second order considerations. Among the master therapists we know, therapy focuses on both, and, as you'll see in Chapter 7, on third order change also. Master therapists have the capacity to expertly maintain a specified treatment focus (on pattern change) while using appropriate interventions to resolve the client's immediate concerns (presenting problems). In other words, they deal with both presenting concerns and the underlying pattern and dynamics.

This chapter focuses on incorporating first order change considerations (presenting problems) in the context of second order change considerations (pattern change). It begins with an overview of first order change. Then, transcription segments from Sessions 3, 4, and 5 illustrate how both orders of change are incorporated with both symptoms and current life problems.

First Order Change

First order change involves reducing symptoms, increasing functioning, or temporarily resolving a current life problem. In this order of change, a therapist helps a client do something different in a specific situation. In terms of patterns, the maladaptive pattern is stabilized or made more tolerable (Fraser & Solovey, 2007). As a result, the client returns to his or her baseline level of functioning. What distinguishes first order from second and third order change, is that efforts to replace the client's maladaptive pattern with a more adaptive pattern are not involved.

For example, an individual with panic attacks may agree to a trial of anti-anxiety medication. This does not change her maladaptive pattern, it reduces the panic symptoms and allows her to continue to function a bit better with the same maladaptive pattern. A cocaine addict may decide to begin attending Narcotics Anonymous for help in achieving sobriety. This intervention is first order change because it can re-stabilize the individual's life without changing the maladaptive pattern. A marriage partner who believes she can no longer tolerate her verbally abusive partner may initiate divorce proceedings. This is first order change because she temporarily resolves a current life problem. However, because her initial pattern has not changed, she might find herself attracted to another partner who is also abusive. Common to all three examples, is that no new and more adaptive pattern is initiated and neither individual dynamics nor systemic dynamics are changed.

While first order change is limiting and inferior to second order change, it nevertheless can play a necessary role in psychotherapy. Unless and until symptoms have been reduced or a life situation has been sufficiently resolved with first order change, the individual may not be receptive or may not be able to engage in second order change activities. The case of Aimee illustrates this. Had she not achieved some level of symptom relief from her feelings of being overwhelmed by learning and practicing meditation, it is unlikely that she would have had the resolve to continue to engage in second order change efforts.

Incorporating First Order and Second Order Change with Symptoms

In the transcription segment that follows, Aimee describes being overwrought with symptoms of fear and worry. Dr. Carlson uses meditation, a first order intervention, to assist Aimee in both reducing and gaining control over her anxiety and ruminative worry. Fortunately, this intervention is quite effective in reducing her symptoms. As it often does, successful first order change efforts increases the client's confidence in the therapist (clinician credibility) and in efficacy of psychotherapy. Then in this and subsequent sessions, Dr. Carlson expertly uses the success of this first order change effort in the service of second order change (i.e., pattern change). He does this by helping Aimee focus on her related thoughts which reflect her maladaptive pattern. This segment illustrates how first and second orders are incorporated.

DR. CARLSON: What strategies have you used before?
AIMEE: I don't know, I really haven't . . . I kind of just let one override the other.

DR. CARLSON: So, would you be interested in looking at one possible way?
AIMEE: Yes.
DR. CARLSON: Now, I'm wondering what would happen if you could become more aware of these thoughts once they start? Because it sounds like once they've started, then they tend to have a life of their own like last night...
AIMEE: Definitely.
DR. CARLSON: As I was hearing you, one after another after another.
AIMEE: Yes.
DR. CARLSON: And there's one strategy that people have found pretty helpful; it's called meditation and I don't know if you've ever learned how to do meditation?
AIMEE: No, but I'm interested in it...
DR. CARLSON: OK, so you wouldn't be opposed to doing some meditation?
AIMEE: No.
DR. CARLSON: What happens with meditation is that you learn to...really learn to breathe, breathing slowly and breathing deeper. Like, right now I see that you're breathing very shallow, did you know that?
AIMEE: Yes.
DR. CARLSON: Can you picture the inside of your lungs are like a jar and when you pour water into a jar you feel the bottom all the way up to the top. So, can you imagine breathing deeply like that where you start and you fill up the bottom and go [*breathes slowly giving an example*] then blow it out the same way and take a slow deep breath. Maybe you learned that when you sang and do this diaphragmatic breathing that singers usually do?
AIMEE: Mhmm.
DR. CARLSON: Where you really use your diaphragm. So, can you practice breathing in slowly and breathing in deeply?
AIMEE: Yes.
DR. CARLSON: And as you do that, you know, maybe you might want to close your eyes and practice right now and see how it goes OK?
AIMEE: OK. [*Closes her eyes and practices deep breathing*]
DR. CARLSON: All the while, while you're breathing in slowly and breathing deeply, that's right. Now, as you breathe in slowly and deeply you'll probably have thoughts that are going to come into your mind, and when these thoughts come into your mind and what I'd like you to do is just to continue to focus on your breathing.
AIMEE: [*focuses on breathing*]
DR. CARLSON: That's right, nice in and out. You might imagine waves on a shore as they flow in and as they flow out and as any thoughts come to

EFFECTING CHANGE: INCORPORATING FIRST ORDER CHANGE

your mind just send them away and go back and focus on the breathing [*pause*]. Breathing in slowly and breathing in deeply and as you're breathing in become aware of all of yourself. [*pause*] Become aware of your body sitting in a chair, become aware of any noises or sounds that you hear, and all the while focusing on your breathing. [*pause*] Breathing in slowly and breathing in deeply. [*pause*] Only you and your breath exist. [*longer pause*]. And, if you could take three more breaths and on the third breath just open your eyes . . .

AIMEE: [*takes three slow and deep breaths, then opens her eyes*]

DR. CARLSON: What was that like for you? Were you able to stay focused on your breathing?

AIMEE: Mhmm.

DR. CARLSON: Did your mind wander or did you have to bring it back.

AIMEE: No.

DR. CARLSON: Wow, that was very good.

AIMEE: It feels really good too.

DR. CARLSON: And see we often don't take the time to become aware of how we're doing and we're finding that as you become aware, when you find yourself getting stressed, as you practice you can just breathe the thoughts away; the thoughts that are the negative thoughts and just be present. So, in your mind when your mom starts to cry, rather than thinking I'm a terrible person now look what I've done, you just go [*breathes deeply*] and choose. I'm sure she'll get over it she's a big person and she's cried before . . ..

AIMEE: Oh, yeah.

DR. CARLSON: I just want my question answered. It's a fair question.

AIMEE: Yeah.

DR. CARLSON: All the while, while you're breathing slowly and breathing deeply. [*pause*]. Now, what I'd suggest is that this is something you can use at any time. At night, for example, when you can't sleep just focus on your breathing [*pause*]. People count backwards from a hundred. On the exhale, you go one hundred, and the next exhale would ninety-nine, and you find that your mind wondered off and you're thinking about school and not being successful, and how you're going to fail, and you just send those thoughts away and come back to one hundred and before you know it you come back down to one. [*pause*]. But, the important part is that you become more and more aware of these thoughts and you have something you can do to send them away if they come back, send them away and send them away again. There's something sort of like a wave . . . you know. . . .

AIMEE: Mhmm.

131

> **DR. CARLSON:** Have you ever seen surfers on a wave when the wave gets higher and higher and higher and then what happens? It breaks.
> **AIMEE:** Yeah.
> **DR. CARLSON:** And those thoughts break too, those thoughts will go right away. It's a way of developing a sense of control and I think when those thoughts come that's when the fear comes, that's where the anxiety comes, that's where the depression comes.
> **AIMEE:** Yeah.

Commentary

In addition to assisting Aimee in achieving a needed measure of relief and a palpable sense of control over daily stressors (first order change), Dr. Carlson is helping her further incorporate her new adaptive pattern in her life (second order change). In other words, first order change is used in the service of second order change, which for the master therapists we know is the main focus of psychotherapy. This is not to say that first order change strategies and interventions like meditation and relaxation training are necessarily inferior to second order change strategies and intervention. Both have their roles in successful psychotherapy. But focusing only on first order change effectively short changes the client by limiting possible treatment outcomes.

Instead, Dr. Carlson focuses on both orders of change, and in so doing amplifies the clinical value of meditation (first order change) by linking it to her new pattern of self-care (i.e., balancing her own needs with those of others without self-criticism and perfectionistic striving).

He specifically embeds thoughts of failure, which reflect her secondary maladaptive pattern of perfectionism. This contrasts the way many trainees and therapists work who view counseling and psychotherapy primarily in terms of problem solving and symptom reduction (first order change).

Dr. Carlson Commentary

Most therapists do skill training or psychoeducation with their clients to create first order change. The question is not whether skill training is done but how well will it is done. Before I began suggesting to Aimee what she might do to reduce her stress and anxiety I wanted to find out what she had tried to do and/or thought about doing. It is important to work with the client's potential solution whenever possible as it increases the likelihood that they will actually comply with the suggestion. When Aimee indicated that she did not know what to do I asked her if she was interested in looking at a possible way.

Obtaining Aimee's permission will increase her compliance. Aimee indicated that she did not know about meditation but was interested in it; allowing me to switch to a teaching mode. When teaching, I attempt to use metaphors that the client can identify such as pouring water from a jar and singing.

Breathing control is so important for clients as it impacts how they feel. When people are stressed and anxious they breathe in a shallow manner and when they are relaxed it is much deeper. This has led some therapists to refer to it as stressing yourself vs. relaxing yourself. I often begin by having clients practice something like meditation for five minutes or less at first and then gradually increase the time of practice as that tends to increase compliance. Sitting with oneself and doing nothing other than breathing is difficult especially for the people who need it most.

 ## Incorporating First Order Change in Second Order Change: Current Life Problem

In the transcription segment that follows, Aimee describes a recurrent life problem involving parenting (breakfast time) that, it soon becomes apparent, reflects her maladaptive pattern. In the process of offering parenting guidance, Dr. Carlson addresses her pattern of meeting the needs of her children while ignoring her own with the accompanying pattern of perfectionism, self-criticism and guilt. Note that this segment occurs near the end of Session 4 in which the first-second order intervention occurs. Session 5 begins with a brief review of the effect of the intervention on both her two sons and on herself.

AIMEE: It is, but then also I feel guilty . . . I have a lot of guilt for having have chosen this person as the father of my kids. I was just a kid myself so umm . . . I feel guilty for it . . . I feel like . . . well I try to do more for them, I try to be like the super parent in order to compensate. I'm like always taking care of them and I need to start letting them do things for themselves, you know letting . . . making them have some responsibility instead of like always . . . I baby them, I really do and they're 13 and 11 now.

DR. CARLSON: What do you mean by baby them?

AIMEE: Umm . . . fix their breakfast and you know cutting up their meat still . . . that's pretty bad, but I do it because I love them and I don't know. I just . . . they need to learn some life skills. You know, I don't want them living with me when they're 25 or 30.

DR. CARLSON: So, you're too good of a mother and because you've been a mother and a father . . .

AIMEE: Mhmm . . .

DR. CARLSON: You've kind of overdone it.

AIMEE: Yes, I have

DR. CARLSON: And if you're going to err by the way, that's the best way to err.

AIMEE: Yeah, I guess it is.

DR. CARLSON: And what would happen if you were to say to them and apologize and say to them I've done you a great disservice that I've done things for you that I know you could do for yourself and now I'm going to start to let you to do more and more things. Let's start with breakfast.

AIMEE: Yeah, I don't know. I've never thought of saying that.

DR. CARLSON: And would you be willing to just get out of the way for breakfast and let them handle the breakfast issue each morning?

AIMEE: Yeah.

DR. CARLSON: And do you think they can?

AIMEE: Yes. Well, my older one he is a little independent because he is the oldest, but still I always have to remind them to do things like picking up their laundry and the usual complaints that I have to.

DR. CARLSON: Well, I don't know if you have to, but you choose to.

AIMEE: Well, I would like to not have to tell them over and over again to clean their room and to do other things.

DR. CARLSON: So, what would happen if we just started out with breakfast?

AIMEE: Breakfast would be the best start. I don't mind doing that every once and a while, but every day I don't work during the day so I'm home so they expect bacon and eggs and pancakes and all of those things, you know, and if I don't then I feel guilty . . . like oh I'm such a terrible mother I didn't make this big breakfast.

DR. CARLSON: Well, how about just doing it one day a week and then the other days just get up and sit with them while they have breakfast.

AIMEE: That would be better for me.

DR. CARLSON: And so you'll still be there and yet let them decide what they want and get them started in preparing it. The one day a week you could do it, you could pick the day.

AIMEE: That would be good. That would take a lot off my mind.

DR. CARLSON: Wow, so we've got exercise that you're going to do and yeah, you'll probably have a little more rest if you're not cooking in the morning. You probably won't be quite so frazzled . . .

AIMEE: Yeah.

DR. CARLSON: And you can maybe get up and get your gear on.

AIMEE: Oh, and another thing I don't think the boys should be eating that kind of food every day any way. I have . . . my younger one, he's a little bit heavy and alright so this is one thing I always pick them up after school and lately I've been not picking them up lately so he walks because he doesn't want to exercise and he's mad at me and he says oh, I had to walk . . . and he makes me feel guilty. He'll say the cars were splashing me and it's like three blocks from the school. So, I always feel like oh there's a part of me that wants to just get in the car and pick him up, but I haven't been doing it lately . . . it's nice to rest though.

DR. CARLSON: How about the rule I mentioned earlier, I'm not going to do things for you that you can do for yourself?

AIMEE: Yeah, I have to tell him that.

DR. CARLSON: Well, you have to tell yourself that, I think, and believe it. Because once we do these things for kids we send the message that I don't think they can.

AIMEE: Yeah.

DR. CARLSON: It sounds like you already believe that he can't walk home from school.

AIMEE: No, I know that he can, but he makes me feel guilty because the minute he walks into the door he's got mud all over his shoes and he does it on purpose too . . . he makes me . . . like oh look at what I have to go through in order to walk home from school . . . when in reality I know the path, I know where he has to walk.

DR. CARLSON: And so what do you say to that?

AIMEE: I say you don't have to go through the mud if you go this way and he'll say well I can't go that way.

DR. CARLSON: Well, what would happen if you were to say, I see you've decided to wash your clothes why don't you take them off now before the mud gets in them.

AIMEE: Yeah, well that would be good. That would be great to say that because then he'd probably stop doing it.

DR. CARLSON: Well, if he has the consequences of doing them rather than letting them fall on you.

AIMEE: Yeah.

DR. CARLSON: Wow, so this could really bring about quite a bit of change in your life. You're talking about becoming more independent in helping your kids become more independent.

AIMEE: Well, because I'm like this big caretaker for everybody else, not only them . . . my father, my grandma, but I wouldn't mind being my grandmother's caretaker though.

DR. CARLSON: But, we're talking about being a better caretaker for yourself and you're doing a better job at that. I mean you got a mother now.

AIMEE: Yeah.

DR. CARLSON: Yeah, and then you're going to talk to your children's grandparents, your in-laws, about what their plan is.

AIMEE: Yeah, I need to know because it's been eating at me the closer I get it gets to release time.

DR. CARLSON: To at least talk about it...

AIMEE: Yeah, exactly.

DR. CARLSON: Because we can't have it like it was before.

AIMEE: Yeah, because I think if I tell them how important it is to me I'd feel so much better. I've gotten things out about and done and all these things have already come out and I don't want to lose that. I don't want to just throw that out of the window because he's back. I value their relationship with me and my kids.

DR. CARLSON: And see my guess is maybe they do too because they haven't had a daughter before and now they've gotten to know you and know the boys and it may be different, but let's find out. And you guys, you're kind of a sure thing, but their son he's kind of a question mark they're not really sure if they want to have a relationship with him.

AIMEE: Yeah.

DR. CARLSON: OK, well, keep putting up those post-up notes and exercise. Maybe you'll do it this week.

AIMEE: Hopefully.

DR. CARLSON: And hopefully you know where.

AIMEE: I know where.

DR. CARLSON: No breakfast but once each week?

AIMEE: Yes, I could do that.

DR. CARLSON: And just tell the kids that and if they say I won't eat you're going to say? That's a choice.

AIMEE: Yeah, that is a choice.

DR. CARLSON: Mhmm... any final thoughts you might have?

AIMEE: I can't think of any right now all these other thoughts and things... I'm kind of drawing a blank, you got me on the spot there.

DR. CARLSON: But you're energy is up so that's great.

AIMEE: Yeah.

DR. CARLSON: I look forward to seeing you again in a couple weeks.

AIMEE: Great.

[SESSION 5]

DR. CARLSON: Aimee it's good to see you again.

EFFECTING CHANGE: INCORPORATING FIRST ORDER CHANGE

AIMEE: It's good to see you.

DR. CARLSON: It's been a couple of weeks; last time we met we talked a lot about your children . . .

AIMEE: Yes.

DR. CARLSON: And some things that you were going to do like a different morning routine.

AIMEE: That has worked. Actually, they've been sort of getting breakfast at school, they have a breakfast program there, so they've opted to do that instead of getting their own breakfast.

DR. CARLSON: OK.

AIMEE: Which is fine with me if it's out there they might as well use it.

DR. CARLSON: OK and how have you been spending your mornings?

AIMEE: Watching the news actually, because I normally never had time to do that you know I don't normally get a newspaper or I don't like the newspaper around town there . . . uhh but anyway that's for political reasons.

DR. CARLSON: So, that's something that you enjoy though, it's kind of taking over something that you like to do?

AIMEE: Yeah, yeah . . . they always have the little updates on what happened yesterday and all of that and I'm usually doing something so I've missed the evening news so it's like a recap of news.

DR. CARLSON: OK, so what was the reaction when you said you're not going to cook breakfast anymore?

AIMEE: Uhh . . . they were pretty mad, at first, I mean they were at first because they thought oh now it's not what are we going to do. That's what my little one says. What are we gonna do now? I said, well you know there's a bowl, there's some cereal, there's some milk, figure it out, you know . . . actually they do know to make their own cereal of course so . . . but umm . . . I didn't think . . . I didn't know that they had the breakfast program. I mean I know they served things like little pastries or whatever, but they have like scrambled eggs and everything there so . . .

DR. CARLSON: So, that works pretty well.

AIMEE: Yeah.

Commentary

This is another excellent illustration of how a therapist can assist a client to deal with an immediate concern and achieve some measure of stability in her life (first order change) while also broadening and extending the impact of her new adaptive pattern on her life (second order change). In viewing and discussing Sessions 4 and 5 with trainees, it is not unusual for them to ask why Dr. Carlson is "wasting" valuable time on parenting issues and the like when he could be doing "real" therapy. Such questions and related comments are welcomed since they provide a powerful teaching moment. Addressing these questions sets the stage to discuss the value of both first order and second order change, particularly when a focus on first order considerations serve to further reinforce the incorporation of the client's new pattern (second order considerations). In addition, assisting a client in dealing with symptoms and current life problems fosters the client's sense that his or her immediate concerns are important to the therapist and will be dealt as they arise.

The issue is not whether the therapist is willing to deal with immediate concerns, but rather the manner in which these concerns are therapeutically processed. The key consideration is treatment focus. Recall that the better a therapist can maintain a treatment focus (treatment focused on pattern change), the more likely the short-term and long-term goals of treatment will be achieved. Dr. Carlson expertly keeps treatment focused and "on track" in all six sessions. No matter what concerns Aimee brings to a particular session, Dr. Carlson processes each concern through the lens of pattern change. It is a powerful learning experience as trainees begin to see the link between what at first appears to be just a "parenting" issue and an additional opportunity to generalize Aimee's new pattern into another area of her life.

Dr. Carlson's Commentary

Aimee was a child who was not "babied" by her parents, and when she had children, she did the opposite to how she was raised. Parents like Aimee do too much for their children in order to be liked. Pampered children with overfunctioning parents tend to become discouraged and underachievers as their parents unwittingly send the message, "I have to do these things for you because I do not think you are able". Aimee understood this problem and saw this as a way to take better care of herself by letting her kids fix their own breakfast. I was so pleased when she stated, "That would be better for me."

Aimee needed to work on pleasing herself as well as others and on self-care. This was one of many indicators of a second order change in her life. Several times in the sessions, Aimee made reference to thinking of herself. Aimee's striving to be perfect provided significant drive for Aimee to make this change. However, during the course of therapy she was able to see that she was looking for satisfaction and happiness and not really a perfect self. Aimee was able to make this insight and to keep her strong drive to make choices that provided her and others a happier more fulfilling life.

Concluding Comment

This chapter focused on incorporating first order change considerations that therapeutically address presenting problems in the context of second order change considerations that therapeutically address pattern change. The transcription segments illustrated how a master therapist effectively incorporates both orders of change in dealing with Aimee's symptoms and a current life problem.

Reference

Fraser, J., & Solovey, A. (2007). *Second-order change in psychotherapy: The golden thread that unifies effective treatments*. Washington, DC: American Psychological Association.

7
EFFECTING CHANGE: INCORPORATING THIRD ORDER CHANGE

In an earlier chapter, the case of a never-employed client with social anxiety disorder was used to illustrate the three orders of change. His family physician prescribed antianxiety medication, which reduced his anxiety symptoms. But, medication could not replace his maladaptive pattern of fearfulness and avoidance, and so he continued to be unemployed. Thereafter, he began therapy with a therapist who would help him to face his fears and avoidance behavior. As a result, a more adaptive pattern replaced his maladaptive one and he was able to find and keep a job. This is second order change. Later, and on his own, he was able to face his fears and engage in an intimate relationship. This is third order change and represents the ultimate goal of therapy because clients become their own therapists. Because master therapists we know are particularly effective with this order of change and because it is essential for effecting changes that last, this chapter focuses on third order change.

For most clients, engaging in third order change efforts does not occur spontaneously after the agreed-on course of therapy is completed. Rather, clients are encouraged and prepared while in therapy to begin taking increased responsibility for effecting change. To the extent to which the therapy process is focused and remains focused, and to the extent to which the therapist encourages clients to become their own therapists, the seeds of third order change are sown and nurtured. This chapter begins with an overview of third order change. Emphasized is the role of self-awareness and how it is fostered. Since therapy that is focused on achieving an agreed-on adaptive pattern is essential in achieving lasting change, the next section is on establishing and maintaining a treatment focus. Next, transcription segments illustrate how Dr. Carlson focuses treatment and keeps it on track. In this process, third order change begins to emerge. To illustrate third order change in action after therapy is completed, segments of a follow-up conversation with Aimee are given. It is noteworthy that Aimee admits that she has become, and continues to be, her own therapist some seven years after completing her six-session therapy with Dr. Carlson.

Third Order Change

Third order change involves self-directed pattern change. In this order of change, clients are able to recognize and change patterns without assistance from their therapists. This means that clients effectively become their own therapist. In essence, third order change is the epitome of self-directed learning and lifelong learning (Beitman & Yue, 1999). It is a basic life strategy necessary for effective functioning in everyday life. It is required and not optional. For that reason, third order change should be the ultimate, long-term goal in therapy.

Inherent in the therapy process are several implicit principles of third order change, which can guide clients in their quest of becoming their own therapist. The most basic principle involves clients learning how to use self-awareness in problematic situations and then to recognize similar situations as they arise in the future and use self-awareness to respond more effectively. It involves them taking a realistic amount of responsibility is all that most solutions require, instead of too much or too responsibility. It also involves practical optimism, which is the belief that amid immediate difficulties there is likely to be a solution (Good & Beitman, 2006).

Related strategies for clients using self-awareness include: "When an unwanted emotional response occurs, try to notice it and stop to examine its source before responding. . . . Think about the consequences of the reaction versus a more thoughtful response. . . . Embrace negative emotions as signals to examine patterns and their associated expectations. . . . Learn from past mistakes by noticing how the current situation appears to be part of a familiar sequence that has led to difficulty. . . . Allow new solutions and new responses to emerge into your consciousness and practice intuitive ranking of the probability of specific responses that may yield the desired results. Learn how to make good decisions and to trust your ability to do so" (Good & Beitman, 2006, p. 145).

The reality is that most clients do not begin engaging in third order change efforts by themselves. Rather, they have been encouraged and prepared by their therapists to start taking responsibility and begin effecting change on their own. The case of Aimee illustrates this phenomenon.

Self-Therapy

A basic premise of this book is that the ultimate goal of treatment is to assist clients in becoming their own therapists (i.e., third order change). But, how do clients become their own therapists? Beck (1995) addresses this question and suggests how clients can develop what she calls a "self-therapy" program. In self-therapy, clients take responsibility for conducting their own therapy much like their sessions with a cognitive-behavioral therapist. That is, they set an agenda, review past homework, address a particular problem and process it, decide on new homework, and schedule their next self-therapy session. For Beck, becoming one's own therapist begins during the last phase of therapy. Here, clients are urged to apply self-therapy as problems or issues arise and then discuss their efforts with their therapist in the next scheduled session. Thus, after termination, a client will already have the experience of doing self-therapy and be able to handle most problems, relapses, or setbacks herself. "If she is unsuccessful, at least she has had an opportunity to use her skills once more. If she does need another appointment, the therapist can help the patient discover what got in the way of her handling the setback or problem independently, and they can plan what the patient can do differently in the future" (Beck, 1995, p. 278).

Establishing and Maintaining a Treatment Focus

From Second Order to Third Order Change

Master therapists that we know seem to excel at effecting second order change efforts while at the same time fostering third order change efforts. Therapists aspiring to increase their therapeutic proficiency would be wise to follow this lead. This, of course, assumes that the therapist recognizes and values third order change. Being mindful of the place of third order change is the starting point. Next, the therapist sets the expectation for third order change. Then, while maintaining the treatment focus, the therapist recognizes and encourages the client's spontaneous efforts to effect change. Finally, in preparation for termination, third order change is discussed and planned.

Establishing a Treatment Focus

Why is a treatment focus necessary? For many years, therapists have been trained to give 'undivided attention' to the client's words, feelings, body language, and concerns. Clinical lore has encouraged and supported this view of practice with the dictum "follow the client's lead," which means that the clinician should provide a nondirective and nonevaluative environment, show interest and respond empathically to whatever the client wants to talk about, and refrain from giving advice. This viewpoint is more attuned to the open-ended, long-term approach to therapy of yesterday than it is to the accountability-based, time-limited therapy that third party payers are currently willing to authorize. Today more than ever, the expectation is that therapists must focus treatment. Accordingly, therapists must also learn "selective attention" or be overwhelmed by the multiple therapeutic rabbits that could be chased. Treatment focus not only provides direction to treatment it also "serves as a stabilizing force in planning and practicing therapy in that it discourages a change of course with every shift in the wind" (Perry, Cooper, & Michels, 1987, p. 543).

How does a therapist specify a treatment focus? The treatment focus is identified in the process of developing a case conceptualization, and the basic theme of the case conceptualization further specifies the focus. Not surprisingly, because the case conceptualization is based on a conceptual map reflecting a theoretical orientation, the focus of treatment is also likely to be informed by the therapist's theoretical orientation. For example, in the interpersonally oriented dynamic therapies the focus is usually the client's maladaptive interpersonal style or pattern. In the cognitive-behavioral therapies, the focus is typically maladaptive thinking and behaviors, and so on.

Maintaining the Treatment Focus

Research is beginning to support the clinical observation that treatment outcomes are significantly improved when therapists maintain a treatment focus (Binder, 2004). However, maintaining that focus is not as easy as it may sound. After all, the lives of clients are complex and changing, and it is to be expected that they will want to discuss and process recent issues and concerns that arise between sessions. Oftentimes, these concerns are not directly related to the focus of treatment. The challenge is for therapists to "track" a treatment focus along "with flexibly modifying the content as new information arises and digressing from the initial focus as circumstances dictate" (Binder, 2004, p. 100). This section briefly discusses the value and challenge of maintaining a focus for treatment.

The primary reason for "staying on track" is that treatment is more likely to achieve the specified treatment goals than if the focus is lost. However, "staying on track" is a considerable challenge for therapists given that clients have a tendency to "shift," consciously or unconsciously, the focus of discussion to a less-threatening or less-demanding topic or concern. Accordingly, treatment can easily be slowed or derailed by that shift therapeutic momentum away from the primary treatment focus. In such situations, therapists face a number of "decision points" in any session in which they can choose various ways of responding to their client. The choice they make directly affects whether the treatment focus is maintained.

Needless to say, staying on track can be a significant challenge, particularly for trainees and beginning therapists. Often because of inexperience and limited familiarity with refocusing strategies, beginning therapists tend to respond to client "shifts" with empathic statements or clarifying questions, which may take the session in a direction different from that of the primary treatment focus. It is only as therapists become aware of such shifts or "decision points" that they can attempt to reestablish the primary focus of treatment.

The reality is that clients do chase "therapeutic rabbits" and that the therapist's role often involves discouraging "a change of course with every shift in the wind" (Perry, Cooper, & Michels, 1987). Typically, clients shift away from the focus because of being overwhelmed with a new life stressor and they feel somewhat compelled to process that situation and reduce their distress. Other times, clients are hesitant to keep on track because resolving a problem or conflict means that they would have to face difficult relationships or responsibilities in their lives for which symptoms or conflicts have safeguarded them from facing. Or, they may want to change but are ambivalent. With effective supervision and experience, therapists learn to discern the various reasons clients divert from the treatment focus.

 ## Focusing Treatment and Effecting Second and Third Order Change

The following transcription segments from Session 3 illustrate how Dr. Carlson establishes and maintains a consistent treatment focus. He maintains or "tracks" the treatment focus themes of choice and empowerment. These themes are central to her more adaptive pattern of taking care of herself while also caring for others, without undue self-criticism and perfectionism. These particular themes present an ironic challenge for him. On the one hand, he wants and needs to foster and promote choice and empowerment by giving Aimee opportunities to make choices within the session. On the other hand, sessions are only fifty minutes long and there are only a limited number of sessions. Accordingly, Dr. Carlson's challenge is to delicately keep the treatment process "on track" by limiting, reframing, and refocusing the client's attempts to shift to another topic or a less salient therapeutic theme before time runs out and therapy is over.

The transcription segments and commentaries illustrate four decision points in which he weighs various therapeutic options. Sometimes these decision points involve deciding whether to stay with the treatment focus when the client shifts the conversation in another direction *or* to go along with the client, at least for a short time. Other times, the decision involves more options.

Aimee came to the third session noticeably dysphoric, and she indicated that she had been "down and depressed all week." Ruminating about difficulties had exacerbated her distress and interrupted her sleep. Since she was unable to control this rumination, the therapist spent about five minutes teaching her controlled breathing and practicing it with good outcomes. Soon after that she said:

AIMEE: Well, I've been really depressed and I'm usually . . . I was in great spirits last week, but I kind of had some setbacks with just thinking about what's next.

Decision Point 1

Since the triggers, predisposing and maintaining factors for her anxious depression were discussed earlier in the session and controlled breathing was offered to reduce rumination and distress, the therapist could go back to further discussion

EFFECTING CHANGE: INCORPORATING THIRD ORDER CHANGE

of *clinical* aspects of depression *or* to maintain the treatment focus on the "pleasing servant" dynamic. The therapist chose to maintain the treatment focus and emphasize *dynamic* aspects of her depressive feelings and other issues that might arise related to the theme of choice and self-empowerment.

DR. CARLSON: Uhuh . . . and sometimes that happens, but it's important that when you have the thoughts that it's important to do the non-depressing things, things that's we talked about.

AIMEE: Yes, uhh . . . when I get depressed it seems like I just don't want to do anything else and the whole world stops. I don't want to put make-up on, I don't want to get off the couch, and I don't want to do the dishes, and . . .

DR. CARLSON: Do you think that's a choice?

AIMEE: Yeah, it's a choice. I choose to do that.

DR. CARLSON: Mhmm . . . and what do you guess is the purpose of choosing depression? I kind of wondered about that before . . . you know, you . . .

AIMEE: Perhaps it's because it's better than feeling or confronting what I want to do. It's a way of retracting, it's procrastinating, you know, and it's an excuse really.

DR. CARLSON: So the purpose, then of depression for you is avoidance?

AIMEE: Yeah.

DR. CARLSON: That was quite a smile you had there.

AIMEE: Yeah, it is that's one way I don't do what I want to do because this is really difficult for me to even think about. And then I had another . . . something happened and I was thinking about what we were going to talk about and I've been down on myself because I chose to do what I would normally do instead of being assertive in this situation. So, it was at my emotional cost again and it happens a lot. I know I don't have to be mean to people, but I'm just not assertive enough to even tell somebody how I feel in a friendly way. I'm just afraid of. So, I'm afraid of it . . . assertiveness, that's what I've been thinking about because I endured it instead of telling this how I felt about it.

DR. CARLSON: And so you're afraid of assertiveness so far?

Decision Point 2

The therapist recognizes that she is beginning to talk about another issue. To shift the focus to another theme (i.e., assertiveness could derail the treatment focus), even if temporarily. Assertiveness is related to empowerment he considered how to proceed. Because his focus was on empowering her and assisting her to make decisions rather than be a "pleasing servant" to others, he reiterated "so far." This is the therapeutic device he initiated in the first session. It's purpose is to cue and prompt the client to take some degree of responsibility in the moment, rather than hopelessly reenacting her "pleasing servant" pattern. Then he shifted back to the primary focus.

AIMEE: Yeah, so far.

DR. CARLSON: Did you find yourself saying "yet" or "so far" at all this week?

AIMEE: Yes, a few times, but like I said I focused on the negative aspect of not doing what I wanted to do.

DR. CARLSON: So, one of the things that you're saying is that you use the depression and the fear to avoid things?

AIMEE: Yeah.

DR. CARLSON: Is that true?

AIMEE: It is true.

DR. CARLSON: I added fear with the depression . . .

AIMEE: It's true.

DR. CARLSON: Then what you do is kind of a negative way for you to not do anything. Can you give yourself permission to not do anything?

AIMEE: Yes.

DR. CARLSON: So, rather than . . .

AIMEE: Yes, but I . . . thinking back on what I'm afraid of most it is to being assertive with other people. It's what I fear most and I've thought of everything and I've thought a lot about it and it scares me to think about being assertive. I don't know why I . . . I just . . . it's like somebody jumping out of an airplane . . . I just don't . . . someone's got to push me.

DR. CARLSON: And I hear you saying that and, I guess I'm not sure why you do it though . . . because it seems like when you do that, again it creates a lot of pain for you.

AIMEE: Oh, it does because . . .

DR. CARLSON: And I'm not sure what about the pain you like . . . and if you not going to do something why don't you go play music? You know, go play the drums rather than lay on the couch or . . . as long as you're not going to do anything go call up a friend or go out and give yourself permission to avoid doing something.

AIMEE: That would be a better choice.

DR. CARLSON: OK well, it would be a less depressing choice . . .

AIMEE: Yes.

> DR. CARLSON: I mean, the one thing is you've got the problem that you're not going to face and another thing is you're going to be depressed. At least we can take care of the problem.
> AIMEE: But I won't... I'm usually not depressed if I have company or...
> DR. CARLSON: Right.
> AIMEE: I'm kind of a loner, I don't have many friends or anything... but uh so I need to make some friends, I guess because I don't really have anybody.

Decision Point 3

Here the focus could have shifted to her lack of friends, and the therapist could have commiserated with her and/or engaged in an assignment to find a friend or work on friendship skills training. Instead, the therapist maintained the primary treatment focus.

> DR. CARLSON: But the purpose of the fear is to not do it.
> AIMEE: Mhmm.
> DR. CARLSON: Alright, and I'm suggesting that you give yourself permission not to do that. I mean, if you're trying to be friends with lots of people, pick one who's maybe more friendly... is there such a person?
> AIMEE: Oh, I'm sure there is out there somewhere, but I feel like afraid to connect. I think that I'm not going to be able to connect with anyone.
> DR. CARLSON: Mhmm... well, especially if you don't try.
> AIMEE: Yeah well, or if you go in it with a negative attitude also because maybe they're reading off me... maybe they sense that and they aren't as friendly towards me as I want them to be. I expect people to throw themselves at me, you know, not throw themselves, but to be the assertive one and I'm just kind of mousey.
> DR. CARLSON: And again all of that becomes a self-fulfilling prophecy when we think that way.
> AIMEE: Mhmm... definitely.
> DR. CARLSON: Now do you think by working on your breathing that that might allow you to make a little bit of a different choice?
> AIMEE: Yes, I need... I need some type of a medium, I've already... I've thought about this too. I need to learn some type of meditation, maybe go to a yoga class something because I don't take... I'll either be depressed or on the couch or I'm doing so much that I don't, you know...
> DR. CARLSON: Right, so you have two speeds.

AIMEE: Yes.

DR. CARLSON: Stop, then . . .

AIMEE: Never have time to just relax and take five.

DR. CARLSON: Unless you're depressed.

AIMEE: Mhmm . . . I don't really have depression too much . . . I don't experience it that often, but like right now it's happening because I don't want to confront these things so . . .

DR. CARLSON: And the things again that you don't want to confront?

AIMEE: Umm . . . Being more assertive . . .

DR. CARLSON: But that's kind of vague to me can we break it down to something specific?

AIMEE: Umm . . . telling family members how I feel about certain things and showing people my true colors . . . getting out of the mask.

DR. CARLSON: Can you . . . do you want to do this all at once or can you do it one step at a time?

AIMEE: No, I could do it one step at a time. That's how I am thinking ahead and always thinking about what I'm going to do next.

DR. CARLSON: It sounds like what you said with your mom is that you, you know, talked to her and got up the courage to do that and now you don't dread her coming over tomorrow.

AIMEE: No.

DR. CARLSON: And I'm wondering if that would be a good formula for you to tell yourself, like we talked about last week, that bringing about change is difficult first, but then it tapers off.

AIMEE: Yes, it seems very difficult right now.

DR. CARLSON: At first.

AIMEE: So far.

DR. CARLSON: At first and so far . . . so is there . . . did you want to work on talking with family a little more or last week it sounded like you wanted to make a friend at the university?

AIMEE: Yeah, I talked to a few people here.

DR. CARLSON: Is there somebody that seems like more interested or less interested in talking to you?

AIMEE: I don't know, I think . . . I can't really . . . I try to strike up a conversation, but it seems like a lot of the time when I do that . . . and I do that out loud in public also, I'm very friendly patron and umm . . . people will kind of look at you like why are you talking to me more than . . . here's your change goodbye.

DR. CARLSON: Friendliness is kind of like that isn't it?

AIMEE: Yeah, it's weird . . . like, it doesn't feel right, but I'm very friendly and it's I don't know . . . maybe people are very leery of that . . . I don't know.

DR. CARLSON: Well, I think at first they are, I think most of us are.

AIMEE: So, I've been talking to a woman and I have her phone number.

DR. CARLSON: Really!

AIMEE: I called her and she never got back to me, but that happens, everybody is busy . . . I'm not thinking oh well, she doesn't like me but it was hard for me to do that.

DR. CARLSON: But another thing that you did.

AIMEE: Yes.

DR. CARLSON: Are you anticipating that if you change it's not going to be difficult?

AIMEE: I don't know, what do you mean by that?

DR. CARLSON: I think my mother used to say "no pain no gain" . . . did you ever hear that?

AIMEE: Oh yes definitely. Well, I've lived for so long by avoiding the issues in one form or another.

DR. CARLSON: I don't know that that's true . . . it seems like what you've done is live for a long time making yourself kind of miserable . . .

AIMEE: Yeah.

DR. CARLSON: But I don't know that you've avoided things . . . I mean, you graduated college, you've turned your papers in, you had some kids, you've been taking care of your dad or grandma, and you've had a job . . . I mean that's not somebody who's avoiding all kinds of things. You confronted your mom . . .

AIMEE: Yeah.

DR. CARLSON: And you ended a marriage; I mean you know you . . .

AIMEE: I think I really need to start to learn to take care of myself, you know and it's hard for me to do that.

DR. CARLSON: Well, it sounds like you're taking care of yourself too.

AIMEE: Yes, but for some reason I view that as kind of being idle or I don't know.

DR. CARLSON: But I see you doing all of these things that you don't acknowledge very much.

AIMEE: No.

DR. CARLSON: And you have a strange way of keeping score.

AIMEE: Yes, I do.

DR. CARLSON: As we talked about last week, you do a paper, you know, you get an A+ and you think it isn't any good.

AIMEE: Yeah.

DR. CARLSON: So, what's the purpose of keeping yourself miserable?

AIMEE: I don't know, I really don't, it's just sort how I've always lived. As a child, I was kind of a melancholy kid.

Decision Point 4

Here the therapist could take several tracks: empathize with the client's bind; explore childhood melancholy; or stay on track and focus on further processing the "pleasing servant" dynamics.

DR. CARLSON: Is that a familiar feeling?

AIMEE: Yeah, it is and I feel like happy-go-lucky jolly me is ... like going to miss something ... screw up or you know not get up or something.

DR. CARLSON: Yeah, uhuh.

AIMEE: Or not turn in the paper because I was busy being happy.

DR. CARLSON: Right. Well, it sounds like you've got all those you's ... you've got the happy you, you've got the melancholy you, you know? You've got that whole gamut of things.

AIMEE: I do, but I know that's how I feel if I'm doing something for me, then I might not be doing something for somebody else and therefore they're disappointed.

DR. CARLSON: OK, well that's a thought.

AIMEE: Yeah.

DR. CARLSON: That's not a feeling.

AIMEE: Yeah, OK.

DR. CARLSON: If I'm doing something for me other people might be disappointed ... that's the thought.

AIMEE: Yeah.

DR. CARLSON: Uhh ... and? What will they do about it?

AIMEE: I don't know. Maybe tell me that I'm selfish or something

DR. CARLSON: And, so if they said why didn't you do that for me you'd say?.

AIMEE: Well, it depends on what it is, but uhh.

DR. CARLSON: I mean, I think isn't it OK to say you're doing something for yourself? I think people get in trouble if they're *just* doing things for themselves.

AIMEE: Yeah.

DR. CARLSON: But I mean it doesn't sound like that's you. I mean you're cleaning your grandmother's house, taking care of your dad, your kids ... I mean you're ...

AIMEE: Sometimes, I think I would like somebody to take care of me for a while. I think that would be nice. Not like doting over me, but like ...

DR. CARLSON: Mhmm ... but you've also said that it's not something that you're very comfortable with.

EFFECTING CHANGE: INCORPORATING THIRD ORDER CHANGE

AIMEE: No, then again, I would probably not accept it I'd feel weird about it . . . you know, so I don't know . . .

DR. CARLSON: Wow.

AIMEE: I would probably not accept it. I'm not very good at taking compliments or praise.

DR. CARLSON: It sounds like that's a much bigger step to do that right now?

AIMEE: Yeah.

DR. CARLSON: I mean that's a much bigger step right now, but that's not something that you're very comfortable with right now?

AIMEE: No, so far.

DR. CARLSON: So far, and that's exactly right so far. You're feeling pretty good though that you talked to your mom?

AIMEE: I was thinking about maybe doing something and I don't know if this sounds corny or not but like just posting little signs around my house and telling me what I've done. Just to kind of remind me of the good things that I've accomplished. Instead of well I didn't do this or I better make sure they're all right.

DR. CARLSON: Mhmm . . . so that's one of those choices about what you think about.

AIMEE: Yeah and at least then it's like . . . I mean I could do all those things in my head, but at least when I turn around it's there behind me . . .

DR. CARLSON: Mhmmm.

AIMEE: And maybe then sooner or later I wouldn't need the signs anymore I would just do it in my head.

DR. CARLSON: Well, it sure sounds like it's worth a try!

AIMEE: Yeah.

DR. CARLSON: I mean, what you're saying is maybe this will help not only break a pattern, but make you aware of the things that you think about. Yeah, I sure think it's worth a try. (pause) And like what would you write on a piece of paper as an example?

AIMEE: Um . . . you're a wonderful mother, uhh, you know, I'm amazed at some of the cars I drive, I mean sometimes . . . I mean anyone can drive a vehicle, but it's a hard job. I don't give myself credit for that.

Commentary

Dr. Carlson was quite effective on tracking and maintaining the treatment focus. It appears that Aimee's efforts to shift the focus to other topics were to avoid dealing with her maladaptive pattern of pleasing and caring for others and putting their needs first. Thus, it was easy for her, being so articulate, to shift away to safer topics. Interestingly, when she was redirected back she rather easily was able to process the core dynamics of her maladaptive pattern.

In this last segment, it is noteworthy how Dr. Carlson links Aimee's depressive and melancholy feelings to her maladaptive pattern. It becomes clearer to her that because of her pleasing pattern she believes that others will not like her and consider herself selfish if she cares for her own needs. As a result, she feels depressed and becomes inactive. Dr. Carlson responds by challenging her to action since behavioral activation (Chartier & Provencher, 2013) is a powerful second and third order change strategy.

Remarkably, Aimee responds with the plan to post "little signs around my house and telling me what I've done. Just to kind of remind me of the good things that I've accomplished." Her idea to use Post-It notes is third order change talk that continues in this and subsequent sessions. The fact that she actually follows through and posts these notes (mentioned near the beginning of Session 4) means that she is not only considering being her therapist but also taking actions such that she effectively has become her own therapist and is a harbinger of lasting change. For this to happen, the therapist needs to recognize, encourage, and incorporate these third order efforts into ongoing therapy. Dr. Carlson recognized and encouraged Aimee's third order efforts and incorporated them into their therapeutic process, including homework assignments, here and in subsequent sessions.

Dr. Carlson's Commentary

A master therapist knows just how important it is to stay on track and to not become sidetracked. Clients often unconsciously try to shift the focus of treatment when it becomes too demanding or threatening to the status quo. As much as Aimee wanted to be empowered and to make her own choices, it was so comfortable letting someone else do it. I was very clear that Aimee needed to realize that even "depression" was a choice since she has other options.

In this section, Aimee showed how she historically has solved one problem by creating another problem such as becoming depressed and then lying on the couch to procrastinate or avoid things. She felt empowered by realizing that she had a choice of either dealing with a situation or doing something she enjoyed.

In psychotherapy, there are many decision points where the master therapist keeps the focus on the therapeutic goals. The therapist not only solves the presenting problems (first order change) but also disrupts the patterned response that created the problem in the first place. This creates a permanent solution. It is also important for therapists to recognize and encourage

EFFECTING CHANGE: INCORPORATING THIRD ORDER CHANGE

clients to create their own solutions. The master therapist asks questions to help clients to create their own solutions. In the session with Aimee, it was rewarding to see her learn to direct her own pattern changes. The master therapist recognizes the importance of helping their client's to create independence and self-caring behaviors.

 ## *Third Order Change and Aimee: Seven Years Later*

In part of her post-therapy conversation with Dr. Carlson, Aimee describes the changes she has made in her life after therapy was completed. She also addresses the role and place of third order change in her life. Chapter 8 contains the rest of this post-therapy conversation.

DR. CARLSON: What other changes have you made in your life since we completed meeting together?

AIMEE: I've made many changes in my life since our meetings but the one thing that stands out the most for me is the awareness of my thought and behavior patterns. I have to constantly be aware of falling into old patterns. It's a challenge. It's just like alcoholics avoiding triggers to drink. I have to avoid certain relationships that steer in the direction of me being the caretaker. I have to stop and think, 'What have I done for myself today?' If I don't exercise this every day, the chances of me falling into a self-destructive pattern increase dramatically.

DR. CARLSON: Are you at all surprised at all these post-therapy changes?

AIMEE: I guess I'm not too surprised at these changes since it's been a trial and error process since we had our last session. Every day is something new and just when you think you've mastered the art of self-care, something else comes your way and you have to catch yourself before you inadvertently fall back into old patterns.

DR. CARLSON: It's been said that a useful indicator of successful therapy is that the client becomes her or his own therapist. Would you say you've become your own therapist?

AIMEE: Yes, I am my own therapist. I definitely go through every day encouraging, motivating, and reevaluating everything that I do. It's a strange phenomenon but it seems as if I am two people. One that actually goes through life, working, living and loving. The other my voice of reason, my therapist so to speak that is constantly there to help me stay aware of my "self."

Commentary

In these transcribed segments from Session 3, it is clear that Dr. Carlson effectively focuses the treatment process on the primary treatment goal, which is to replace Aimee's maladaptive pattern with a more adaptive one. By keeping this goal foremost and managing to keep the therapy process on track, the primary goal is achieved within the space of six sessions and Aimee integrates the adaptive pattern within her being.

Based on her post-therapy comments, the change effected endures seven years later, largely because she has become her own therapist. It is noteworthy that she manages, on a daily basis, to maintain her new pattern. She uses self-awareness in anticipating potentially problematic situations. As noted in the discussion of the third order change strategies, self-awareness is the basic principle for achieving and maintaining such change (Beitman & Yue, 1999).

Dr. Carlson's Commentary

Aimee's comments seven years later were affirming of the second and third order changes that were developed in our sessions. I was pleased to see that Aimee saw herself as her own therapist; however, I also know that many therapists would have a hard time not receiving credit for such outcomes.

Concluding Comment

Third order change has been described and illustrated. The main take-home point of this chapter is that third order change–that occurs within therapy and following termination—typically evolves from second order change efforts. The more therapy is focused, the more second order is likely to occur, and in the midst of it, third order change efforts are likely to arise. To the extent to which the therapist understands the importance of third order change, the more likely the client's self-generated efforts at third order change will be recognized, encouraged, and incorporated into the therapy process. At some level, master therapists know this and act upon it.

References

Beck, J. (1995). *Cognitive Therapy: Basics and beyond*. New York, NY: Guilford Press.
Beitman, B., & Yue, D. (1999). *Learning psychotherapy*. New York, NY: Norton.
Binder, J. (2004). *Key competencies in brief dynamic psychotherapy: Clinical practice beyond the manual*. New York, NY: Guilford.

Chartier, I., & Provencher, M. (2013). Behavioural activation for depression: Efficacy, effectiveness and dissemination. *Journal of Affective Disorders*, *145*, 292–299.

Good, G., & Beitman, B. (2006). *Counseling and psychotherapy essentials: Integrating theories, skills, and practices.* New York, NY: Norton.

Perry, S., Cooper, A., & Michels, R. (1987). The psychodynamic formulation: Its purpose, structure, and clinical application. *American Journal of Psychiatry*, *144*, 543–551.

8
EFFECTING CHANGE: MONITORING, EVALUATION, AND TERMINATION

The last session is critical in the therapy process, and almost as important as the first session. As the treatment process winds down and formally ends, the therapist's role is to focus on evaluating the therapeutic alliance and treatment outcomes and preparing the client for life after therapy ends. This chapter addresses each of these factors. The transcribed segments from Sessions 4 and 6 illustrate how the therapist monitors treatment progress at the midpoint and at the end of therapy, and prepares the client for termination. Also, included is a segment of the post-therapy conversation between Aimee and Dr. Carlson, some seven years after their last session.

Treatment Evaluation

In this age of accountability, the expectation is that therapists will not only provide effective treatment but also be able to demonstrate that their treatment is and has been effective. Such an expectation has given rise to two different perspectives on how to achieve such evidence. One perspective emphasizes "evidence-based practice," which is based on the premise that specific treatment interventions must have been empirically demonstrated to be effective with specific psychological problems. The other perspective emphasizes "practice-based evidence," which is based on the premise that effectiveness is more a function of therapist–client collaboration than of specific treatment interventions (Sperry, Brill, Howard, & Grissom, 1996). This second perspective places a premium on assessing specific treatment processes and outcomes measures and requires therapists to monitor treatment processes and outcomes. This chapter focuses on the second perspective. Until recently, the focus of research and clinical practice was on the final or overall assessment of treatment outcomes. More recently, the focus has shifted to ongoing assessment (i.e., session-by-session monitoring of therapeutic progress). Arguably, both forms of assessment are necessary and clinically valuable.

When it comes to evaluating clients' responses to treatment, therapists are not particularly good at predicting the effectiveness of their client–therapist relationship or of treatment outcomes. Rather, research reveals that client ratings of the client–therapist alliance are more accurate and a better predictor of client involvement in treatment than therapist ratings (Orlinsky, Rønnestad, &

Willutzki, 2004). Research also shows that a client's subjective experience of change early in the treatment process is the better predictor of treatment success compared with all other measures and predictors (Orlinsky, Rønnestad, & Willutzki, 2004). So, how can therapists know and evaluate a client's response to treatment? The answer is simple: monitor treatment outcomes.

The basic premise of treatment outcome research is that therapists need feedback (Sperry, Brill, Howard, & Grissom, 1996). Research consistently shows that when therapists receive feedback on their work with clients, their therapeutic relationships and treatment effectiveness increase significantly. One study showed that when therapists had access to outcome and therapeutic alliance information, their clients were less likely to drop out of treatment, were less likely to deteriorate, and were more likely to achieve clinically significant changes (Whipple et al., 2003). Another study evaluated client–therapist relationships that were at risk of a negative outcome. It found that therapists who received formal feedback were 65% more likely to achieve positive treatment outcomes than therapists who did not receive such feedback (Lambert et al., 2001). A third study of more than 6,000 clients found that therapists who used ongoing, formal feedback measures had markedly higher retention rates and a doubling of overall positive effects compared with therapists without such feedback (Miller, Duncan, Brown, Sorrell, & Chalk, 2006). While not a randomized controlled trial (RCT), the results of this study are noteworthy given the very large number of clients involved. Finally, data from Shimokawa, Lambert, and Smart (2010) have reviewed the effect of feedback on clients who were predicted to be treatment failures as well as clients who were on-track for a positive therapeutic outcome. This meta-analytic and mega-analytic review combined data from six well-designed RCTs that compared treatment-as-usual with feedback-assisted treatments in which the same therapists offered both conditions to more than 4,000 clients. Results indicated that feedback to therapists and clients had a powerful effect over treatment-as-usual with cases that were predicted to be treatment failures, some 20% to 30% of clients. Such feedback enabled therapists to identify and intervene differently than in treatment-as-usual. The results of this feedback were rather substantial in that they further reduced deterioration rates to 5.5%.

In short, when both therapist and client know how the client rates the therapeutic relationship and treatment outcomes, three things can be predicted: an effective therapeutic relationship is more likely to be developed and maintained; the client will stay in treatment; and positive treatment outcomes result. Thus, ongoing monitoring of the treatment process and outcome appears to be essential to effective therapy. This section identifies various ways of assessing the therapist–client relationship and monitoring treatment progress and outcomes.

Measuring Treatment Outcomes

Among the many psychometrically sound outcome measures available, the following are quick—called ultra-brief measures taking less than two minutes—and easy to evaluate instruments for monitoring and evaluation of treatment outcomes.

Session Rating Scale

The Session Rating Scale (SRS) (Duncan et al., 2003) is a short and easy to administer measure of therapeutic alliance that consists of four items. The instructions are simple and straightforward. The client is given a sheet of paper on which four horizontal lines 10 cm long are printed. On the first line, the client rates how well understood and respected he or she felt in the just completed therapy session. On the second line, the client rates how much the client and therapist worked on what he or she wanted to talk about. On the third line, the client rates how good a "fit" the therapy approach was for him or her and rates his or her social and work life. On the fourth line, the client rates how satisfied he or she felt about the session. The scale is completed by the client immediately after the session has ended (Miller, Duncan, Brown, Sorrell, & Chalk, 2006). Use of the SRS is free of charge to individual mental health practitioners by license agreement found at www.heartandsoulofchange.com.

Outcomes Rating Scale

The Outcomes Rating Scale (ORS) (Miller & Duncan, 2000) is a short and easy to administer outcomes measure consisting of four items. The instructions are simple and straightforward. The client is given a sheet of paper on which four horizontal lines 10 cm long are printed. The client is asked to mark with a pen stroke, somewhere along each horizontal line, how things went in the past week. On the first line, the client indicates how he or she had felt. On the second line, the client rates his or her relationships. On the third line, the client rates his or her social and work life. On the fourth line, the client rates his or her well-being. The scale is typically completed by the client immediately before the session begins, although it may be administered after the first meeting (Miller, Duncan, Brown, Sorrell, & Chalk, 2006). Use of the ORS is free of charge to individual mental health practitioners by license agreement found at www.heartandsoulofchange.com.

Besides improving treatment, there are other reasons for collecting client feedback. Such feedback permits therapists to not only monitor the client's progress but also plot the therapists' own cumulative career development in three ways. As a result, therapists can identify their effectiveness and whether they have improved and then can reflect on what they can do to grow as a therapist (Duncan, 2012).

Termination

Termination is the last phase of treatment and represents both an event and a process. As an event, termination means client–therapist contact ends, and as a process it means that the client's level of responsibility increases as the nature of the client–therapist relationship changes. Facilitating the process of terminating and preparing the client for it form the therapist's primary focus in the last phase of treatment. Preparing for termination is a time for clients to express their thoughts and feelings about what the therapeutic process and the therapist has meant to them, as well as an opportunity to review their progress in achieving treatment goals. It is also a time to plan for maintaining treatment gains and anticipate the inevitable lapses and setbacks that may ensue. Finally, when preparing for termination, one may refect upon what remaining therapeutic tasks clients might work on in the future, and what additional therapeutic contact with the therapist or other treatment might be indicated.

Too often the clinical competency of preparing for termination has been neglected or downplayed in training programs and in textbooks. The situation has not improved appreciably in the past 30 years since training programs were criticized: "Not only are criteria and techniques for termination not taught and discussed, but termination as a valuable therapeutic opportunity is undoubtedly neglected" (Weddington & Cavenar, 1979, p. 1303). An indicator of this neglect is high dropout rates from psychotherapy. Premature termination rates are approximately 50% (Clarkin & Levy, 2003; Wierzbicki & Pekarik, 1993) but appear to be much higher in training programs. A recent study found that the rate of premature termination observed in a training clinic was 77% (Callahan, Aubuchon-Endsley, Borja, & Swift, 2009)! Nevertheless, effective and competent psychotherapy practice assumes the capacity to deal effectively with termination issues. Accordingly, this competency is addressed in this chapter as well as the related competency: maintaining treatment gains. This section begins with a discussion of maintaining treatment gains and relapse prevention before discussing the competency of termination.

Maintaining Treatment Gains

Making progress in therapy usually consists of some combination of gaining insights, being less symptomatic, feeling better, thinking more positive, or acting in more adaptive ways. There is no guarantee that such progress or treatment gains will be maintained. Progress in therapy can be additive but just as often regressions occur. The client's challenge is to stay the course and continue to practice and apply the skills and strategies learned in the course of therapy. Such ongoing efforts are essential for maintaining gains (therapeutic change). Relapse prevention and self-therapy are important components of the early and middle phases of therapy and are critical components of the final phase of therapy when preparing the client for termination. CBT, in particular, has been shown to help clients to make lasting changes; when clients have a plan and the skills to prevent relapse, are motivated, and have a plan for continued growth, the treatment effect is likely to be maintained and even increased (Gloaguen, Cottraus, Cucharet, & Blackburn, 1998). In other words, relapse prevention is a key factor in maintaining treatment gains.

Preventing Relapse

Relapse prevention is a self-control strategy for assisting clients in how to anticipate and cope with the problem of relapse or recurrence of symptoms or problematic behaviors (Daley, 1989). While it was initially developed as a treatment adjunct with addictive behaviors (Marlatt & Gordon, 1985), it has been applied to smoking cessation, pain control, weight management, sleep disorders, as well as to most psychiatric disorders (Sperry, Lewis, Carlson, & Englar-Carlson, 2003). In short, relapse prevention is a strategy for anticipating and reducing the likelihood of relapse.

Relapse prevention planning (Marlatt & Gordon, 1985) begins with the assessment of a client's likely interpersonal, intrapersonal, environmental, and physiological risks for relapse and specific stressors and situations that may precipitate it. Once these potential triggers and high-risk situations are identified, cognitive and behavioral techniques are implemented that incorporate both specific interventions to prevent or manage them if they do occur. It also involves a discussion of more global strategies to address lifestyle balance, craving, and cognitive distortions that could expose the client to high-risk situations where relapse is most likely. Such a relapse plan is likely to increase the client's sense of self-efficacy and effectiveness in maintaining treatment gains (Carroll, 1996).

Self-Therapy

Chapter 7 described self-therapy from a CBT perspective. The basic idea is that during the last phase of therapy, clients are urged to practice being their own therapists between sessions as problems arise. They then discuss their efforts with their therapist in the next scheduled session. This experience prepares clients to handle most problems, relapses, or setbacks after termination (Beck, 1995).

Preparing for Termination

While preparing a client for termination is usually considered a key task of the final phase of therapy, some approaches such as cognitive therapy consider it a task that begins much earlier (Beck, 1995). As noted previously, the treatment formulation component of the case conceptualization serves as a guide to both specifying treatment outcomes and anticipating obstacles and challenges to achieving those outcomes. More specifically, it assists the therapist in anticipating particular difficulties a specific client may experience with termination. Thus, the therapist will not be surprised when a particular client experiences difficulty with termination because of a history of losses or a pattern of clinging or dependency on others (Cucciare & O'Donohue, 2008).

Indicators of Readiness for Termination

Different therapeutic approaches describe theory-specific criteria for determining when termination is indicated. However, there are also some general indicators common to these various approaches which are useful in assessing a client's readiness for termination from treatment. These include (1) the client's presenting problem is essentially resolved or symptoms are reduced or alleviated; (2) the client has developed sufficient insight to understand the problem and patterns that lead to treatment; (3) the client's coping skills are sufficiently improved for dealing with life circumstances; and (4) the client has more capacity to plan and work productively (based on Heaton,1998).

During the course of a planned termination several activities and processes are commonly observed. These include: "a retrospective look at how therapy has proceeded, sharpening of client's future plans for life without the therapist, discussion of possible return appointments, and a statement of appreciation by both client and therapist" (Good & Beitman, 2006).

The therapist does well to begin the process by asking the client to recount the most important changes the client has made in the course of treatment. "Reviewing progress with patients may enable them to more clearly see the significance of their treatment gains, potentially motivating them to continue maintaining gains and building on the progress that they have made during treatment (Dobson & Haubert, 2008, p. 314).

Termination Considerations

In short, the objectives of termination are to provide clients with a healthy ending to therapy and the therapeutic relationship, to review clients' progress and growth, and to prepare clients for future challenges. When therapy has been focused on both presenting problems and on pattern change, preparation for termination is relatively straightforward. It begins with a review of client progress in terms of both resolution of the presenting problem(s) and the extent of pattern change.

The termination phase provides additional opportunities to address specific pattern issues. Clients may have difficulty ending relationships because they lack healthy models for interpersonal relating. Their developmental histories may include experiences of unexpected loss, abandonment, or abuse and neglect by parents or caretakers, which makes the prospect of moving beyond the safety of therapy difficult. A useful marker of progress achieved in such circumstances is the relative ease of coping with planned termination.

 Monitoring Treatment Progress: Case of Aimee

As noted earlier in this chapter, monitoring treatment progress can be accomplished in different ways. While some therapists use ultra-brief self-report instruments to measure client progress and record these scores on a progress chart, Dr. Carlson provides his own session-by-session evaluations as well as seeking Aimee's evaluations of the therapy process at the fourth and sixth sessions.

In his initial reflection on and evaluation of Session 1, Dr. Carlson noted that Aimee has a reasonably good intellectual understanding of her problems, particularly her social relationships, but is not able to resolve them. She recognizes her pattern of taking good care of others, but at the price of not taking care of herself. This first interview seems to confirm her scores on the Kern Lifestyle Scale in terms of needing to please others, of victimizing herself by not speaking up, and of surrounding herself with others who are self-centered and demanding. Despite her history of physical abuse and dependency on others, Dr. Carlson suggests that Aimee is a good candidate for brief, focused therapy that will focus on second order change.

Dr. Carlson's initial evaluation of Session 2 is that Aimee is committed to the therapeutic process and reasonably well engaged in it. She has some difficulty accepting her assets and strengths. Several between-session assignments were given that can increase her assertiveness, self-acceptance, and self-care. He notes that while she left the session feeling empowered, it appears that she is also experiencing some tension between the comfort of enacting her maladaptive pattern and the discomfort of a more adaptive pattern, particularly as her self-talk has been disrupted.

In his initial reflection on Session 3, the midway point of this six-session therapy, Dr. Carlson notes that while Aimee experienced a setback in her efforts to be more assertive with her mother, setbacks are not uncommon in therapy, and that therapeutic change comes not only from making progress but, just as importantly, from learning from setbacks. She shows some indications that she has learned much about herself as a result of it. He assesses the meditation intervention as an effective strategy that has fostered awareness of her negative thoughts and how she can neutralize them.

Dr. Carlson's initial evaluation of Session 4 is that Aimee is much more positive and decisive, presumably because of her positive experience of being assertive and connecting with her mother. She is more energetic and less depressed. Several problems and solutions were addressed regarding her mother, ex-husband, in-laws, parenting, and beginning an exercise program. He notes that Aimee seems to be responding favorably to empowerment-focused interventions and is more easily recognizing that she has the resources that are necessary to live a happier, more satisfying and confident, and interdependent life.

In his initial reflection on Session 5, Dr. Carlson noted that Aimee continues to show that she understands how her actions keep her stuck in relationships. She developed some strategies for being with men in an honest fashion, and then introduced her present relationship dilemma. In sum, Aimee continues to demonstrate that she has benefitted from therapy with increased functioning and better self-confidence.

EFFECTING CHANGE: MONITORING, EVALUATION, AND TERMINATION

In his initial reflection on Session 6, Dr. Carlson concluded that Aimee has achieved all the specified treatment goals. She has also met her own stated expectation for therapy, which was to deal with her anger and resentment toward her mother. Furthermore, it appears she has developed sufficiently effective strategies that will allow her to maintain her therapeutic gains.

At the beginning of the fourth session, Dr. Carlson engages Aimee in a mid-therapy evaluation. They have already completed three of their planned six sessions and have three more to go.

DR. CARLSON: It's been three weeks since we last talked, and before we move into tonight's content, what we'll be talking about, I was just wondering how this is going, our talking together. Whether it's meeting your needs or its doing the kinds of things you'd hope to have done.

AIMEE: It's been great, so far. I've changed you know not dramatically or anything, but everybody in my family seems to notice it . . .

DR. CARLSON: Oh, wow.

AIMEE: That I'm not as frazzled as I usually am . . .

DR. CARLSON: Is there anything else that you can think that I could do that might be helpful that I'm not doing?

AIMEE: No, not that I know of . . . I haven't really thought about that.

DR. CARLSON: Well, if you do please feel free to bring it up.

Commentary

While this is a brief exchange, Aimee's words here seem to accurately reflect her sentiments, words, and actions in subsequent sessions. In short, Dr. Carlson's inquiry provides an opportunity for her to verbalize her evaluation of the previous three sessions. It would also have been interesting to have the results of a brief or ultra-brief paper-and-pencil evaluation instrument such as the SRS and the ORS (Miller & Duncan, 2000; Duncan, Miller, Parks, Claud, Reynolds, Brown & Johnson, 2003).

Dr. Carlson's Commentary

I was happy to see Aimee's excitement and satisfaction about what she has been able to accomplish as a result of her work in therapy. I also asked her to comment on my work as a therapist as I wanted her to know that the feedback goes both ways and that I valued her thoughts. I was not surprised by Aimee's response that she had not really thought about it. She is more concerned with whether or not she is being a good client.

The form that I used with Aimee before each session, where she wrote her responses to what has been different, what has improved, and what did she want to work on today, has become a helpful tool for monitoring the treatment process. Since my sessions with Aimee I have added a 1-to-10 scale for clients where they also check where they are before each session in regard to friends, work, family, and health. This feedback has been very useful as it allows me to discuss issues that could possibly have been overlooked.

 Progress Reflected in a Recent Dream

In their sixth and final session, Aimee describes dreams that she has been experiencing. Dreams, like early recollections, reflect an individual's basic pattern and positive changes in patterns and dreams reflect core psychological change (Mosak & DiPietro, 2006). Accordingly, Dr. Carlson inquires about dreams and recent changes in them.

AIMEE: Yeah, it is and it's actually inspired me to start journaling because I have a lot of dreams and vivid dreams too . . . I remember like almost like a movie in my head.

DR. CARLSON: Really.

AIMEE: But I never wrote them down, I don't know why I didn't do that either. I always feel like I'm too busy for myself to do that so I started to do that as well.

DR. CARLSON: Are the dreams changing at all?

AIMEE: Uhh . . . some of them. It's usually always centered around conflict which is sometimes I run from a lot, but umm. . . .

DR. CARLSON: Yeah, do you have one that you can remember?

AIMEE: Yeah, I do actually, I had this one a couple days ago and it was about all these girls in high school and I wasn't exactly the most popular girl in school, I wasn't the dork or anything, but girls were mean to me . . . the popular girls. I was kind of an outcast so I confronted them and I was yelling at them and . . . I mean not being . . . saying profanities, but actually telling them . . . giving them a piece of my mind.

DR. CARLSON: So, the dream of the high school girls who picked on you were picking on you?

AIMEE: Well, they were like talking and whispering which is what they used to do . . .

DR. CARLSON: And . . .

AIMEE: About how I was dressed and whatever. . . . so I was just like . . . it was just like a bunch of people they don't even . . . some of them were outside of high school like some of them were my mother's friends that she . . . she kind of has these materialistic friends that they talk about me because I'm into counseling and I'm not a business major you know and all their kids are like into business and making money and . . .

DR. CARLSON: So, they talk down at you too?

AIMEE: Yeah . . . it was like an audience like they were all there.

DR. CARLSON: Right, but all these people who sort of look down on you or picked on you and historically what have you done . . . not in the dream but in real life?

AIMEE: Nothing, oh I'll always shine it on like . . . because they'll say some rude things to me not blatantly, but you know any windows about my career choice or whatever the way I live.

DR. CARLSON: And in the dream what happens?

AIMEE: I told them how I felt but I can't really explain . . . it was like this great thing from *The Breakfast Club* or something I was like I had this great speech about you know I'm doing something worthwhile and just because I don't care about money that doesn't mean that I'm worthless and . . .

DR. CARLSON: You know, this is so interesting because when I look at dreams, dreams to me are rehearsals did you know that . . . and symbolically this is people have picked on me and I've let them and in this dream you're rehearsing standing up. It sounds a lot like taking this position and also standing up and putting it out there for others to have.

AIMEE: Yeah, you're right it's just funny because I thought like if I've never done that like I'd go off and I didn't go off. I made the speech about who I was. They don't know who I am. They just know like this person that laughs at them when really inside I think that's really ignorant of you to say that. So, um it felt good and I didn't feel like bad or like oh I'm going to hurt their feelings. I just sort of . . .

DR. CARLSON: Yeah, so you're really more of a participant than a victim.

AIMEE: Yeah, definitely.

> **DR. CARLSON:** Wow!
>
> **AIMEE:** And there was background music and everything.
>
> **DR. CARLSON:** That must be the musician in you.
>
> **AIMEE:** Something . . . yeah there was really something I tell you and then I woke up and I felt really good the whole day. I had this great day and it was really great. I loved it. That was a good dream.
>
> **DR. CARLSON:** Yeah, it sounds like a very powerful one too.
>
> **AIMEE:** Yeah, I also think because, in the near future, I'm going to probably be confronting some of these friends. Actually, my mother's friend, it's her daughters, I went to school with them and they're all like in this little clique, you know, and she's having this get together at my aunt's house and it's like I think that's kind of why I started thinking about it. So I know they're going to be there and I know they're going to be like so what are you doing . . . and well I don't have a job right now and because I'm unemployed at this point and . . .
>
> **DR. CARLSON:** It sounds like you're going to stand up for yourself. Is that the message?
>
> **AIMEE:** Yeah.

Commentary

That Aimee reports becoming more assertive in her dreams is another indication of second order change. Her dreams reflect a shift in her basic pattern of being pleasing and unwilling to meet her needs and to communicate assertively, to being more in meeting her own needs and in communicating more assertively. Dr. Carlson points out that dreams are a rehearsal for subsequent action. It is noteworthy that as Session 6 continues, Aimee talks about how she is planning to confront these girls at a upcoming social event.

Dr. Carlson's Commentary

Aimee's dream was a powerful verification of the changes she had been making in therapy. Her changed position in her dream from being a victim to being a person with a voice was very encouraging. Aimee felt her new empowerment and talked in an excited fashion. I have found dreams to be accurate indicators of what someone is rehearsing and this seems to fit Aimee's movement in the area of social empowerment, having a voice and standing up for herself.

Preparing for Termination

It might be useful to review Dr. Carlson's original treatment plan here. That plan included four treatment goals or outcomes: First, empower her and have her view herself in a more positive, less perfectionistic way. Second, realize she has the resources that are necessary to live a happier and a more satisfying life. Third, help her to be more confident and independent. Fourth, take better care of herself. These treatment goals directly reflect a more adaptive pattern of caring for others and also caring for herself. In the process of achieving these four goals she effectively dismantled her maladaptive behavior of caring for others but not caring for herself.

Several intervention strategies were seamlessly combined to achieve this new pattern and four treatment goals.

As noted earlier in this chapter, in a planned termination, the therapist's role in preparing for termination is to review progress achieved and address the potential for relapse. It also includes a discussion of the near future and potential areas of concerns on which the client might focus (as third order change), and the possibility of additional therapy involving first and/or second order change considerations.

DR. CARLSON: OK, we can kind of take a minute because this is the last time we're going to meet and we had agreed to meet for six times. So, I wanted to go over a few things and see where this journey has taken you.

AIMEE: OK.

DR. CARLSON: And it seems like a lot of change has taken place since we began, even in the way you look and feel . . .

AIMEE: Mhmm . . .

DR. CARLSON: You had indicated, when we began, that your goal coming here was to deal with anger and resentment that you had towards your mother and it seems like you were able to talk to your mom . . .

AIMEE: Mhmm . . .

DR. CARLSON: Where's the anger and resentment now?

AIMEE: It's not there, not towards my mother. I don't really have any anger or resentment anymore.

DR. CARLSON: And so now you've got a mother that you didn't have . . .

AIMEE: Yeah.

DR. CARLSON: And you've started to give yourself permission to do some things that you've wanted to do

AIMEE: Mhmm . . .

DR. CARLSON: And you started to do things that you wanted to accomplish like talking to other people and wanting to take some action and not be so alone . . .

AIMEE: Yes.

DR. CARLSON: You were going to find a mentor and you've learned how to use the word yet.

AIMEE: Yes.

DR. CARLSON: In putting closure on some of the things that you were dealing with . . . I can't do this yet. You found that you really liked having a mother and that you needed to start doing things and analyze and think less.

AIMEE: Yes.

DR. CARLSON: It seems like you're doing that. And you've talked about meditation and how you didn't acknowledge the positive in the things that you do, but there's so many now to look at.

AIMEE: Yeah.

DR. CARLSON: And you seem to be seeing them?

AIMEE: Yeah, definitely. I'm not as hard on myself than I normally am . . . I just sort of wake up and you know if something goes wrong I used to . . . sometimes that would be the downfall of the day like alright this is screwed up so like today with the paper I could've like freaked out and been crying at the computer that's happened to me a lot of times during finals . . .

DR. CARLSON: Yeah, but it didn't happen today.

AIMEE: No, I just said alright I guess I'll try to do this hopefully I could make it here on time and it all worked out at my cool . . . I was doing my breathing exercises while I was typing it out.

DR. CARLSON: Wow!

AIMEE: And I could type pretty fast so it didn't take me that long.

DR. CARLSON: And then, we could probably publish this idea these post-up notes.

AIMEE: Yeah.

DR. CARLSON: Another use for post-up notes is that they could turn your life around . . . you found those reminders really helpful.

AIMEE: Yes, I still have them around my bed . . . this morning I was reminded to think positive and I have to remind myself because sometimes I'll wake up in a bad mood, but it reminds me that I can refuse to feel this way.

EFFECTING CHANGE: MONITORING, EVALUATION, AND TERMINATION

DR. CARLSON: Wow... so that gets you going in the right direction each day. Good, and you talked about exercising and it's interesting that although it took you a while you did it and you did it in steps, but you did it.

AIMEE: I actually went there one day and I walked out this was like two weeks ago, not too long after we met that last time and I walked in there and I wanted this woman to go with me and for some reason that was my way of not doing it... I'm like alright she's not here that's it I'll do it another day.

DR. CARLSON: So, you really did do it... that's one more step I didn't know about.

AIMEE: So, like about a week ago is when I went in I think it's been a week now.

DR. CARLSON: Wow, that's...

AIMEE: And I felt really ridiculous...

DR. CARLSON: Sometimes it may take you awhile to get started, but once you get going you're going.

AIMEE: Yeah because I can't fail I don't want to fail like if I start something and I don't finish that to me is like yeah alright why did I do that... I can't fail.

DR. CARLSON: Well, that's probably something that we could talk some more about you know if we were meeting about failure in your life and that it's probably OK to make mistakes, but not for you right now.

AIMEE: Mhmm...

DR. CARLSON: And then we also talked about you in relationships with other guys and we've talked about that you were kind of a crockpot or slow cooker and not like microwaves and how you were going to work and have you had any opportunities to...

AIMEE: I haven't had any opportunities to be any one of those things so...

DR. CARLSON: Right, but my guess is that will happen.

AIMEE: Yeah, like right now I'm really focused on me right now which is amazing because I never was focused on me... it was always all these other things you know. Before, I tried not to think about me.

DR. CARLSON: Yeah, because you were always focused on the world.

AIMEE: Yeah.

DR. CARLSON: Except yourself.

AIMEE: Mhmm...

DR. CARLSON: And now you're doing what we talked about last time which is practicing standing up for yourself and speaking up for yourself and taking care of yourself.

AIMEE: Mhmm...

DR. CARLSON: Wow! That's a lot that has been accomplished!

AIMEE: Yeah!

DR. CARLSON: What do you think you need to be working on next? If you were to not be so hard on yourself, but maybe had the courage to be imperfect.

AIMEE: Yeah, that would probably be the next step and you know maintaining where I'm at now. I don't want to slip up, but I haven't only a few times and said I'm feeling kind of down and what am I doing type of thing but . . .

DR. CARLSON: Have you gotten a hold of a way to keep from slipping up?

AIMEE: Usually, it's just me I have to recognize it.

DR. CARLSON: That's interesting, now is it possible to use those post-up notes?

AIMEE: Oh yeah, definitely.

DR. CARLSON: I mean maybe to put up those kinds of things like meditate, exercise, speak up, take care of self . . .

AIMEE: Yes, I guess I could do that. I still have a few of them up not all of them, but like the hardest ones for me to remember like when I get up I'm going to be in a good mood and not think about oh well the car is broke down or this that and the other.

DR. CARLSON: That you have a choice.

AIMEE: Yeah.

DR. CARLSON: You can think about the broken car or the sunny sky.

AIMEE: Yes, exactly.

DR. CARLSON: They're both true.

AIMEE: Yeah, but one looks a lot nicer.

DR. CARLSON: There you go . . . and so maybe having that formula written . . .

AIMEE: Yeah, that might be a good idea for a formula.

DR. CARLSON: Well, it's been very nice talking with you Aimee. I'm positive that you really got a jump start on the next step in your life.

AIMEE: I'm very proud of myself which I don't say very often. I'm honestly at the best place in my life right now.

DR. CARLSON: And you know what the best part about it is you created it.

AIMEE: You're right.

DR. CARLSON: It's your choice, your world. Good luck!

AIMEE: Thank you!

Commentary

Aimee's evaluation of the therapy process and outcomes is that she has made significant changes. Second order change has occurred. She indicates that she has improved most in being better able to take care of herself and meet her own needs. Specifically, she experiences a resolution of her main presenting problem—a recurring relational issue—which was to deal with her anger toward her mother. This success can be attributed to a major shift in her dominant pattern from being pleasing and unassertive to being more assertive in communicating her needs to her mother in a reasonably conscientious manner. However, because she says she still fears failure, there has been less of a shift on her secondary pattern of perfectionism. It is interesting to note that she does not give a specific answer to Dr. Carlson's question about what she might work on after therapy. She agrees with him that she needs to work on having the courage to be imperfect. This, of course, directly reflects her secondary pattern of perfectionism. As Dr. Carlson indicates, if therapy were to continue beyond the agreed upon six sessions, this would be the treatment focus.

Dr. Carlson's Commentary

As I prepared for the final session with Aimee, I was surprised at all of the areas that we had covered in our time together. Aimee was "beaming" in this session and actually able to accept the positive feedback she was receiving because the feedback was related to specific areas of change and not vague platitudes. Feedback needs to be specific, honest, and tailored to the individual client. If I would have stated, "I liked the way you have become a happier person or changed your style of living," she would not have responded so enthusiastically.

In terminating therapy, I find it helpful to go over what has been accomplished and what is unfinished. It is also important to identify future areas of challenge where relapse might be more likely to occur and to obtain some commitment from the client to keep moving toward their goals. For Aimee, it was a major breakthrough when she stated that she was proud of herself as that was a strong sign that she was concerned with her own care and not just caring for others.

Post-therapy Evaluation

In this post-therapy conversation, Aimee comments on her impressions of her therapy experience. She describes in some detail the changes—first and second order changes—that occurred as a result of these six sessions. This conversation is a continuation of the follow-up interview reported in Chapter 7 where she describes additional changes she had made and how she has become her own therapist (third order change).

DR. CARLSON: As you look back at our work together, what stands out most?

AIMEE: The aspect of our work that stands out most was the challenge to confront my mother. There was valuable time spent discussing my animosity toward her, but what seemed most effective was the confrontation. I hesitate to use the word confrontation but that's how it felt when I was faced with it. It was more of an overdue expression of feelings; however, it felt confrontational because I had lived my life never truly expressing how I felt about her neglect and lack of motherly instinct. Even as I was faced with telling her how I felt, I kept reverting back to how it would make her feel. It's a classic thought pattern of a child of an alcoholic. I hesitated even in the face of true progression because I felt it was at the expense of my mother's feelings. Once I got over that, it felt great to have that off my chest.

DR. CARLSON: What are the main changes that you made during our therapy work together?

AIMEE: The main changes that I made during our work together were to begin living my life with my mental health in mind. I needed to learn to be mindful of my needs instead of others'. Additionally, I needed to begin to forgive my mother for the experiences I had in childhood. Once I began to forgive her, I felt as if I had begun to start healing from deeply embedded emotional wounds within me. I started attending ACOA [Adult Children of Alcoholics] meetings and it changed my life significantly. I think children with addicted parents often feel isolated and alone in the world. When I went to my first ACOA meeting, I cried as if I was attending a funeral and in a sense I did. The funeral was for my old way of life and it's hard to say goodbye to life-long patterns no matter how destructive they may be. The beauty of it is I found a sort of surrogate family in the other ACOA members. It was an epiphany. I was not alone. There was a reason for my irrational thoughts and behaviors and I began to understand why.

DR. CARLSON: Are you at all surprised at all these changes?

AIMEE: I am completely surprised by these changes. I guess the most surprising aspect is that there is another way of life. I don't have to be wounded forever by my childhood. Out of suffering comes wisdom and I've been handed a valuable gift as a result.

DR. CARLSON: On a scale from 1 (Dissatisfied) to 10 (Highly Satisfied) what number would you rank our sessions?

AIMEE: I would rank our sessions as a nine. I would have given it a ten but the one thing that was extremely difficult for me was the push to actually express how I felt toward my mother. I know that's the purpose of the therapy but regardless it was a real challenge for me.

DR. CARLSON: Are there any additional thoughts that you might have regarding our sessions or anything that was particularly helpful that was not mentioned above?

AIMEE: Since our sessions, I wrote my mother a letter expressing how I felt as well. I felt inspired to use writing as a means of communicating since it has always been a skill of mine. I was shaking when I wrote it. The emotions I felt as I put the pen to the paper were overwhelming but I was driven by the other "self" to do it. Afterwards, I felt relieved but I also knew that this letter was intended for me not for her. I knew that ultimately my mother would not come to some sort of understanding about herself at all. But that was OK. That is the level of understanding that I gained through therapy. It's not about reaction but action. If she was hurt by it, so be it. I wasn't going to hide behind a smile any longer and that was liberating. I wish that I would have thought of the letter while we had our sessions together but I did act as my own therapist to process it. I grew from the experience and moved on.

Commentary

As she reports on the seven years following termination, her comments are primarily about the shift that has occurred in her dominant pattern. Third order change is most prominent in this post-therapy conversation. In answer to the question about being her own therapist [in her quote reported in Chapter 7], she quickly and decisively agrees that she has continued the process of change after her final session with Dr. Carlson. Furthermore, in her touching portrayal of the letter she wrote, but did not send to her mother [above], she not only expresses deeply felt feelings but has found another useful and effective "treatment strategy" for third order change: her writing ability. It was a liberating and transforming experience for her just as her decision to use the post-it notes had been during her therapy. Commenting on the impact of the letter and her new change strategy she says: "I did act as my own therapist to process it. I grew from the experience and moved on."

It is also noteworthy that she points to how difficult it was "to say goodbye to life-long patterns no matter how destructive they may be" and compares the experience to being at a funeral. The reality is that changing maladaptive patterns is not easy and the reality is also that Aimee has had the courage and perseverance to maintain her hard won changes. That she is involved in ACOA is not surprising given the family history of alcoholism. This involvement provides her with both social support and a greater understanding of herself and her family of origin. This experience seems to both reinforce the changes that she made in her therapy with Dr. Carlson and extend them.

Dr. Carlson's Commentary

I was surprised by the clarity of Aimee's memories of our time together. She clearly remembered the main focus of our work and seemed just as proud today as seven years ago. I was pleased to learn that Aimee had created ways to maintain the gains of therapy and to find ways to be her own therapist. This single case of just six sessions shows the power of psychotherapy to make deep, significant and long lasting change.

Concluding Comment

The importance of the last session cannot be overstated. The process of evaluating the treatment process and preparing for termination is a necessary part of highly effective therapy. Based on the transcribed segments and the post-therapy conversation, it is clear that major changes had been effected in her six-session therapy. Because of her early history of neglect and abuse and later abuse by her ex-husband, many therapists would not consider Aimee an ideal candidate for very brief, time-limited therapy. Nevertheless, as was noted in the case conceptualization (Chapter 4), there were therapy-promoting factors, including previous successful change efforts, a high level of self-control, resilience, and motivation for treatment that Aimee brought to therapy. This plus Dr. Carlson's expertise, a high level of clinician credibility, an effective therapeutic alliance, and significant corrective relational experiences both inside and outside therapy sessions, resulted in significant first, second, and third order changes.

References

Beck, J. (1995). *Cognitive therapy: Basics and beyond*. New York, NY: Guilford.

Callahan, J., Aubuchon-Endsley, N., Borja, S., & Swift, J. (2009). Pretreatment expectancies and premature termination in a training clinic environment. *Training and Education in Professional Psychology, 3*, 111–119.

Carroll, K. (1996). Relapse prevention as a psychosocial treatment: A review of controlled clinical trials. *Experimental and Clinical Psychopharmacology, 4*, 46–54.

Clarkin, J., & Levy, K. (2003). Influence of client variables on psychotherapy. In M. Lambert (Ed.), *Handbook of psychotherapy and behavior change* (5th ed.). New York, NY: Wiley.

Cucciare, M., & O'Donohue, W. (2008). Clinical case conceptualization and termination of psychotherapy. In M. O'Donohue & W. Cucciare (Eds.), *Terminating psychotherapy: A clinician's guide*. (pp. 121–146). New York, NY: Routledge.

Daley, D. C. (1989). *Relapse prevention: Treatment alternatives and counseling aids*. Blaze Ridge Summit, PA: TAB Books.

Dobson, K. & Haubert, L. (2008). Termination with persons with depressive disorders. In M. O'Donohue & W. Cucciare (Eds.), *Terminating psychotherapy: A clinician's guide* (pp. 303–324). New York, NY: Routledge.

Duncan, B. (2010). *On becoming a better therapist.* Washington, DC: American Psychological Association.

Duncan, B. (2012). The partners for change outcome management system (PCOMS): The heart and soul of change project. *Canadian Psychology, 53,* 93–104.

Duncan, B., Miller, S., Parks, L., Claud, D., Reynolds, L., Brown, J., & Johnson, L. (2003). The Session Rating Scale. Preliminary properties of a "working" alliance measures. *Journal of Brief Therapy, 3,* 3–12.

Gloaguen, V., Cottraus, J., Cucharet, M., & Blackburn, I. (1998). A meta-analysis of the effects of cognitive therapy in depressed patients. *Journal of Affective Disorders, 49,* 59–72.

Good, G., & Beitman, B. (2006). *Counseling and psychotherapy essentials: Integrating theories, skills, and practices.* New York, NY: Norton.

Heaton, J. (1998). *Building basic therapeutic skills: A practical guide for current mental health practice.* San Francisco, CA: Jossey-Bass.

Lambert, M., Whipple, J., Smart, D., Vermeersch, D., Nielsen, S., & Hawkins, E. (2001). The effects of providing therapists with feedback on patient progress during psychotherapy: Are outcomes enhanced? *Psychotherapy Research, 11*(1) 49–68.

Marlatt, G., & Gordon, J. (1985). *Relapse prevention: Maintenance and strategies in the treatment of addictive behaviors.* New York, NY: Guilford Press.

Miller, S., & Duncan, B. (2000). *The Outcomes Rating Scale.* Chicago, IL: Author.

Miller, S., Duncan, B., Brown, J., Sorrell, R., & Chalk, M. (2006). Using outcome to inform and improve treatment outcomes: Making ongoing, real-time assessment feasible. *Journal of Brief Therapy, 5,* 5–23.

Mosak, H., & DiPietro, R. (2006). *Early recollections: Interpretive method and application.* New York, NY: Routledge.

Orlinsky, D., Ronnestad, M., & Willutzi, U. (2004). Fifty years of psychotherapy process-outcome research: Continuity and change. In M. Lambert (Ed.), *Bergin and Garfield's handbook of psychotherapy and behavior change* (5th ed., pp. 307–389). New York, NY: Wiley.

Shimokawa, K., Lambert, M. J., & Smart, D. W. (2010). Enhancing treatment outcome of patients at risk of treatment failure: Meta-analytic and mega-analytic review of a psychotherapy quality assurance system. *Journal of Consulting & Clinical Psychology, 78,* 298–311.

Sperry, L., Brill, P., Howard, K., & Grissom, G. (1996). *Treatment outcomes in psychotherapy and psychiatric interventions.* New York, NY: Brunner/Mazel.

Sperry, L., Lewis, J., Carlson, J., & Englar-Carlson, M. (2003). *Health promotion and health counseling: Effective counseling and psychotherapeutic strategies.* Boston, MA: Allyn & Bacon.

Weddington, W., & Cavenar, J. (1979). Termination initiated by the therapist: A countertransference storm. *American Journal of Psychiatry, 136,* 1302–1305.

Whipple, J., Lambert, M., Vermeersch, D., Smart, D., Nielsen, S., & Hawkins, E. (2003). Improving the effects of psychotherapy: The use of early identification of treatment and problem-solving strategies in routine practice. *Journal of Counseling Psychology, 50,* 59–68.

Wierzbicki, M., & Pekarik, G. (1993). A meta-analysis of psychotherapy dropout. *Professional Psychology: Research and Practice, 24,* 190–195.

9

EFFECTING CHANGE: BECOMING A MASTER THERAPIST

We regularly get asked three questions about master therapists. What is a master therapist? How do master therapists work? How does one become a master therapist? Chapter 1 has already addressed the first question, while Chapters 2 through 8 have addressed the second one. This chapter focuses on the third question. In this era of accountability, it is not unreasonable for trainees and therapists to be concerned about achieving the status of master therapist. Presumably, there are criteria for determining master therapist status and ways of being recognized for having met those criteria. Do therapists demonstrate that they are master therapists by receiving a certificate from an Internet organization after filling out a form and paying a fee? Does it require publishing a psychotherapy book or a psychotherapy video? Does it result after putting in 10 years or 10,000 hours of psychotherapy practice—the so-called Ericsson's 10,000-hour rule (Ericsson & Lehmann, 1996)? Does it involve being peer-nominated (i.e., formally recognized by several of your colleagues)? Peer-nomination, by the way, is the method used in many studies to identify master therapists (Ronnestad & Skovholt, 2013).

At indicated in Chapter 1, there is no consensus as to what criteria constitutes expertise and mastery in psychotherapy. That means that current discussions about the criteria for identifying clinical expertise and mastery in psychotherapy are necessarily tentative. Nevertheless, this chapter suggests some research-based indicators of mastery. The chapter begins by distinguishing psychotherapy expertise from competence and specifies the level of knowledge, skills, professional judgment, and personal and interpersonal qualities associated with expertise in psychotherapy practice. Next, it describes some developmental stages and phases, developmental tasks, and developmental themes and markers of mastery in psychotherapy. Then it describes key strategies for increasing expertise and mastery, emphasizing reflection, supervision, and deliberate practice.

Expertise, Competence, and Psychotherapy

Expertise is best viewed as high level proficiency and competence beyond a minimal level of proficiency and competence (Sperry, 2010a). It represents extraordinary rather than adequate performance. Expertise involves a superior level of knowledge, skills, professional judgment, and personal and interpersonal qualities. While minimal competence represents adequate performance in each of these areas or domains, expertise involves superior performance in all of them.

More specifically, expertise requires extensive knowledge of facts and theories of human development, personality, psychopathology, and change processes. Expertise also requires well-honed general clinical skills in diagnostic interviewing, empathic listening and responding, and the ability to establish a strong therapeutic alliance, particularly with difficult clients. But it also requires high-level clinical skills and experience in pattern recognition, case conceptualization, the capacity to deal effectively with treatment interfering factors such as transference, countertransference, ambivalence, alliance ruptures, and sensitivity to intrapsychic, relational, social, and cultural factors that might affect the psychotherapy process (Sperry, 2010b). Such expertise requires a level of professional judgment necessary to navigate through most ethical dilemmas, and to avoid complications that could arise through dual relationships, professional impairment, harm-threatening clients, and working beyond the limits of one's competence. It also requires a high level of personal and interpersonal competence that includes ease in relating effectively with a wide range of clients and others, professional demeanor, professional maturity, self-regulation, resilience, and an awareness of one's own physical health and capacity for self-care.

Expertise is a lifelong process of continued development extending over several years of professional practice. More specifically, it requires years of professional training, professional experience, and professional challenges to be confronted and overcome on the path to expertise. Furthermore, it requires an awareness of one's professional limitations, which motivates the professional to continue learning and developing throughout their career (Skovholt & Jennings, 2004).

While there is no consensus as to what constitutes mastery in psychotherapy, it may be useful to identify the kind of criteria that demonstrate expertise in psychotherapy. While none have specifically been identified for psychotherapy, five criteria have been proposed for evaluating clinical expertise among clinical psychologists (Overholser, 2010). Modified to the practice of psychotherapy the criteria might be (1) possession of a terminal degree in a psychotherapy discipline, (2) at least 10 years of progressive clinical experience in the direct provision of psychotherapy, (3) advanced training or credentialing in a specific area of psychotherapy, (4) visibility in the professional community at a national level, and (5) demonstrated evidence of superior clinical skills in psychotherapy. Of course, criteria 4 and 5 are considerably more difficult to quantify and document compared with the first three criteria. In the absence of agreed-on criteria, the following sections describe a number of research-based markers and indicators of mastery and the developmental processes that accompany it.

Stages of Expertise

The process of developing expertise in psychotherapy involves a developmental trajectory of acquiring and refining the core competencies of psychotherapy. This trajectory and the stages associated with it are just beginning to be studied in the mental health professions. These stages appear to be similar to the five developmental stages of expertise identified in other professions (Dreyfus & Dreyfus, 1986). A description of these stages has been modified to reflect training for and the practice of psychotherapy (Sperry, 2010a).

Beginner

At this stage trainees possess a limited knowledge and understanding in analyzing problems and intervening. Such trainees are reliant on basic principles and techniques, are rule-bound, and are usually too inexperienced to flexibly apply these principles and techniques.

Advanced Beginner

In this stage trainees possess a limited capacity for pattern recognition and application of interventions but have difficulty generalizing this capacity to different clients and new situations. Rules and principles previously learned now become guidelines. Trainees at this stage inevitably need considerable support and clinical supervision.

Minimally Competent

At this stage psychotherapists can function independently albeit at a minimal level of competence, which is the level required for licensure as an independent practitioner. Psychotherapists at this stage are likely to be consciously aware of long-range goals and plans for their clients and can adapt to the changes in the client with appropriate changes in the intervention plan. They typically can recognize patterns more easily and begin to tailor intervention. They usually experience a feeling of mastery and are able to cope with and handle crises or other problems as they arise. Furthermore, they can more easily integrate theory and research into every aspect of their practice applications.

Proficient

At this stage psychotherapists possess a more integrative understanding of their clients, and their performance is guided by flexibility and a clear understanding of the nuances of therapeutic interventions and the impact of the intervention on the client and others. At this stage, psychotherapists are typically able to effectively train and supervise others in intervention skills.

Expert

At this stage psychotherapists possess an intuitive grasp of the clinical situation and can rapidly assess problems and design appropriate interventions. They quickly recognize, usually intuitively, when interventions are not working and are able to modify treatment accordingly. Typically, these individuals have integrated their personal and professional lives, are highly effective in their professional endeavors be it therapy, consultation, or supervision. They are usually masterful in relating to others and value human relationships above personal needs. Not surprisingly, they are admired by their clients, and are considered master therapists by their peers, even though they continue to be lifelong learners. Expert psychotherapists, also referred to as master therapists (Skovholt & Jennings, 2004), routinely practice highly effective therapy (Sperry, 2010a).

Developmental Phases in a Therapist's Career

There have been some general and specific criticisms of the stage model advocated by Dreyfus and Dreyfus (1986). Chief among the general criticisms is the that the problem of expert fallibility is underplayed and that differences between styles of decision making between experts and lay people have been underestimated. A specific criticism is that the development of trainees and therapists is better represented by overlapping phases rather than discrete stages (Ronnestad & Skovholt, 2013). Based on Ronnestad and Skovholt's extensive qualitative research on how psychotherapists develop over the course of their careers, a five-phase model was derived. Beyond specifying the characteristics of each phase, these researchers also articulated the developmental tasks associated with each phase. From an educational perspective, developmental tasks provide useful learning targets to meet as the individual progresses from phase to phase. Following is a brief description of these phases and their developmental tasks (Ronnestad & Skovholt, 2013).

Novice Student Phase

The novice phase is defined as the time frame between the beginning of graduate training through the second year of training. This usually encompasses the first practicum experience. Generally, this phase is representative of the younger, less-experienced individual who has not experienced extensive personal stressors. The older, more experienced individuals are likely to have confronted many of the following four developmental tasks: (1) to make some sense of an extensive amount of conceptual knowledge that will be acquired from graduate classes and the professional literature, (2) to demonstrate in practicum sufficient procedural competence (i.e., sufficient mastery of assessment and therapy/counseling skills), (3) to handle the intense emotional reactions that ensue from seeing their first clients in practicum, and (4) to maintain an openness to information and theory at a meta-level, while also engaging in the "closing off" process of selecting therapy theories and techniques to use.

Advanced Student Phase

This phase is defined as the last part of graduate training in which the student functions as a trainee in an advanced practicum, internship, or clerkship site and is receiving regular and formal supervision. It is critical in the process of forming the identity of a psychotherapist.

Five developmental tasks have been derived: (1) to learn more complex conceptual knowledge that meets the criteria set by the training institution, (2) to demonstrate procedural competency, that is, sufficient mastery of assessment and therapeutic skills as assessed by supervisors in particular, (3) to maintain an openness to information and theory at a global level, while also engaging in the "closing off" process of selecting therapy theories and techniques to use, (4) to modify unrealistic and perfectionistic images of psychotherapy and of the role and identity of the psychotherapist, and (5) to manage the bewilderment that comes from seeing the practice of psychotherapy as increasingly complex.

Novice Professional Phase

This phase is defined broadly as the first two to five years of professional practice after graduation. Presumably, the individual will qualify and become licensed during this phase. Typically, these years are experienced as highly intensive and engaging as the new professional faces many challenges and decisions. This phase is critical in consolidating the identity of a psychotherapist. Four developmental tasks are identified: (1) to develop an identification with the profession and commitment to the practice of psychotherapy, (2) to succeed in the transformation from the dependency of graduate training to the independence that is expected after completing professional training, (3) to master any disillusionment with training, self, and the profession that may have emerged some time after graduation, and (4) to continue exploring and defining one's work role.

Experienced Professional Phase

This phase is the least precise in its definition. Basically, the therapist has been practicing for several years. During this time frame, the therapist is likely to have experience in different work settings, have utilized different treatment modalities, and worked with different types of clients. Three developmental tasks have been derived: (1) to maintain a sense of professional growth and resiliency while avoiding burnout and stagnation, (2) to integrate one's personal self into a coherent professional self, and (3) to create a work role that is experienced as highly coherent with the psychotherapist's coherent professional self.

Senior Professional Phase

This phase is defined as having practiced psychotherapy for a minimum of 25 years following graduate training. Many have practiced longer, and continue to practice or have retired. Of all the phases, this is the one in which individuals designated as master therapists are most likely to reside. Three developmental tasks have been derived: (1) to maintain a sense of profession growth and resiliency while avoiding burnout and stagnation, (2) to maintain a work role that is experienced as highly coherent with the psychotherapist's coherent professional self, and (3) to adapt—when the time comes—to partial or full retirement approaching, adjust client load, and prepare clients for this change.

Themes of Profession Development in Psychotherapy

While this phase model offers a most useful longitudinal perspective of the psychotherapist's career trajectory, it is necessarily limited. What follows is a more thematic and cross-sectional view of the process of becoming a psychotherapist. Ten themes summarize the findings of several qualitative studies (Ronnestad & Skovholt, 2013).

1. Optimal Development Requires the Integration of Personal and Professional Selves

With increasing experience one's sense of personal self becomes integrated into a coherent professional self. In its optimal expression this integration is likened to Carl Rogers' concept of congruence wherein experiences are consistent with the self.

2. The Modes of Therapist Functioning Shift From Internal to External to Internal

Three shifts are noted in the therapist's developmental trajectory. First, in the pretraining mode, the individual is not socialized into the professional helping culture. Second, in the training mode, the individual accommodates and assimilates the external and rigid model of socialization. Third, in the post-training period, the individual experiences loosening and a more internal model of socialization.

3. Continuous Reflection Is a Prerequisite for Optimal Learning and Development

Reflection is a continuous and focused search for a more comprehensive, nuanced, and in-depth understanding of oneself and others. The increasing capacity for ongoing reflection has been found to be essential in avoiding professional stagnation. Three types of reflection have been identified: reflection-in-action (present), reflection-on-action (past), and reflection pre-action (future). Studies of master therapists find that the more proficient the therapist, the more types of reflection are operative.

4. Professional Development Is a Lifelong Process

Learning to integrate theory and practice occurs over a lifetime of immersion in therapy practice and in having reflected on its difficulties and challenges. Professional development also includes involvement in roles as a supervisor, teacher, and consultant that fuel this integration and overall development.

5. Professional Development Is a Continuous Process but Intermittent and Cyclical

Professional development is generally experienced as a continuous sense of competence and mastery, a process that may be barely noticeable. However, it can also occur as repeated cycles with sequences of hope, self-doubt, anxiety, dejection, exploration, and integration.

6. An Intense Commitment to Learning Propels the Developmental Process

A commitment to learn, reflect, and take ethically appropriate risks is characteristic of those with experience a growing sense of enthusiasm about doing therapy. Research shows that it involves a renewal of morale and motivation needed for therapeutic work rather than leading to burnout or compassion fatigue.

7. Initial Anxiety in Their Professional Work Is Mastered by Most

Anxiety is not uncommon among those in training. However, it tends to decrease after six months of practice. Both the trainee's personality and the culture of the training program can reduce or increase the level of anxiety. This is particularly the case when training balances support with the expectation for growth.

8. Interpersonal Sources of Influence Largely Propel Professional Development

Just as distressed clients experience therapeutic relationships as therapeutic because they are caring and securely protective, the professional growth of therapists is impacted by interpersonal experiences of supervisors, teachers, and mentors. Nevertheless, trainees may experience some disillusionment with their training and the dichotomy between theory research and practice.

9. Not All Therapists Develop Optimally

There are many factors that influence professional development. These include talent, training, personality, cognitive and affective capacities, and interpersonal skills. A consistent research finding is that therapists with poor interpersonal skills and lack of a genuine commitment to the welfare of clients are less likely to develop optimally than those with good interpersonal skills and a more genuine commitment to client welfare.

10. There Is a Realignment From Self-Therapist as Powerful to Client as Powerful

Over time, as therapists feel more professionally confident and recognize their limitations and are able to integrate these blows to their ego, they tend to become more humble as therapists. Simultaneously, they increasingly realize that therapeutic change takes place to the extent to which they are able to foster client empowerment. In other words, a change in perspective occurs. It involves the shift from the therapist as expert and hero to client as expert and hero.

The Developmental Path to Becoming a Master Therapist

While these ten themes characterize the general development of psychotherapists in general, they do not characterize the specific development of master therapists. What follows is a summary of the markers or indicators of the developmental trajectory of master therapists. These markers are based on the findings of several qualitative studies (Ronnestad & Skovholt, 2013).

In addition to markers of the developmental path or trajectory there are markers of the preconditions or prerequisites. In others words, if these prerequisites are not present at the outset of the journey, it is unlikely that the master therapist status is achievable.

Necessary Preconditions Before Beginning the Journey Toward Mastery

1. Being Relationship Oriented

The individual's fundamental orientation is toward others in contrast to a primary orientation toward to objects. Attachment bonds are important in becoming a master therapist, as well as being drawn toward others and the themes in their lives.

2. Drawn to Uncertainty

Unlike careers in which well-defined parameters, linear thinking, and intellectual mastery are essential, therapy is replete with ill-defined situations that are seldom resolved with sequential, rational problem solving. Those who thrive in this work are confident in searching for clarity while remaining comfortable with the uncertainly and complexity of the human condition.

3. Being Affectively Attuned to the Needs of Others

Learning to become empathic begins early in attachment bonds as one's own welfare becomes tied to the capacity to care for others. Affective expertise grows over the years as one learns how to care for others and develop finely tuned affective sensitivity.

Developmental Markers on the Path Toward Mastery

1. Intense Desire for Mastery

Master therapists manifest a deep intrinsic motivation to master the domain of psychotherapy. Over an extended period of time and despite periods of failure and discouragement, this motivation only increases in intensity. "The development of genuine expertise requires struggle, sacrifice, and honest, often painful self-assessment. There are no shortcuts" (Ericsson, Prietula, & Cokely, 2007, p. 15).

2. Deliberate Practice Over Many Years

Neither the amount of experience nor mindless practice alone is sufficient in increasing psychotherapy competency. Rather, structured, progressively more challenging practice sessions in which feedback is provided and incorporated lead to mastery. Estimates are that at least 10 to 15 years of such mindful, progressive practice are characteristic of master therapists.

3. Open to Feedback but Not Derailed by It

Being open to accurate feedback is essential to mastery, whereas avoiding inaccurate feedback since it can derail progress. Openness to feedback is essential to deliberate practice as is self-reflection and self-monitoring. Having these feedback loops is essential to mastery. Lacking such feedback loops, many practitioners fall victim to not learning from their experience and stagnate.

4. Deep Coaching Attachments

Mastery requires the recognition that professional development extends well beyond graduate training. It also requires a willingness to seek coaching and consultation from supervisors and mentors who can provide accurate feedback as well as encouragement. Effective coaching changes over the developmental path, such that a more demanding style of coaching is needed as the novice therapist develops skills and confidence, followed by a less demanding style. Overall, development is optimally fostered when the coach's support and challenge are in balance given the therapist's level of mastery.

5. Humility

The experience of integrating failure and humiliation into one's professional sense of self is important for mastery. It continually opens the individual to learn and to improve while developing the cognitive schema of expertise. It is the opposite of narcissism which can effectively negate openness to feedback necessary for growth.

6. Balance Between Other-Care and Self-Care

Master therapists are individuals who by nature and training can readily demonstrate affective attunement to the needs of others. However, such concentrated focus can be exhausting if the therapist has not learned self-care skills. Master therapists have learned these skills and incorporate them in caring for their own physical, emotional, and spiritual needs. As a result, they are able to maintain a vibrancy and passion for their work through balancing a deep giving of themselves with expertise in meeting their own needs.

7. Cultural Competence

Mastery requires a commitment and considerable skill in accurately understanding and constructing a map of the client's worldview. This form of competence includes all the factors that weave a pattern of individual differences such as socioeconomic status, age, gender, ethnicity, religious and spiritual perspective, sexual orientation, generation, and nationality. Besides sensitivity to cultural factors, master therapists are able to provide appropriate spiritually sensitive interventions when indicated or provide a referral for such interventions.

Strategies for Increasing Expertise and Mastery

The description of these markers of development and mastery provides the background for a discussion of strategies for fostering expertise and mastery. We begin with a brief overview of modes of learning and modes of practice. Then, we describe the use of reflection, supervision, and deliberate practice.

Modes of Learning

The process of developing the requisite knowledge, skills, and competencies of psychotherapy expertise involves a mix of three kinds of learning: declarative, procedural, and reflective (Bennett-Levy, 2006). Declarative learning involves conceptual, and technical, and interpersonal knowledge. This kind of learning is largely facilitated by lectures, presentations, discussions, and reading. Procedural learning is the application of knowledge to the clinical practice and is largely facilitated by clinical experiences and supervision. It occurs when declarative knowledge become actualized in practice and refined. Procedural learning is essentially skill-based, clinical learning. Reflective learning differs markedly from declarative and procedural learning. It involves reflecting on declarative and procedural knowledge and come to a decision about a course of action. Various processes are involved in this type of learning. They include analyzing experiences, comparing them with others, identifying a plan of action as necessary, and possibly changing previous information and insights in the light of the analysis. In clinical training, the reflective system is mostly facilitated by client and supervisor feedback of therapist performance in addition to therapist self-evaluation (Bennett-Levy, 2006).

When it comes to developing mastery and expertise in psychotherapy, all three types of learning are involved. Research show that the interaction of these three types of learning is required to develop and master a competency(Bennett-Levy & Thwaites, 2006).

This three-pronged view of learning further clarifies the difference between a skill and a competency. Skill learning involves primarily procedural learning, although some declarative learning may also be involved. In contrast, competency learning involves all three types of learning since it involves knowledge (i.e., declarative learning), skills (i.e., procedural learning), and attitudes, and values, and standards (i.e., reflective learning). It appears that reflective learning is essential to becoming highly proficient and effective as a therapist (Bennett-Levy & Thwaites, 2006; Schön, 1983).

Modes of Practice

It has been noted that highly effective therapists think, act, and reflect differently than less effective therapists (Binder, 2004; Binder & Betan, 2012; Sperry, 2010a). The result of what is essentially a different mode of practice is evident in both therapeutic alliances and clinical outcomes achieved by highly effective therapists. Recently, these differences are increasingly being confirmed by research (Skovholt & Jennings, 2004). This section briefly summarizes these observations in terms of the way in which these therapists characteristically think, act, and reflect.

Think

So how do master therapists think differently? They seem to quickly and intuitively know if they are connecting with clients and are guided by cognitive maps that assist them in incisively assessing, conceptualizing, and planning intervention. In addition, they quickly and intuitively know if their case conceptualization is accurate. How is this possible? For one, highly effective therapists engage in more nonlinear thinking than linear thinking. Linear thinking is the familiar and characteristic thinking pattern in which an individual approaches life and problems. In contrast, nonlinear thinking "requires therapists to see and understand the client's characteristic, old, 'personally' linear pattern; envision a new alternative way (or pattern) of seeing and behaving; and communicate that new way to the client" (Mozdzierz, Peluso, & Lisiecki, 2009, p. 5).

Act

Master therapists act differently than other therapists with regard to all the core competencies. That means they easily develop and maintain effective therapeutic alliances and work with clients in ways that are qualitatively different than beginning and minimally competent therapists. On observation, it becomes clear that they listen, respond, assess, formulate, plan interventions, and manage treatment issues differently than other therapists. Largely, this is because they are guided by cognitive maps in focusing and implementing treatment interventions. They continually seek feedback from clients by observation and questioning, and are more likely to assess progress with outcome measures. Thus, they quickly know if treatment is on target and change and modify it based on that feedback. It has been observed that master therapists easily and effortlessly are able to improvise and change therapeutic direction and methods as treatment circumstances change (Binder, 2004). As a result of these capabilities, master therapists rather consistently excel in dealing with complex clinical situations and difficult clients (Lambert & Okishi, 1997).

Reflect

Finally, they reflect differently than other psychotherapists. Although the domain of reflection may seem more subtle and difficult to observe than thinking and action, it may be well be that expertise in this domain actually inspires, drives, and gives direction to how these master therapists think and act. Reflective practice is a continuous process and involves the learner considering critical incidents in his or her life experiences. As defined by Schön (1983), reflective practice involves thoughtfully considering one's own experiences in applying knowledge to practice while being coached by professionals in the discipline. It is the process by which therapists reflect on their own therapeutic methods in order to more fully understand the client and the optimal strategies and tactics for fostering goal attainment and client growth.

Reflection

Reflection, also called reflective practice, can be three-fold for the psychotherapist. The therapist can self-reflect, can reflect with a supervisor, peer, or consultant, or can reflect with the client. Master therapists are likely to regularly engage in all three, in contrast to less effective therapists. Over the years of being involved in the training and supervision of therapists, we have noted major differences in reflection and reflective activity among trainees and practicing psychotherapists.

Self-Reflection

Self-reflection, which is also referred to as self-supervision, can be done with or without a written account such as a journal. Some trainees and practicing psychotherapists keep a journal of encounters with clients in which they reflect on what they have learned from their mistakes, implementation of their supervisor's suggestions and directives, countertransferences, etc. They are also likely to ponder client issues between sessions and to prepare themselves for subsequent sessions. In contrast, other trainees and practitioners demonstrate little or no interest in keeping such a reflection journal, and are less likely to spend time contemplating client issues between sessions. These differences are noteworthy because research demonstrates that therapist self-reflection involving journal keeping does translate to improved therapeutic alliances as well as clinical outcomes (Bennett-Levy & Thwaites, 2006).

We have noticed that highly effective psychotherapists tend to regularly reflect on the details of their performance with one or all of their clients on a given day and are more likely to identify specific actions and alternate strategies for reaching their goals. They will focus on controllable factors such as "I probably should have done this instead of that," or "I forgot to do this and will do it next session." For example, "Instead of organizing today's session on his drinking behavior, it would have made more sense to focus on getting his driver's license back, because that's what he seems to be really concerned about. Next session, I'll focus on what the client really wants and then pursue that."

In contrast, when less effective psychotherapists reflect on a past session they are more likely to attribute failure to external and uncontrollable factors: "This client is just not motivated to change," "She's just so resistant," "I guess I had a bad day," or "I wasn't feeling very well today." They are also more likely to focus on failed strategies in the belief by understanding the reasons why an approach did not work will lead to better outcomes. Subsequently, unlike highly effective therapists, they spend less time focusing on strategies that might have been more effective.

Supervision as Reflection

Highly effective supervisors tend to view supervision as a reflective process in which both supervisee and supervisor reflect on individual and systemic dynamics affecting the client, session dynamics between client and supervisee, as well as supervisor–supervisee dynamics. They are likely to consider reflection essential in their development as effective therapists. In such a context, supervisees are likely to carefully prepare case material such as process notes, transcriptions, and tapes and are eager to receive the supervisor's feedback. Supervisors are likely to reflect on the trainee's level of training and experience as the basis for assigning clients.

They are also likely to reflect on the past supervision sessions in light of the optimal balance of support and challenge needed to promote trainee development. The next section on "Supervision" continues this discussion.

Reflection Involving Clients

In terms of therapists engaging in reflection with clients (i.e., seeking feedback from clients on the therapy process and progress as well as about the therapeutic relationship), differences among trainees is also evident. When therapists actively seek out such feedback verbally or with ultra-brief feedback instruments, the therapeutic alliance improves, as do treatment outcomes and the likelihood of premature termination decreases significantly. Our experience and that of other therapy trainers and supervisors match the findings of a growing body of research pointing to both statistical and clinically significant differences between therapists who engage in such feedback-reflection with clients and those who do not (Reese et al., 2009).

Supervision

Over the past few years, psychotherapy supervision has changed considerably. In the past the primary goals of supervision were to teach supervisees how to conceptualize clinical material, to select and apply therapeutic intervention, to develop professional believe and values, and to adhere to ethical standards of conduct (while all of these goals are still important, supervision has increasingly become competency-based, evidence-based, and accountability-based; Watkins, 2012). It is increasingly being understood as transformational learning (Carroll, 2010). According, it currently is being described as "an educative process by which and through we as supervisors strive to embrace, empower, and emancipate the therapeutic potential of the supervisees with whom we have the privilege to work" (Watkins, 2012, p. 193). While learning case conceptualization, treatment selection, professional values, and adhering to ethical standards are necessary conditions to practice psychotherapy, they are not sufficient to achieve mastery and expertise. It is our belief that the process of becoming a master therapist is facilitated by highly effective supervisors who "emancipate therapeutic potential of supervisees" and create an environment for "transformational learning."

Supervisor Self-Reflection

Such supervisors will also expect and foster self-reflection in their supervisees. "In conjunction with supervisee self-reflection, supervision self-reflection also bears equal mention and consideration as a sine qua non for the instigation of an effective supervision process as well" (Watkins, 2012, p. 199). The implication is that unless psychotherapy supervisors regularly engage in self-reflection they cannot provide the kind of high-level supervision needed to foster mastery and expertise in their supervisees.

Table 9.1 Comparison of Psychotherapy and Case Management Supervision

Psychotherapy Supervision	Case Management Supervision
Main focus is to increase the trainee's psychotherapy core competencies (alliance; therapy assessment; case conceptualization; interventions—primarily *second order change*; monitor effected change; termination, etc.)	Main focus is to increase the trainee's case management skills (communication; behavioral assessment; coordination of services; case planning; counseling—*first order change*; etc.)
Ongoing review of a single case from intake to termination [other cases are briefly reviewed re: case management mode]	Regular review entire caseload with an emphasis on clients with safety; unmet ADL (basic self-management issues), etc.
Review video (audio/process notes) re: content *and* process; encourage and evaluate trainee personal—professional growth	Review charts re: content; review and evaluate trainee skills, liability issues; little or no emphasis on personal—professional growth
Regularly address transference—countertransference issues	Seldom, if ever, address transference—countertransference issues
Fosters self-reflection	Unlikely to foster self-reflection

Psychotherapy Supervision Versus Case Management Supervision

An unfortunate trend that effectively undercuts the path to psychotherapy expertise and mastery in supervisees is providing case management supervision under the guise of providing psychotherapy supervision. This is a particular concern in clinics and agencies that regularly assign chronic and highly complex clients who are more likely to respond to effective case management than to psychotherapy. Trainees with a caseload of such difficult clients do need case management supervision, and that is often what trainees receive. Unfortunately, clinic and agency administrators and supervisors too often view the supervision they provide as psychotherapy supervision. The reality is that case management supervision cannot and does not foster the development of basic psychotherapy skills, much less foster psychotherapy expertise. Table 9.1 distinguishes these types of supervision.

Deliberate Practice

Expertise in complex professional domains like psychotherapy requires many hours of deliberate practice for expertise to emerge (Jennings, Skovholt, Goh, & Lian, 2013). Deliberate practice refers to the time devoted to reaching for objectives just beyond one's level of proficiency (Ericsson & Lehmann, 1996). Deliberate practice involves using specific interventions, mastering particular strategies, and getting feedback from clients to optimize their treatment. In other words, becoming a master therapist and achieving therapeutic success is a function of therapists' capacity to incorporate deliberate practice and self-reflection in their professional lives.

Deliberate practice involves three components: the performance of well-designed tasks at an appropriate level of difficulty, useful feedback, and opportunities for repetition and correction of errors (Ericsson & Lehmann, 1996). In learning new skill sets and competencies, deliberate practice involves engaging in increasingly difficult elements of the skill or competency. Setbacks and frustration are a necessary part in developing expertise. Persistence and learning through failure, although unpleasant, are also necessary. Seeking constant feedback in various forms is another essential component of deliberate practice. This includes directly asking clients for feedback as well as using standard assessments and performance measures to assess clients' progress. Then, it means implementing or using the feedback to alter the course or direction of treatment. "Being open to feedback is part of deliberate practice. Another part of turning experience into expertise is the use of reflection. . . . There must be a feedback loop so that the individual can learn from the practice. When therapists are fully licensed and working alone, they can fall victim to not learning from their own practitioner experience if there is no deliberate practice feedback system that includes self-reflection and self-monitoring of oneself as a practitioner" (Jennings, Skovholt, Goh & Lian, 2013, p. 241).

Practicing Deliberate Practice

Deliberate practice is essential to developing expertise, it is not optional. Trainees often ask how they can use and incorporate deliberate practice in learning to become more proficient therapists. Adopting one or more of the following activities for a given time frame (e.g., a semester) is a good place to begin. Consider these activities to be deliberate practice targets toward which you direct your efforts.

1. Observe and identify clients' dominant maladaptive patterns within the first five minutes of watching several video cases; then watch further to confirm or revise the pattern.
2. Practice identifying more adaptive patterns within two minutes of identifying maladaptive patterns (in Target No. 1).
3. Develop and draft clinical formulation statements (from a biopsychosocial, CBT, dynamic, Adlerian, or solution-focused perspective) on all your current (and past) clients. Aim to increasingly decrease the time required so that you can derive a written formulation statement within 10 minutes. Compare your statement to the clinical formulation statements for each of the therapeutic orientations (Sperry & Sperry, 2012).
4. Develop and draft cultural formulation statements and treatment formulation statements on all your current (and past) clients. Aim to increasingly decrease the time required so that you can derive an written formation statement within 10 minutes.

5. Develop and draft Mini-Mental Status Exam statements—within 10 minutes—for all your current clients.
6. Draft "verbatims" (transcriptions from memory) for every session with a particular client; add a third column for commentary. Aim to increasingly decrease the time required so that it is no longer than the scheduled session, so that you can derive an written formulation statement within 10 minutes.
7. Plan ahead how you would handle negative transference for several of your current clients.
8. Plan ahead how you would handle an eroticized transference for one or more of your current clients.
9. Draft out how you would handle a client's threat to harm a third party for one or more clients.
10. Pick out a repetitive verbalization (e.g., "Ah") or ineffective strategy (e.g., leading the client) and plan exactly how you will refrain or replace it in subsequent sessions and then implement it.
11. Reflect and subsequently continue to reflect (in your daily journal entries) on a specific issue until it is resolved.
12. Plan and draft scenarios (minimum of 15 minutes) of how you would use motivational interviewing.
13. Practice with particular clients so that your self-scored ratings are at or above 6.5/10.0. Start with Profile II-III clients and move to Profile III clients, then to Profile III-IV clients (Cf. Chapter 1).
14. Practice a specific therapeutic intervention with given clients so that their ratings on the Session Rating Scale (SRS) are consistently at or above 38/40. Discuss their ratings and use feedback to make appropriate changes in therapy process.

Concluding Comment

There is yet to be consensus on the criteria for assessing psychotherapy expertise and mastery and the designation of master therapist. Nevertheless, the chapter has described several research-based indicators of mastery. It has also discussed three strategies for increasing psychotherapy expertise: reflection, supervision, and deliberate practice. Presumably, these chapters have increased the reader's awareness and appreciation of psychotherapy expertise and mastery. Hopefully, this book will increase the resolve of trainees and therapists to become master therapists.

References

Bennett-Levy, J. (2006). Therapist skills: A cognitive model of their acquisition and refinement, *Behavioural and Cognitive Psychotherapy, 34,* 57–78.

Bennett-Levy, J., & Thwaites, R. (2006). Self and self-reflection in the therapeutic relationship. In P. Gilbert & R. Leahy (Eds.), *The therapeutic relationship in the cognitive behavioral psychotherapies* (pp. 255–282). London, UK: Taylor & Francis.

Binder, J. (2004). *Key competencies in brief dynamic psychotherapy: Clinical practice beyond the manual.* New York, NY: Guildford.

Binder, J., & Betan, E. (2012). *Core competencies in brief dynamic psychotherapy.* New York, NY: Routledge.

Carroll, M. (2010). Supervision: Critical reflection for transformational learning (Part 2). *The Clinical Supervisor, 29,* 1–19.

Dreyfus, H., & Dreyfus, S. (1986). *Mind over machine.* New York, NY: Free Press.

Ericsson, K. A., & Lehmann. A. (1996). Expert and exceptional performance: Evidence of maximal adaptation to task constraints. *Annual Review of Psychology, 47,* 273–305.

Ericsson, K. A., Prietula, M., & Cokely, E. (2007). The making of an expert. *Harvard Business Review, 85,* 114–121.

Jennings, L., Skovholt, T., Goh, M., & Lian, P. (2013). Master therapists: Exploitations of expertise. In M. Ronnestad & T. Skovholt (Eds.), *The developing practitioner: Growth and stagnation of therapists and counselors* (pp. 213–246). New York, NY: Routledge.

Lambert, M., & Ogles, B. (2004). The efficacy and effectiveness of psychotherapy. M. Lambert (Ed.), *Bergin and Garfield's handbook of psychotherapy and behavior change* (5th ed., pp. 139–193). New York, NY: Wiley.

Lambert, M., & Okishi, B. (1997). The efficacy and effectiveness of psychotherapy supervision. In C. Watkins (Ed.), *Bergin and Garfield's handbook of psychotherapy and behavior change* (5th ed., pp. 139–193). New York, NY: Wiley.

Mozdzierz, G., Peluso, P., & Lisiecki, J. (2009). *Principles of counseling and psychotherapy: Learning the essential domains and nonlinear thinking of master practitioners.* New York, NY: Routledge.

Overholser, J. (2010). Clinical expertise: A preliminary attempt to clarify its core elements. *Journal of Contemporary Psychotherapy, 40,* 131–139.

Reese, R., Usher, E., Bowman, D., Norsworthy, L., Halstead, J., Rowlands, S., et al. (2009). Using client feedback in psychotherapy training: An analysis of its influence on supervision and counselor self-efficacy. *Training and Education in Professional Psychology, 3,* 157–168.

Ronnestad, M., & Skovholt, T. (2013). *The developing practitioner: Growth & stagnation of therapists & counselors.* New York, NY: Routledge.

Schön, D. (1983) *The reflective practitioner.* New York, NY: Basic Books.

Skovholt, T. M., & Jennings, L. (2004). *Master therapists: Exploring expertise in therapy and counseling.* Boston, MA: Allyn & Bacon.

Sperry, L. (2010a). *Core competencies in counseling and psychotherapy: Becoming a highly competent and effective therapist.* New York, NY: Routledge.

Sperry, L. (2010b). *Highly effective therapy: Developing clinical competencies in counseling and psychotherapy.* New York, NY: Routledge.

Sperry, L., & Sperry, J. (2012). *Case conceptualization: Mastering this competency with ease and confidence.* New York, NY: Routledge.

Watkins, E. (2012). Psychotherapy supervision in the new millennium: Competency-based, evidence-based, particularized, and energized. *Journal of Contemporary Psychotherapy, 42,* 193–203.

BIBLIOGRAPHY

The following references are offered as primary resources for further exploring the world of the master therapist and the phenomenon of psychotherapy expertise and its determinants.

Baumeister, R., & Tierney, J. (2011). *Willpower: Rediscovering the greatest human strength.* New York, NY: Penguin.

Castonguay, L., & Hill. C. (Eds.). *Transformation in psychotherapy: Corrective experiences across cognitive-behavioral, humanistic, and psychodynamics approaches.* Washington, DC: American Psychological Association.

Cummings, N., & Cummings, J. (2013). *Refocused psychotherapy as the first line intervention in behavioral health.* New York, NY: Routledge.

Duncan, B. (2010). *On becoming a better therapist.* Washington, DC: American Psychological Association.

Duncan, B., Miller, S., Wampold, B., & Hubble, M. (Eds.). (2010). *The heart and soul of change: Delivering what works* (2nd ed.). Washington, DC: American Psychological Association.

Ericsson, K. A., Charness, N., Feltovich, P., & Hoffamn, R. (Eds.). (2006). *The Cambridge handbook of expertise and expert performance.* New York, NY: Cambridge University Press.

Fraser, J., & Solovey, A. (2007). *Second-order change in psychotherapy: The golden thread that unifies effective treatments.* Washington, DC: American Psychological Association.

Greene, R. (2013). *Mastery.* New York, NY: Viking.

Kottler, J., & Carlson, J. (2002). *Bad therapy: Master therapists share their worst failures.* New York, NY: Routledge.

Kottler, J., & Carlson, J. (2004). *Their finest hour: Master therapists share their greatest success stories.* Camarthan, UK: Crown House Publishers.

Kottler, J., & Carlson, J. (2009). *Creative breakthroughs: Tales of transformation and astonishment.* New York, NY: Wiley.

Kottler, J., & Carlson, J. (2013). *Helping beyond the fifty minute hour.* New York, NY: Routledge.

Kottler, J., & Carlson, J. (2014). *On being a master therapist: Practicing what we preach.* New York, NY: Wiley.

Orlinsky, D., & Ronnestad, M. (2005). *How psychotherapists develop: A study of therapeutic work and professional growth.* Washington, DC: American Psychological Association.

Ronnestad, M., & Skovholt, T. M. (2013). *The developing practitioner: Growth and stagnation of therapists and counselors.* New York, NY: Routledge.

Skovholt, T. M., & Jennings, L. (2004). *Master therapists: Exploring expertise in therapy and counseling.* Boston, MA: Allyn & Bacon.

Sperry, L. (2010). *Core competencies in counseling and psychotherapy: Becoming a highly competent and effective therapist.* New York, NY: Routledge.

Sperry, L., & Sperry, J. (2012). *Case conceptualization: Mastering this competency with ease and confidence.* New York, NY: Routledge.

INDEX

abuse 44
acceptance 105–7, 124
accountability 1, 2, 142, 156, 189
acculturation level 77, 82
acculturative stress 77
adaptive patterns 13, 76, 79, 89, 96–7, 101–2, 126
advanced beginner stage 178
advanced student phase 180
advice giving 80
affective sensitivity 184
alcohol dependence 104
alliance ruptures 21
ambiguity 6
ambivalence 21
anxiety 182
anxiety disorders 104, 105
assertiveness 114–15, 124, 145–6
assessment: ongoing 156; of outcomes 2, 156–8
avoidance 104, 105, 114, 124, 126
avoidant personality 90

beginner stage 178
behavioral activation 105
biological interventions 81
biological vulnerabilities 76
blocking 105–6, 107, 124
borderline personality 90
boundaries 7
breathing 112–13, 130–2, 133

career phases 179–81
case conceptualizations 14, 74–99; about 74; clinical formulation 76–7; commentary 94–8; components of 75–83; cultural formulation 77; development of 44, 87–91; diagnostic formulation 75–6; establishing treatment focus in 142–3; explanatory power of 83–4, 85–7; predictive power of 84–7; provisional 94–5; transcription 92–4; treatment formulation 78–83
case management supervision 190
CBT *see* cognitive-behavioral therapy (CBT)
change: facilitation of 14; orders of 14, 102–3; pattern 101–2, 128, 141; zero order of 103; *see also* first order change; second order change; third order change
choice 144, 145
clients 3; awareness of 12–13; creating solutions 152–3; deficits of 22–5; expectations of 12, 20, 24, 44, 126–7; motivations of 12; perceptions of 22; reflection with 189; resources of 3, 22–5, 44–5; self-efficacy of 7; strengths 46; subjective experience of 157; trust in 7–8
client-therapist relationships 156–7, 159; *see also* therapeutic alliance
clinical conditions, second order change view of 104
clinical expertise 1–2
clinical formulation 76–7
clinical skills 177
clinician credibility 22, 45, 82, 129
coaching 184
cognitive-behavioral therapy (CBT) 82, 105, 159
cognitive complexity 6, 9–10, 74
cognitive domain 5
cognitive maps 186, 187
cognitive restructuring 80, 107
competence 176–7
competencies 4

197

complexity 6, 9–10, 74
contextual factors 22–3
continuous reflection 181
controlling involvement 10
coping skills 161
core competencies 4
core treatment strategy 106–7
corrective experiences 13, 49–52, 70–3, 81; defined 50; emotional 50–1, 81; relational 51–2; types of 50–1; use of 124
countertransference 7, 21
cuento therapy 82
cultural competence 8, 185
cultural explanatory model 77
cultural formulation 77
cultural identity 77, 82
culturally sensitive treatment 81–3
cultural norms 20
current life problems 133–8

decision points 143–53
declarative learning 185
deframing 106
deliberate practice 74, 184, 190–2
dependent personality 91, 97
depression 104, 105, 113–16, 144–5, 152
desensitization 105
diagnostic formulation 75–6
diaphragmatic breathing 112–13, 130–2
dreams 164–6

EBP *see* evidence-based practice (EBP)
EBTs *see* evidence-based treatments (EBTs)
emotional domain 5
emotional receptivity 6
emotional well-being 6, 7
empathy 184
empirically supported treatment (EST) 1, 2
empowerment 144–6
EST *see* empirically supported treatment (EST)
etiological factors 76–7
evaluation: post-therapy 171–4; of treatment 156–8, 161–4
evidence-based practice (EBP) 1–2, 156
evidence-based treatments (EBTs) xvii
expectations 12, 20, 24, 44, 126–7
experience 6
experienced professional phase 180

expertise 176–7; clinician credibility and 22; criteria for 177; psychotherapeutic 4–5; research on 1, 3–4; stages of 178–9; strategies for increasing 185–92
expert stage 179
explanatory model 82
explanatory power, of case conceptualizations 83–7
exposure 80, 105, 107, 124

facilitators 90
familismo 82
feedback 157, 171, 184, 187, 191
first order change 128–40; about 128–9; commentary 132–3; defined 102; description of 103; facilitation of 14; goals 78, 87, 89; incorporation of 129–39; session transcription for 129–37
first session 19–47; case study/transcription of 25–43; client resources/deficits, profiling 22–4, 25; clinical credibility and 22; commentary 44–7; effecting change in 24–5, 45, 47; structure of 19; tasks for 19; therapeutic alliance and 19–21
framing 106

goals 20, 78, 89–90, 141
guidance 80
guilt 133

habituation 80
healing involvement 10–11
histrionic personality 91
human nature 7
humility 185

impasses 21
intelligence 22
interpersonal influence 22
interpretation 80–1, 107
interventions 2, 8, 73, 105–6; *see also* treatment

Kern Life Style inventory 26, 97, 162
knowledge domains 5

learning: commitment to 182; lifelong 5–6, 141, 177, 182; modes of 185–6; transformational 189
lifelong learning 5–6, 141, 177, 182
linear thinking 186–7

INDEX

loneliness 97
long-term goals 78, 141

maintaining factors 77
maladaptive patterns 13–14, 76, 79, 87–9, 96, 101–2, 126–9
master therapist 1, 3; becoming a 176–92; characteristics of 5–8, 16; criteria for 176, 177; developmental path to becoming 183–4; expertise and 176–9; profile of 4–11; self-reflection by 10; work processes of 11–14, 16–17
mastery 15, 177, 184–92
measurement, of outcomes 157–8
medication 81, 107
meditation 111–13, 116, 122, 129–33, 140
metacognition 9–10, 74
minimally competent stage 178
Morita therapy 82
movement 88

narcissistic personality 91
negative emotions 141
negative self-talk 71, 72
nonlinear thinking 186–7
novice professional phase 180
novice student phase 179

obsessive-compulsive personality 91
openness 6
orders of change 14, 102–3; see also first order change; second order change; third order change
other-care 185
outcomes 2–4, 83, 90, 143, 156
Outcomes Rating Scale (ORS) 158

panic attacks 12, 105–6, 129
paradoxical suggestion 25
parenting issues 133–8
patterns: about 75–6; adaptive 13, 76, 79, 89, 96–7, 101–2, 126; changing 101–2, 128, 141; identifying 13–14, 87, 88; maladaptive 13–14, 76, 79, 87–9, 96, 101–2, 126–9
peer-nomination 176
perfectionism 98, 144
perpetuants 77
personal boundaries 7
personal experience 6
personalismo 82

personality styles 88, 90–1
personal life experiences 8–9
personal self 181
positive expectations 12
positive reframing 71
post-therapy conversation 153
post-therapy evaluation 171–4
practice: deliberate 184, 190–2; modes of 186–7
practice-based evidence 156
precipitants 75, 87–8
predicting 106, 124
predictive power, of case conceptualizations 84–7
predisposition 76–7, 89
premature termination 159
prescribing 106
presentation 75, 87–8
procedural learning 185–6
professional boundaries 7
professional development 5–6, 177, 181–3
professional experience 6
professional judgment 177
professional self 181
proficient stage 178
Profile I 23, 24
Profile II 23
Profile III 23–4, 46
Profile IV 24
Profile V 24
prognosis 23, 24, 44–5
progress 159–64
protective factors 22, 25
psychoeducation 80, 105, 107, 125, 132–3
psychological vulnerabilities 76
psychotherapeutic expertise 4, 5; see also expertise
psychotherapy: current context of 1–4; effective xvii, 156; EST movement in 2; expertise and mastery in 1, 176–9; professional development in 181–3; supervision 189–90; termination of 158–64; training 4

randomized clinical trials (RCTs) xvii
reflection 181, 187–90
reflective learning 186
refocusing strategies 143
reframing 106, 124
regression 102, 159
relapse prevention 159, 160

199

INDEX

relational domain 5
relationship orientation 183
relationship skills 7
replacement 79–80, 107
resistance 21
reversal 104, 105, 107, 124

second order change 100–27, 140; commentary on 124–6; core treatment strategy and 106–7; corrective experiences as 13; defined 102; description of 103; facilitation of 14; goals 78, 87, 89–90; incorporating first order change in 129–39; session transcription for 107–23; strategies and interventions 105–6; transitioning to third order change 142; view of clinical conditions 104
second session 49–73; commentary on 70–2; corrective experiences and 49–52, 70–2; transcription of 52–70
selective attention 142
self-awareness 10, 140, 141, 154
self-care 132, 138, 177, 185
self-control 22
self-criticism 144
self-directed change 141; *see also* third order change
self-efficacy 22, 160
self-empowerment 144–6
self-other schemas 70, 126
self-reflection 10, 74, 181, 187–90
self-therapy 141–2, 159, 160
senior professional phase 180–1
Session Rating Scale (SRS) 158
short-term goals 78
silent expectations 20
situational factors 10–11
skill training 107, 132–3, 186
social vulnerabilities 76–7
Society for Psychotherapy Research/ Collaborative Research Network (SCR/CRN) 10
solutions, client-created 152–3
strategic questioning 94
strategies, second order change 105–6
strengths, focusing on 46, 71
stressful involvement 10, 11
student phase 179–80
substance dependence 104
supervision 74, 188–90

support 79, 107
supportive therapy 79
symptoms 129

10,000-hour rule 176
termination 158–64; considerations 161; indicators of readiness for 160–1; maintaining treatment gains after 159–60; premature 159; preparing for 160, 167–71
therapeutic alliance xviii–xix, 2–3, 7; effective 20–1, 187; enhancement of 11–12; establishing 20, 44, 71; first session and 19–21; importance of 19; maintaining productive 21; therapist and 20–1
therapeutic bond 20
therapeutic objectives 20, 78
therapeutic skills 7
therapist effect xvii, 3, 45
therapists: abilities of xvii–xviii; client perceptions of 22; clients as own 141–2; developmental phases in career of 179–81; role of 3–4; situational factors influencing 10–11; stages of expertise for 178–9; therapeutic alliance and 20–1; *see also* master therapist
third order change 102, 173; about 140–1; commentary on 151–3, 154; description of 103; facilitation of 14; incorporating 140–55; self-therapy 141–2; session transcription for 144–51, 153; transitioning from second order change to 142; treatment focus and 142–53
thought processes 186–7
time-limited therapy 142
training programs 4
transference 7, 21, 192
transformational change *see* second order change
transformational learning 189
treatment: core treatment strategy 106–7; culturally sensitive 81–3; empirically supported 1, 2; evaluation 156–8, 161–4; goals 20, 78, 87, 89–90; interventions 81–3, 89; maintaining gains made in 159–60; monitoring progress in 161–4; obstacles 83, 90–1; outcomes 2, 3–4, 83, 90, 143, 156–8; second order change and 106–7; strategy 79–81; termination of 158–64

treatment focus 14, 78–9, 142–53
treatment formulation 78–83
treatment-interfering factors 21
trustworthiness 22
12-step programs 104

uncertainty 183

well-being 6, 7
working alliances 7

zero order change 103

HOW MASTER THERAPISTS WORK

How Master Therapists Work engages the reader in experiencing what really happens in therapy with master therapists: who they are, what they do, and how they bring about significant change in clients. It examines one master therapist's actual six-session therapy (also available on DVD) that transformed a client's life, resulting in changes that have been sustained for more than seven years. Session transcriptions directly involve the reader in every aspect of the therapeutic change process. This is followed by the commentary of a master therapist–psychotherapy researcher, who explains how these changes were effected from a psychotherapy research perspective. Next, the master therapist who effected these changes explains what he was thinking and why he did what he did at key points in the therapy process. Then, the client shares her thoughts on this life-changing therapeutic experience. This is a must-have, one-of-a-kind book that will greatly enhance the therapeutic understanding and skills of both practicing therapists and therapists-in-training.

Len Sperry, MD, PhD, ABPP, is professor of mental health counseling at Florida Atlantic University and clinical professor of psychiatry and behavioral medicine at the Medical College of Wisconsin. He has practiced, researched, and taught psychotherapy for more than 40 years. He has more than 600 publications, including more than 60 books, mostly on psychotherapy. He has collaborated with Dr. Carlson on several articles, book chapters, books on psychotherapy, and other projects.

Jon Carlson, PsyD, EdD, ABPP, is distinguished professor of psychology and counseling at Governors State University and a psychologist at the Wellness Clinic in Lake Geneva, Wisconsin. He has practiced and taught psychotherapy for more than 40 years. He has authored 160 journal articles and 60 books and created over 300 professional trade videos and DVDs with leading therapists and educators. He is the recipient of several awards for his contributions to psychotherapy.